FUN PUZZLES AND BRAIN TICKLERS

MORE THAN 250 Word and Number Games, Trivia Quizzes, and much more!

Previously published as *Brain Games for Brain Power*

Reader's Digest

New York / Montreal

A READER'S DIGEST BOOK

Individual puzzles are the copyrighted property of the puzzle authors.
BrainSnack® is a registered trademark.

Cover image: Fourleafover/Getty Images

Copyright © 2021 Trusted Media Brands, Inc.
All rights reserved. Unauthorized reproduction, in any manner, is prohibited.
Reader's Digest is a registered trademark of Trusted Media Brands, Inc.

ISBN 978-1-62145-565-3

Printed in China

10 9 8 7 6 5 4 3 2 1

Note to Readers

The consultants, writers, editors, and proofreaders have taken all reasonable measures to confirm and verify the accuracy of the information contained in this title. However, some statements of fact can be open to interpretation. Similarly, new information and research often reveal that long-held beliefs are not true. We welcome your input on any answers for which you have sound evidence may be incorrect.

INTRODUCTION

These days, it seems like much of our free time is filled with technology; we're always watching TV or scrolling on our smartphones. While those things can be fun, they won't necessarily help you build your smarts. This book gives you, the clever adult reading this, the best of both worlds—a delightful distraction that'll also beef up your brain.

No matter what kind of brainteasers you like, you'll find it in *Fun Puzzles and Brain Ticklers*. In addition to classics like word searches, crosswords, and sudoku (as well as *Reader's Digest*'s well-loved, vocabulary-expanding Word Power quizzes), you'll be entertained by less familiar puzzle types like Kakuro, Number Clusters, Weather Charts and much, much more, all at different levels of difficulty. These puzzles feature unique themes, bright colors and plenty of opportunities for learning, no matter if you're a numbers person, a word whiz, or a trivia aficionado.

So, go ahead. Put your comfy clothes on, grab a pencil and some snacks, and kick back and relax with a form of entertainment that doesn't require a charger or power cord. Your brain will thank you for it.

About the Puzzles

Brain Games for Brain Power is filled with a delightful mix of classic and new puzzle types. To help you get started, here are instructions, tips, and some examples.

WORD GAMES

CROSSWORD PUZZLES

Clues are the deciding factor that determines crossword-solving difficulty. Many solvers mistakenly think strange and unusual words are what make a puzzle challenging. In reality, crossword constructors generally try to avoid grid esoterica, opting for familiar words and expressions.

WORD SUDOKU

The basic sudoku puzzle is a 9 x 9 square grid, split into nine square regions, each containing nine cells. You need to complete the grid so that each row, each column, and each 3 x 3 frame contains the nine letters from the black box above the grid.

There is always a hidden nine-letter word in the diagonal from top left to bottom right.

EXAMPLE   SOLUTION

WORD POWER

These quizzes test your knowledge of grammar and language and help you develop a better vocabulary. Find out where you stand on the Word Power scale by using the simple rating system included on the answer pages.

WORD SEARCHES

In a word search, the challenge is to find hidden words within a grid of letters. Words can be found in vertical columns or horizontal rows or along diagonals, with the letters of the words running either forward or backward.

NUMBER GAMES

SUDOKU

The basic sudoku puzzle is a 9 x 9 square grid, split into nine square regions, each containing nine cells. Complete the grid so that each row, each column and each 3 x 3 frame contains every number from 1 to 9.

EXAMPLE   SOLUTION

In addition to classic sudoku puzzles, you'll find **SUDOKU X** puzzles, where the main diagonals must include every number from 1 to 9, and **SUDOKU TWINS** with two overlapping grids.

KAKURO

These puzzles are like crosswords with numbers. There are clues across and down, but the clues are numbers. The solution is a sum that adds up to the clue number.

Each number in a black area is the sum of the numbers that you have to enter in the next empty boxes. The empty boxes that make up the sum are called a run. The sum of the across run is written above the diagonal in the black area, while the sum of the down run is written below the diagonal.

Runs can contain only the numbers 1 through 9, and each number in a run can be used only once. The gray boxes contain only odd numbers and the white, only even numbers.

EXAMPLE	**SOLUTION**

LOGIC PUZZLES

BINAIRO

Binairo puzzles look similar to sudoku puzzles. They are just as simple and challenging, but that is where the similarity ends.

There are two versions: odd and even. The even puzzles feature a 12 x 12 grid. You need to complete the grid with zeros and ones, until there are 6 zeros and 6 ones in every row and every column. No more than two of the same number can be next to or under each other. Rows or columns with exactly the same combination are not allowed.

EXAMPLE   **SOLUTION**

The odd puzzles feature an 11 x 11 grid. You need to complete the grid with zeros and ones until there are 5 zeros and 6 ones in every row and column.

KEEP GOING

In this puzzle, start on a blank square of your choice and connect as many blank squares as possible with one single continuous line.

You can only connect squares along vertical and horizontal lines, not along diagonals. You must continue the connecting line up until the next obstacle—i.e., the rim of the box, a black square, or a square that has already been used.

You can change direction at any obstacle you meet. Each square can be used only once. The number of blank squares left unused is marked in the upper square. There may be more than one solution, but we include only one solution in our answer key.

EXAMPLE   **SOLUTION**

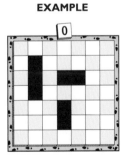
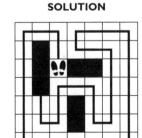

About the Puzzles (continued)

NUMBER CLUSTER

Number cluster puzzles are language-free, logical numerical problems. They consist of cubes on a 6 x 6 grid. Numbers have been placed in some of the cubes, while the rest are empty. Your challenge is to complete the grid by creating runs of the same number and length as the number supplied. So, where a cube with the number 5 has been included on the grid, you need to create a run of five number 5's, including the cube already shown. The run can be horizontal, vertical, or both horizontal and vertical.

EXAMPLE	SOLUTION

WORD PYRAMID

Each word in the pyramid has the letters of the word above it, plus a new letter.

Using the clues given, answer No.1 and then work your way to the base of the pyramid to complete the word pyramid.

SPORT MAZE

This puzzle is presented on a 6 x 6 grid. Your starting point is indicated by a red cell with a ball and a number. Your objective is to draw the shortest route from the ball to the goal, the only square without a number. You can move only along vertical and horizontal lines, but not along diagonals. The figure on each square indicates the number of squares the ball must be moved in the same direction. You can change direction at each stop.

EXAMPLE	SOLUTION

CAGE THE ANIMALS

This puzzle presents you with a zoo divided into a 16 x 16 grid. The different animals on the grid need to be separated. Draw lines that will completely divide up the grid into smaller squares, with exactly one animal per square.

EXAMPLE	SOLUTION

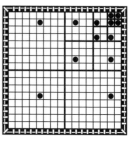

TRIVIA

TRIVIA QUIZZES & TRIVIAL PURSUITS

Trivia in a variety of formats and topics will probe the depth of your knowledge of facts. Questions and answers will tempt, tease, and tickle.

VISUAL PUZZLES

Throughout you will find unique mazes, visual conundrums, and other colorful challenges. Each comes with a new name and unique instructions. Our best advice? Patience and perseverance. Your eyes will need time to unravel the visual secrets.

BRAINSNACK® PUZZLES

To solve a BrainSnack® puzzle, you must think logically. You'll need to use one or several strategies to detect direction, differences, and/or similarities, associations, calculations, order, spatial insight, colors, quantities, and distances. A BrainSnack® ensures that all the brain's capacities are fully engaged. These are brain sports at their best!

WEATHER CHARTS

We all want to know the weather forecast, and here's your chance to figure it out! Arrows are scattered on a grid. Each arrow points toward a space where a weather symbol should be, but the symbols cannot be next to each other vertically, horizontally, or diagonally. A symbol cannot be placed on top of an arrow. You must determine where the symbols should be placed.

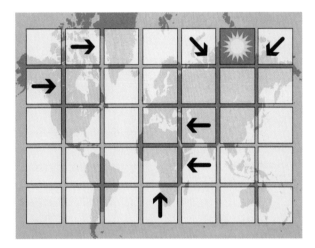

BRAINTEASERS

You'll also find short brainteasers scattered throughout these pages. These puzzles will give you a little light relief from the more intense puzzles while still challenging you.

Signs of Spring

ACROSS

1 Speech impediment
5 Popular '70s hairstyle
9 Male sheep
12 Child's boo-boo
13 Great Barrier ___
14 Word of discovery
15 Days of ___ (the past)
16 Flowering sign of spring
18 Events of a story
20 ___ Vincent de Paul
21 Materialize
24 Earns
25 Strange
26 Extend out
27 You buy them by the dozen
28 Awful
29 Ridicule
33 Total
34 What you do to a turkey or pumpkin
35 Marked with stripes
39 Holy
40 Got up
41 Crick in the neck
42 Nest ___, spring chore for the birds
44 *Sesame Street* character
48 Stomach muscles, for short
49 Tied
50 An amphibian
51 *Norma* ___
52 Hair colorings
53 Castle material

DOWN

1 Actress Myrna ___
2 ___ Jima
3 Word of address for a gentleman
4 Spring ___ (certain vocal frogs)
5 Passion
6 Achievement
7 Sports official, for short
8 Counterbalance
9 More than one radius
10 "Give me ___!" (request for a clue, 2 words)
11 Shakes
17 Paddle
19 Boy
21 Amazement
22 Square ___ in a round hole
23 Porker
24 Spring rains and thawing bring this
26 Preserve, jelly
28 Spring plant blossom
29 Short spring coats
30 Blunder
31 Adam's mate
32 Crimson
33 Planted a lawn
34 Open a ___ of worms
35 Storybook elephant
36 Caribbean island
37 Loud sound
38 Internet access type (abbrev.)
39 Stop and yield
41 Leg joint
43 ___ League school
45 Hawaiian volcano Mauna ___
46 Big ___ on campus
47 25 Across synonym

Sudoku

Fill in the grid so that each row, each column and each 3 x 3 frame contains every number from 1 to 9.

6				5	2			
2		9		1		6	3	
7	1		3				4	
5	9							
		4	1	7	5	9		
							8	3
	2				7		6	9
	5	8		3		1		4
			9	4				8

do you KNOW?

What is the world's smallest state?

_____

_____

UNCANNY TURN

Rearrange the letters of the phrase below to form a cognate anagram, one which is related or connected in meaning to the original phrase. The answer can be one or more words.

THIRTY ROOMED

Cage the Animals

Draw lines to completely divide up the grid into small squares with exactly one animal per square. The squares should not overlap.

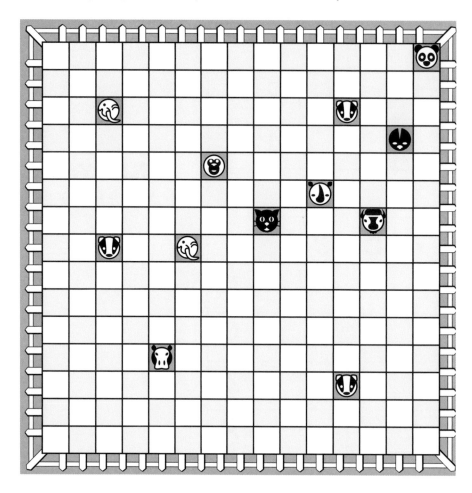

LETTERBLOCKS

Move the letterblocks around so that words are formed on top and below that you can associate with condiments. In some blocks, the letter from the top row has been switched with the letter from the bottom row.

CROSSWORD # Up and Down

ACROSS

1 "... nine, ten, ___ fat hen"
5 Printing daggers
10 *Candida* playwright
14 Bubkes
15 Like a mare
16 Scheherazade offering
17 Jerry Lewis movie
19 Sword with a bowl-shaped guard
20 Larry, Curly and Moe
21 Broke loose
23 ___ Gatos, CA
24 Panel layer
25 Rock concert buys
29 Blotto
33 De la Garza of *Law & Order*
34 Still-life objects
36 Literary adverb
37 Puppy pick-up spot
38 *The Communist Manifesto* is one
39 "No problem!"
40 Pup's sound
41 Gigi's sister
42 Mall features
43 Day or night
45 Counseled
47 Cause of road accidents
48 Serpentine fish
49 Gulf of Tonkin country
53 Up to date with
57 *Lost ___ Mancha* (2002 documentary)
58 "Yes, I'm sorry to say"
60 Be a couch potato
61 Squash variety
62 Spam containers
63 Duck genus
64 Araby VIP
65 Trees sacred to Druids

DOWN

1 *Them!* monsters
2 Thai money
3 Word form of "thought"
4 Molotov cocktail component
5 "That's the ___ trick in the book!"
6 Quick kiss
7 *Bambi* aunt
8 Doily trim
9 Ticks off
10 Shoplifts
11 "Special" times at the bar
12 Out of the wind
13 Garden trespasser
18 Ancient mall
22 P&L preparers
25 Bond girl Roberts
26 Whacked
27 Frank Loesser's *The Most ___*
28 Shopaholic's indulgence
29 Pelvis parts
30 *Rocky III* actor
31 Hair-raising
32 Fright
35 ___ de toilette
38 Golfer Lehman
39 Small dagger
41 Finalize a check
42 Forestall
44 Wrecks
46 Expose a fraud
49 Bob who hosted *This Old House*
50 Part of the plot
51 Gray and Whitney
52 Speed-of-sound number
53 Hillside dugout
54 Operatic song
55 Done for
56 Dick Tracy's love
59 Mrs. kangaroo

Textiles

All the words are hidden vertically, horizontally or diagonally—in both directions. The letters that remain unused form a sentence from left to right.

```
T E X T S W A N S K I N T I L
S S L O O W W E N T C L O T H
N E C M E C E R E M H S A C A
O N Y A S A I D L L T R H A T
T F E I R S N R E T W O E V E
T L S J N L B A T E L U M A U
U E R T E T E N T H W I E T D
B E E E R A I T E R M T U A A
L C J H S K N O R D A E Y Q M
S E I G S N A S R T E T R T A
S T E K N A L B Y F T A T E S
B R C B T I C H C R A T S V K
V U R I A H O M L N P S U L T
B E A K S N H A O E E T D E A
E L L U T A D R T N S E N V M
P I E O A D T A H I T E I I N
S D A D U I F I G L R F E R E
E D A C O R B N N E Y T W A Y
```

- BANDAGE
- BLANKET
- BROCADE
- BUCKSKIN
- BUTTONS
- CASHMERE
- CLOTH
- DAMASK
- FLEECE
- INDUSTRY
- JEANS
- JERSEY
- LINEN
- MOHAIR
- MULETA
- NEW WOOL
- PLAIT
- QUILT
- SATIN
- SCARLET
- SHEET
- SILK
- STARCH
- SUEDE
- SWANSKIN
- TAPESTRY
- TARTAN
- TERRY CLOTH
- THREAD
- TRICOT
- TULLE
- TWEED
- VELOUR
- VELVET

Keep Going

Start on a blank square of your choice and connect as many blank squares as possible with one single continuous line. You can only connect squares along vertical and horizontal lines, not along diagonal lines. You must continue the connecting line up until the next obstacle, i.e., the rim of the box, a black square or a square that has already been used. You can change direction at any obstacle you meet. Each square can only be used once. The number of blank squares that will be left unused is marked in the upper square. There is more than one solution. We only show one solution.

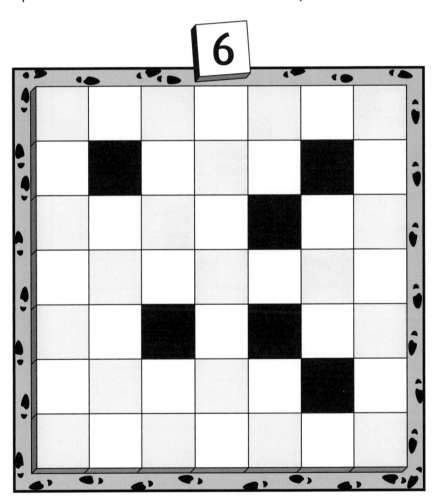

Over the Rainbow 1

ACROSS

1 Pair of mules
5 Tavis Smiley's network
8 Elbow bone
12 "Stepping Stone" singer White
13 Censor's insert
15 Declared
16 Elvis ___ Presley
17 Like Hooterville
18 Volcano near Messina
19 Dr. Seuss story
22 Nail at a slant
23 Camp bed
24 Meeting schedule
27 Lousy cars
30 Binge
31 Hunk
33 Timetable abbr.
35 Celebrate a victory
39 Excellent service?
40 Baserunner's goal
41 Lindley in *The Heartbreak Kid*
42 College try
45 Edit
47 Venezuelan river
48 Legal point
49 Anthony Burgess novel (with *A*)
58 City in a CCR song
59 Correct copy
60 Standard
61 Nutmeg husk
62 Zellweger in *Jerry Maguire*
63 Cherrystone
64 Construction wood
65 This instant
66 Effortless

DOWN

1 Steel mill residue
2 Henry VIII's sixth wife
3 Islands of the Moluccas
4 Not quite a score
5 Free advertisement
6 *Titanic* sinker
7 The Red and the Black
8 Familiar with
9 Plastering board
10 *Black Swan* heroine
11 First lady's man
13 Dog show category
14 Sugar pill

20 Musical group
21 ___ de plume
24 On the double
25 Misery
26 ___ *in the Dark* (1964)
27 After a while
28 Cybergeeks
29 Cubic meter
30 ...vian, e.g.
32 Sci-fi author Stanislaw
34 Helen Hayes in *Airport*
36 Javelin competitor
37 Show indecision
38 Pain

43 Effortless
44 Mork's planet
46 Decrease, as support
49 Keep time, in a way
50 Singer in *Footloose*
51 Hagar's war god
52 Straw in the wind
53 R.E.M.'s "All the Way to ___"
54 Was familiar with
55 *Show Boat* heroine
56 Pâté de foie ___
57 TV award

Maddening Maze

Here's another intricate pathway to confound and confuse you. Once again, start at the arrow and follow your feet to the center of the maze. Try to complete the puzzle within 5 minutes.

Word Sudoku

Complete the grid so that each row, each column and each 3 x 3 frame contains the nine letters from the black box below. The hidden nine-letter word is in the diagonal from top left to bottom right.

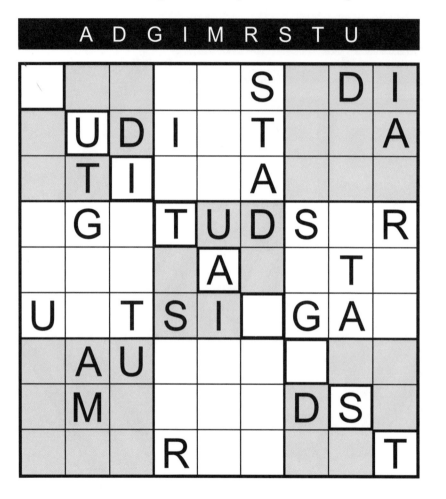

A D G I M R S T U

					S		D	I
	U	D	I		T			A
	T	I			A			
	G		T	U	D	S		R
				A			T	
U		T	S	I		G	A	
	A	U						
	M					D	S	
			R					T

do you KNOW?

What was the name of Little Lord Fauntleroy?

_____

_____

SANDWICH

What four-letter word belongs between the word on the left and the word on the right, so that the first and second word, and the second and third word, each form a common compound word or phrase?

HUNCH _ _ _ _ PACK

WORD POWER # Decorator's Delight

It's time to shake off the decor doldrums and set your inner home stylist free. Before you start testing paint chips and fabric swatches, test yourself with words you might encounter while sprucing up.

. . . .

1. cabriole *n.*—A: china cabinet. B: curved furniture leg. C: tea cart.

2. trug *n.*—A: shallow basket. B: triangular jug. C: padded footrest.

3. bolster *n.*—A: comforter cover. B: bed skirt. C: long pillow.

4. pilaster *n.*—A: column jutting from a wall. B: ornate molding on ceiling. C: recessed cubbyhole.

5. torchère *n.*—A: propane fireplace. B: stand for a candlestick. C: wall-mounted light.

6. grommet *n.*—A: sliding drawer. B: eyelet to protect an opening. C: anchor chain for hanging lamps.

7. pounce *v.*—A: transfer a stencil design. B: add light. C: combine fabrics.

8. patina *n.*—A: weathered look of copper or bronze. B: two-toned floors. C: high-gloss surface.

9. finial *n.*—A: ornament at the tip of a lamp or a curtain rod. B: pull string. C: metal drawer handle.

10. organdy *n.*—A: polka-dot pattern. B: insulating lining. C: transparent muslin.

11. newel *n.*—A: sunny nook. B: central post of a circular staircase. C: arched doorway between adjoining rooms.

12. bergère *n.*—A: upholstered chair with exposed wood. B: one-armed couch. C: semicircular occasional table.

13. ceruse *n.*—A: eye-catching color. B: table runner. C: pigment composed of white lead.

14. Bauhaus *adj.*—of or relating to … A: rococo style. B: a German school of functional design. C: an eco-friendly house.

15. incise *v.*—A: prune. B: slice. C: engrave.

Over the Rainbow 2

ACROSS

1 Jet pioneer
5 Heavy footfall
10 Shakespeare's river
14 *Brokeback Mountain* heroine
15 Gretzky was one
16 Anger
17 Duke Ellington classic
19 Spooky sound
20 Riviera wear
21 Pardon from guilt
23 "Stop filming!"
24 Swiss waterway
25 "Money, Money, Money" musical
29 Ton's 2000: Abbr.
30 Channel for old films
33 Berry in *X-Men: The Last Stand*
34 Cads
36 "Big Band," for one
37 ___ Dhabi
38 Diet guru Craig
39 ___ Kippur
40 "May ___ of service?"
41 Sagal in *8 Simple Rules ...*
42 Steel joist
44 Pep-rally sound
45 *Songs ___ Minor* (Keys album)
46 General pardon
48 Busy as ___
50 Suffix for pay
51 But
54 Spanish nobleman
58 River in Bavaria
59 Harry Belafonte hit
61 Kind of check or coat
62 Stethoscope sounds
63 Archer in *Fatal Attraction*
64 Toledo's lake
65 Variety show host
66 Bullyboy

DOWN

1 Petting zoo animal
2 *The Time Machine* race
3 In a crazed way
4 Fanatic
5 This evening, on marquees
6 Relieves of a burden
7 *Mamma Mia!* role
8 Prefix for phone
9 Most likely
10 Armadillo's protection
11 Elizabeth Taylor's trademark
12 Name of five Norwegian kings
13 Maui bird
18 Case-harden
22 Be fresh with
25 Committee head
26 Limerick rhyme scheme
27 Elvis Presley film
28 Iota preceder
29 Lotte in *Semi-Tough*
31 Certain Balkan
32 Pappy Yokum's mate
35 About 2 o'clock on a compass
38 Charlotte Brontë heroine
41 Ukraine capital
42 Acquired relative
43 Dog bed, often
47 In a sour mood
49 Capital of Switzerland
51 Sign on
52 Glacial ridges
53 Twenty quires
54 Jubilance
55 Snorkasaurus of Bedrock
56 Composer Dohnanyi
57 Barbara in *I Dream of Jeannie*
60 Inc. relative

Sport Maze

Draw the shortest way from the ball to the goal. You can only move along vertical and horizontal lines, not along diagonal lines. The figure on each square indicates the number of squares the ball must be moved in the same direction. You can change direction at each stop.

2	4	1	5	1	2
1	0	4	4	3	5
4	3	1	2	2	3
5	3	0	3	2	5
5	1	3	3	2	1
3	4	1	2		3

do you **KNOW**?

Who wrote and recorded
"I Am…I Said"?

_____

_____

UNCANNY TURN

Rearrange the letters of the phrase below to form a cognate anagram, one which is related or connected in meaning to the original phrase. The answer can be one or more words.

SURE CITY

Spot the Differences

Find the nine differences in the image on the bottom right.

tri**v**ia

- What beetle feeds on aphids and is named after the Virgin Mary?

_____

do you **KNOW**?

What is the capital of Slovenia?

_____

_____

CROSSWORD Hollywood Glamour

ACROSS

1 *Dinner at Eight* bombshell Harlow
5 Despair
10 Talk
14 ___ Major
15 Astrid Lindgren's Longstocking
16 *MASH*'s Jamie
17 NFL star Flutie
18 Bare teeth
19 Butter bean
20 High school assignment
22 Fellows
24 Ornamental fish
25 Butterfly catchers
28 Fashion icon Audrey
30 Elegant Lake of *The Blue Dahlia*
34 ___ *and Peace*
35 Perfect serve
36 Celebrities
38 Related to birth
42 Place for wood or a lawn mower
44 Pecking ___
46 ___ *With the Wind*
47 Coin
49 Type of boom
51 At this time
52 Cover
54 Quick-talking Russell of *His Girl Friday*
56 Monroe of *Bus Stop*
60 Singer McEntire
61 Symbolized by Uncle Sam
62 Biblical son of Seth
64 Spread open
68 Small, medium or large
70 Degrade
73 Finished
74 ___ of March
75 Type of lemon
76 Prefix for eight
77 Relinquish control
78 Jimmy of *Superman*
79 Actress Lillian of *The Birth of a Nation*

DOWN

1 Beatles' "Hey ___"
2 Greek god of love
3 Computer brand
4 Site of the '98 Winter Olympics
5 Electronic mapping device (abbr.)
6 *Hamilton* composer ___-Manuel Miranda
7 October birthstone
8 "Queen of all media"
9 Shower problem
10 Lightbulb type (abbr.)
11 A 17-syllable poem
12 A knight's mail
13 Locomotive
21 Desires
23 Bridge
26 Musician Puente
27 Injury reminders
29 Boast
30 Like the ocean
31 Word before chamber
32 Stink
33 Fervor
37 Mexican mister
39 Nobelist Morrison
40 Unnamed (abbr.)
41 Obscene
43 Lunch counter
45 Ascend
48 River in Egypt
50 Taxis
53 Someone with a lot of energy
55 Cuddly pup
56 The M in MTV
57 Stage direction
58 Tore down
59 Last name in prizes
63 Speaks
65 Sets of points, in math
66 Hill dwellers
67 Slangy affirmative
69 Opposite of WNW
71 Observe
72 Seabird

Sudoku

Fill in the grid so that each row, each column and each 3 x 3 frame contains every number from 1 to 9.

	2	6			9			1
				4		5	2	
	1		7					4
9			6	2			4	8
	4						7	
2	8			7	3			9
1					8		3	
	9	4		6				
7			3			2	9	

TRIANAGRAM

Three-word groups of anagrams are also called triplets or trianagrams.
Complete the group:

T R A I N E R _ _ _ _ _ _ _   _ _ _ _ _ _ _

WORD SEARCH Roman Empire

All the words are hidden vertically, horizontally or diagonally—in both directions. The letters that remain unused form a sentence from left to right.

```
L T H E R O A S M E A N I K S
Z E N O E I U M M P E I I B R
E P G R V I O P B G A N E A D
L B L I D Y I B A E G L P I I
C U L U O R T H A D P M M T C
E T A O E N T E O S O L O E T
A L R G G R S M U E E T P R A
C N F R A N K S O T B E E C T
B H O C O N S U L A O B E U O
P A O C R O A P E R I N E L R
V N R R I C L T H T E Y S G O
E N E B I B A V O S L A V E S
S I N R A N U P R I N C E P S
U B F E E R R R A G R I P P A
V A N S E E I D C A E S A R A
I L N D P M R A E M O T E C T
U R E D R U M E N S U T U R B
S U T I T S D H I S P A N I A
```

- AFRICA
- AGRIPPA
- BARBARIANS
- BRUTUS
- CAESAR
- CARTHAGE
- CLAUDIUS
- CONSUL
- DICTATOR
- EMPIRE
- FRANKS
- GAUL
- HANNIBAL
- HISPANIA
- HORACE
- KINGDOM
- LEGIONS
- LIVIA
- LUCRETIA
- MAGISTRATES
- MURDER
- NERO
- PLEBS
- POMPEII
- PRINCEPS
- REMUS
- RUBICON
- SENATE
- SENECA
- SLAVES
- TEUTONS
- TIBER
- TITUS
- VESUVIUS
- ZENO

Good Arrows

Robin, Marion, and Little John were practicing archery in the forest one day. Each fired six shots and each scored 142 points. Robin's first two shots scored 44 points. Marion's first shot scored 6 points. Who scored a bull's-eye? The 18 shots are marked on the target.

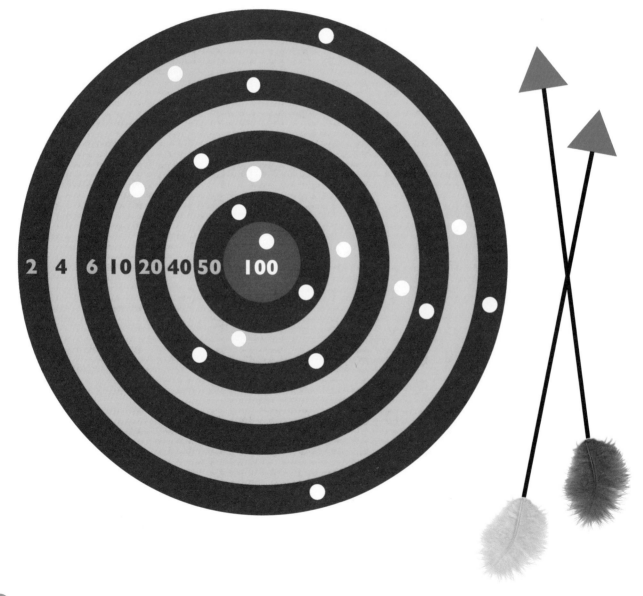

Target Practice

Six archers each fire three arrows that hit a target. Alison beats Keith by two points, Keith beats Charles by two points, Charles beats Jill by two points, Jill beats Martin by two points, and Martin beats Jonathan by two points. What were the scores of the six players?

6 8 15 21 35

Form the words that are described in the brackets with the letters above the grid. An extra letter is already in the right place.

TERRY SLEEP (Oscar Best Actress 2012)

M										

Petite

ACROSS

1 Eli Manning aerial
5 A ___ for sore eyes
10 Kind of beetle or party
14 Springfield Elementary's Krabappel
15 Wickerwork material
16 Dale's companion
17 Superboy's hometown
19 German duck
20 First mate's superior
21 *You've Got Mail* star
23 Intimate
24 Stretch of time
25 Big-top safety gear
27 Painting medium
31 Cary in *The Princess Bride*
34 Top-40 deejay Casey
36 "___ little teapot ..."
37 Little piggies
38 "Me too!"
39 Sing like Cleo Laine
40 In agreement
41 Dead duck
42 Comes off as
43 Fun City
45 Golf tourney
47 Greed or craft ender
48 40th president
52 Peter in *Murder by Death*
56 Billings locale
57 Unmitigated ___
58 Generation Xer's progenitor
60 Lady Antebellum, for one
61 Steaming
62 Lacoste founder, _____ Lacoste
63 Bunch
64 Audible breaths
65 Frequent flyers, once

DOWN

1 Joe in *My Cousin Vinny*
2 Madison Avenue exec
3 Goes postal
4 Freebies with soup
5 Part of USSR
6 "Love ___ the Air" (1978 hit)
7 Indy 500 winner de Ferran
8 Steering station
9 Arbor Day honoree
10 Spanish wine
11 Edward Albee play
12 Ski area near Salt Lake City
13 "Galveston" singer Campbell
18 Stows in a hold
22 Antiseptic's target
26 Florida lizard
27 Jetson pooch
28 Corp. VIP
29 Muslim leader
30 Musical based on a T.S. Eliot book
31 Wellington's alma mater
32 Isolated
33 Keeler or Winkie
35 Raided the icebox
38 Palme ___ (Cannes Film Festival award)
39 Ottawa hockey team
41 *Rango* director Verbinski
42 "I ___ reason why ..."
44 Coldplay hit
46 Examines
49 Arcade attractions
50 About
51 Nasal openings
52 Noncoms: Abbr.
53 Rank of British nobility
54 Baseball stats
55 Delhi dress
56 Folktale
59 Popcorn purchase

Horoscope

Fill in the grid so that every row, every column and every frame of six boxes contains six different symbols: health, work, money, happiness, family and love. Look at the row or column that corresponds with your sign of the zodiac, and find out which of the six symbols are important for you today. The symbols appear in increasing order of importance (1–6). It's up to you to translate the meaning of each symbol to your specific situation.

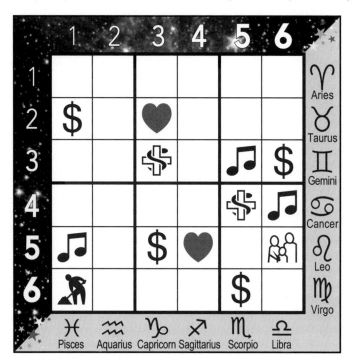

do you KNOW?

What are the names of Titania's fairy servants?

_____

_____

END GAME

The words you are seeking all have the letters END in them in the position indicated. When you have found all of the answers with help from the clues on the right, one column will reveal the END GAME word, which is a call for a drive.

— — — — — — **E N D**   In love with a girl

E N D — — — — — —   Examination by tube

— — — — — — **E N D**   Express disapproval

— — — **E N D** — — —   An attachment

Sunny

Where will the sun shine? With the knowledge that each arrow points to a place where a symbol should be, can you locate the sunny spots? The symbols cannot be next to each other vertically, horizontally or diagonally. A symbol cannot be placed on top of an arrow. We show one symbol.

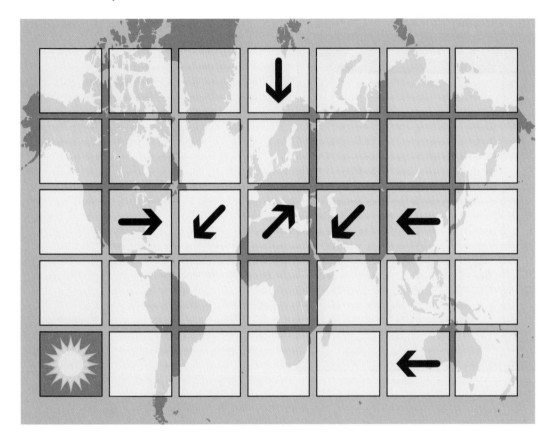

BLOCK ANAGRAM

Form the words that are described in the brackets with the letters above the grid. Extra letters are already in the right place.

INJURED DNA (Oscar Best Actor 2012)

CROSSWORD **Gardening Gear**

ACROSS

1 Hawaiian dish
4 Chevy ___ (2 words, with 18-Across)
7 Chicago airport
12 The law has a long one
13 Time period
14 Tennis great Federer
15 Garden cutters for twigs and small branches
17 Dietary supplement brand name
18 See 4-Across
19 Medical abbreviation
21 Kneeling ___ for gardening
22 Water carrier for gardening
24 Be nosy
25 Erase
26 Run-___ (sentences lacking connections)
27 Capital of the Bahamas
29 Tool for unwanted plants
31 Hand tool for digging in the garden
35 Type of energy
37 Quarterback Manning
38 Captain in *Moby Dick*
41 Fond du ___, Wisconsin
42 Long-handled gardening implement
43 Garden tool with teeth
44 Slangy agreement
45 School vehicle
46 Outline
48 Garden clippers
52 Aired again
53 Facial appendage
54 Ignited
55 Signs
56 Family room
57 Secret agent

DOWN

1 Buddy
2 Gold in Guatemala
3 Deadlock
4 Root ___
5 Flub
6 Beams of light
7 Spheres
8 Flat-bladed gardening gear
9 Mouth open in surprise
10 Related to kidneys
11 Wear away
16 Baked dessert
20 Village in Connecticut
22 In what way
23 Single
24 Conditional release
25 Pair
27 Web
28 Part of a circle
30 Gentle touch
32 Animals similar to ferrets
33 Large type of deer
34 Fib
36 Plotted
38 Spacey prefix
39 Group of wives
40 Knowledgeable
42 Jog
44 Cravings
45 Char
47 Watering ___ for the garden
49 Singer Carly ___ Jepsen
50 Tombstone abbreviation
51 Pigpen

Number Cluster

Cubes showing numbers have been placed on the grid below, with some spaces left empty. Can you complete the grid by creating runs of the same number and of the same length as the number? So, where a cube with number 5 has been included on the grid, you need to create a run of five number 5's, including the cube already shown. The run can be horizontal, vertical, or both horizontal and vertical.

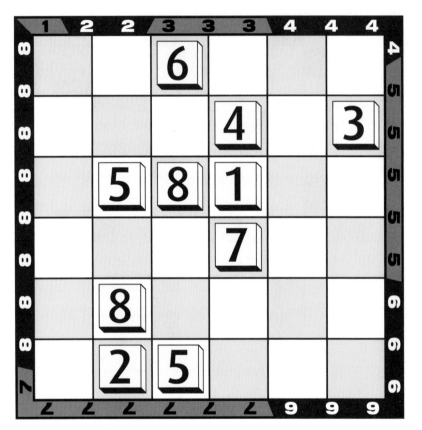

do you KNOW?

What kind of car did Starsky and Hutch drive?

_____

_____

DOODLE PUZZLE

A doodle puzzle is a combination of images, letters and/ or numbers that represent a word or a concept. If you cannot solve a doodle puzzle, do not look at the answer right away. Think hard—and outside the box.

Word Pyramid

Each word in the pyramid has the letters of the word above it, plus a new letter.

I
(1) Rhode Island
(2) gentle wind
(3) water falling in drops
(4) fairy bluebird
(5) aviators
(6) vivid red
(7) inhabitant of the U.S.

do you **KNOW**?

How did Cleopatra kill herself?

_____

_____

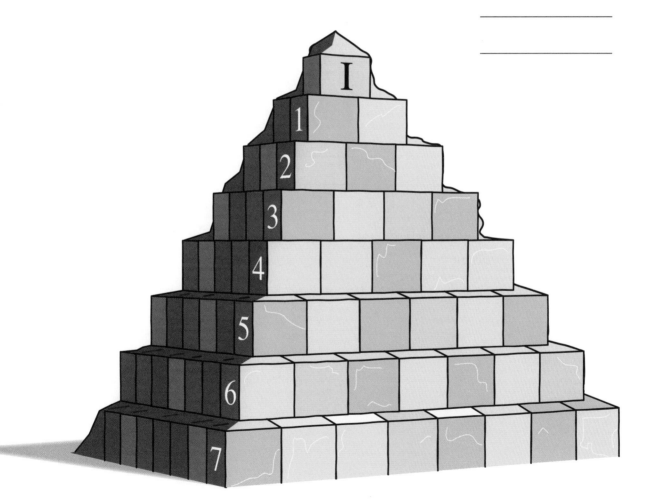

Not So Petite

ACROSS

1 Mascara target
5 Oboe forerunner
10 Partly open
14 "Thought" prefix
15 Eagle nest
16 Sushi fish
17 *Pee-wee's Big Adventure* trucker
19 Leave out
20 NBA All-Star Game side
21 Take a spill
23 Orinoco tributary
24 Ipanema site
25 TV witch
29 Mr. Met and others
33 Stale
34 Van Susteren or Garbo
36 Zorro's letter
37 Bad toupees
38 Gossipy woman
39 542-year-old Smurf
40 Flow's counterpart
41 Awareness
42 Spit in the Ocean's game
43 Least aloof
45 Narratives
47 Ump's call
48 Likely
49 New Testament author
53 *The Lady Eve* director
57 Employee-safety org.
58 Endangered Chinese mammal
60 Proofer's "never mind"
61 Countermand
62 Fleming and McKellen
63 Fabled race loser
64 Duck
65 "Jabberwocky" opener

DOWN

1 Have a sweet melody
2 Mother of Jabal and Jubal
3 Wizened
4 Harry Potter's alma mater
5 Biblical strong man
6 LeBron James' team
7 SFO info
8 Toupees
9 Assemble
10 Energy type
11 Japanese golfer
12 Kapoor in *Slumdog Millionaire*
13 Tag with a "PG-13"
18 Kafkaesque
22 Celestial bear
25 Spread widely
26 Vacation island near Curacao
27 *Nineteen Eighty-Four* dictator
28 ICM employee
29 ___ and bounds
30 One day ___ time
31 Wigwam
32 Kenmore's company
35 Dr. colleagues
38 "You got it!"
39 The "Mona Lisa" is one
41 Rogen in *The Green Hornet*
42 Easy out
44 Change genetically
46 Squeal
49 Pit at a rock concert
50 *The Thin Man* dog
51 "My word!"
52 Bowery bum
53 Really comfortable
54 Mimic a mouse
55 Krabappel of *The Simpsons*
56 Fresh talk
59 To boot

TRIVIA QUIZ A Special Occasion

Each holiday brings its own distinctive food to the table, from America's Thanksgiving pumpkin pies to the plum puddings that define a British Christmas.

ENJOY A SEASONAL TASTE OF THESE HOLIDAY-SPECIFIC FOODS FROM AROUND THE WORLD.

1. What time of year do Spanish people traditionally eat the honey and almond delicacy called *turrón*?

2. What's the Swedish word for a laden table of special-occasion foods?

3. What noble cheese, made with the same mold as French Roquefort, is considered a necessity for the British Christmas season?

4. Hanukkah is often celebrated with potato latkes and jelly doughnuts fried in oil. What's the significance of the oil used in cooking?

5. Following Ramadan, the fasting season in the Muslim calendar, there is a celebratory feast called Eid ul-Fitr. For how many days do people feast?

6. Heart-shaped cookies made of what are sold at fairs throughout Germany in the autumn?

7. Why is Britain's classic Christmas pudding called "plum" when there are no actual plums in it?

8. During what season do Orthodox Russians consume a sweet cheesecake-like dessert called *paska* or *pashka*?

9. During Diwali, the Hindu holy festival of lights, a celebration that falls in October or November each year, families make and share great quantities of what type of food?

10. Why should you not cut the noodles in the dish before serving them during Chinese New Year?

Sudoku Twin

Fill in the grid so that each row, each column and each 3 x 3 frame contains every number from 1 to 9. A sudoku twin is two connected 9 x 9 sudokus.

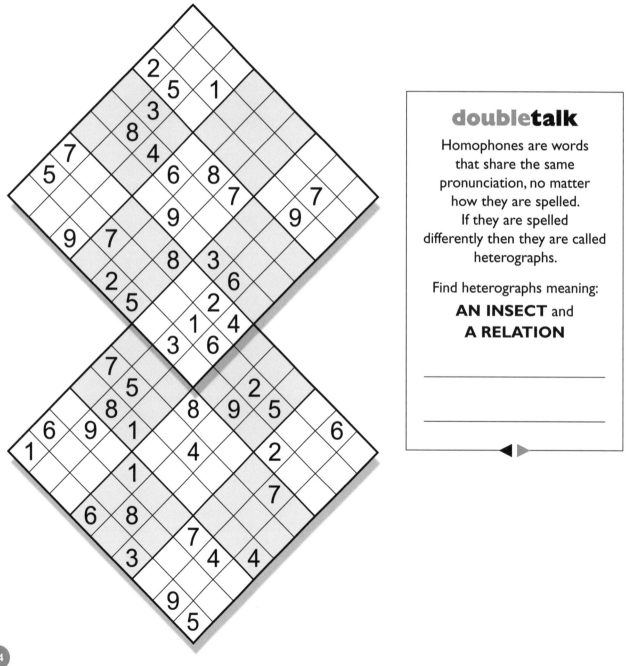

doubletalk

Homophones are words that share the same pronunciation, no matter how they are spelled. If they are spelled differently then they are called heterographs.

Find heterographs meaning:
AN INSECT and **A RELATION**

_____

_____

CROSSWORD Apple Varieties

ACROSS

1 Spasm of pain
5 Speed competition
9 Branch
12 Margarine
13 Tennis player Lendl
14 Hawaiian flower necklace
15 Take the skin off an apple
16 Great apple for fruit kabobs
18 University bigwig
20 Buenos ___, Argentina
21 Humiliate
24 Fate
25 Spy
26 Mild yellow-red apple
27 ___ and arrow
28 ___ ed. (school subj.)
29 Make a mistake
32 Apple first cultivated in Japan
34 Concur
36 Tempting songstresses in Greek myth
39 Freeway entrance lane
40 Early video game maker
41 Sicilian volcano
42 One of the most popular apples in North America since 1811
44 A financial market (abbrev.)
48 Interjections
49 Sea bird
50 12 p.m.
51 Sailor's "yes"
52 Buck or doe
53 Christmastime

DOWN

1 Flavored soda
2 Ginger ___
3 Word in a wedding announcement
4 ___ delicious, popular yellow apple
5 Puerto ___ Benicio Del Toro, for one
6 Makeup brand
7 Auto
8 Involve
9 Five- ___ chili
10 Actress Zellweger
11 Center
17 Mona ___
19 Dine
21 Small drop
22 Sense of self
23 Kitten's cry
24 Mary ___ cosmetics
26 Letters after DEF
28 Jammies (abbr.)
29 Time period
30 Stage of sleep (abbr.)
31 Sales ___
32 Shade-loving plant
33 Joined
34 ___ Taylor clothing store
35 ___ Smith, tart green apple
36 South Pacific islands
37 Like a rash
38 Rear children
39 "In ___ words..."
41 Laborer of old
43 Native metal
45 "I love ___!"
46 Name for the sun
47 Direction opposite WSW

Keep Going

Start on a blank square of your choice and connect as many blank squares as possible with one single continuous line. You can only connect squares along vertical and horizontal lines, not along diagonal lines. You must continue the connecting line up until the next obstacle, i.e., the rim of the box, a black square or a square that has already been used. You can change direction at any obstacle you meet. Each square can only be used once. The number of blank squares that will be left unused is marked in the upper square. There is more than one solution. We only show one solution.

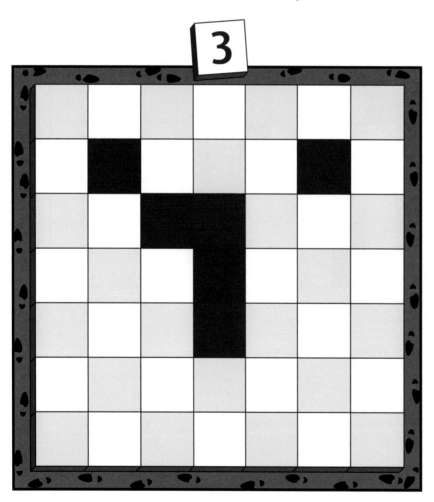

WORD SEARCH # Volcanos

All the words are hidden vertically, horizontally or diagonally—in both directions. The letters that remain unused form a sentence from left to right.

```
T K H E E V E S U V I U S R D
I A C T I V E U P T J I O I A
I M N O F A S E U P U E O A C
E C R E C R U S T V F R M D I
P H E O X L C A N N I G U G T
M A O L H T A E D T A O E E E
O T G C A A I N E M L Y A O T
P K G R W N L N D C S N H L L
A A A V A E D A G E C A T O A
A R B S I N E N R U S T R G S
A O B P I L I H O M I I I Y A
C C R C T W O T N I S S T E B
I Q O N O U E N E C S E H E S
R A A L T N A M R O D S N E D
E M G L E T A A D L E F I E D
M E V I S O L P X E T O A M N
A E W I C B N I A T N U O M E
E A G C R A T E R J E L A V A
```

- ACTIVE
- ALARM
- AMERICA
- ANDESITE
- ARARAT
- BASALT
- CRATER
- CRUST
- DACITE
- DEATH
- DIORITE
- DORMANT
- EIFEL
- EMISSION
- ETNA
- EXPLOSIVE
- EXTINGUISHED
- FUJI
- GABBRO
- GEOLOGY
- GEYSER
- GLOWING CLOUD
- GRANITE
- HAWAII
- ICELAND
- JAPAN
- KAMCHATKA
- LAVA
- MAGMA
- MANTLE
- MOUNTAIN
- POMPEII
- TOBA
- VESUVIUS

'60s Hits

ACROSS

1 Race length
5 Hurdles for doctors-to-be
10 Soldering tool
14 Ireland, in poetry
15 *Air Music* composer
16 *Peter Pan* dog
17 "Soul Man" duo
19 Does Easter eggs
20 Their motto is "Can Do!"
21 Unlawful
23 Celtic god of the sea
24 Jacob's first wife
25 Revised
29 Like a junior miss
32 Audible dashes
33 Executed a gainer
35 Like much of Saudi Arabia
36 Suffix for Capri
37 ___ *for Corpse*: Grafton
38 *Love Story* composer
39 "Queen of Country" McEntire
41 Fender-bender results
43 Teller's partner
44 Built
46 Maine capital
48 At the vertex
49 Guy's mate
50 Dovish
53 Term of endearment
57 Thin necktie
58 "Oh, Pretty Woman" singer
60 Kid Rock hit
61 Kind of union
62 St. Petersburg river
63 1979 Polanski film
64 Church council
65 Stretch out

DOWN

1 Army chow
2 "Dies ___" (Requiem Mass hymn)
3 Peru capital
4 Allows
5 Called for a pizza
6 Curtain hardware
7 Lofty altar
8 Eshkol of Israel
9 Seemed funny
10 Hoosier State
11 "Hit the Road Jack" singer
12 R.E.M.'s "The ___ Love"
13 GOP Elephant creator
18 When pigs fly, to poets
22 Marvin in *Cat Ballou*
25 Flip over
26 Some time after
27 "She Loves You" group
28 Cubed
29 Kernel's coat
30 "Jack and the Beanstalk" heavy
31 Jennifer's *Ab Fab* role
34 Car ID
40 They speak louder than words
41 Exits the premises
42 Sweetened
43 Taffy-making step
45 Ski lift
47 Distinctive clothing
50 Blind as ___
51 Iditarod Trail's end
52 Irish golfer McIlroy
53 Extinct bird
54 Czech river
55 De ___ (from square one)
56 Chew like a beaver
59 PBS chef of *Can Cook* fame

Cage the Animals

Draw lines to completely divide up the grid into small squares with exactly one animal per square. The squares should not overlap.

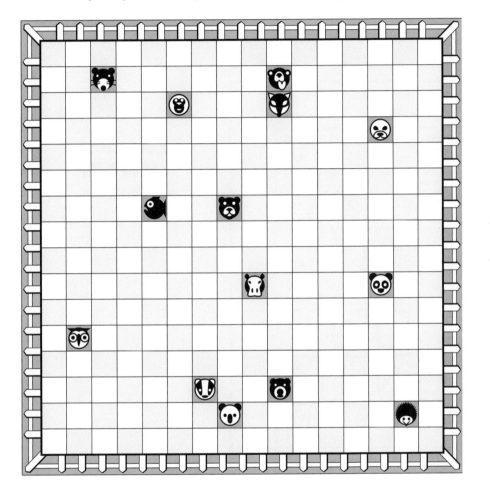

do you KNOW?

In *Finding Nemo*, what kind of fish is the teacher?

_____

_____

LETTERBLOCKS

Move the letterblocks around so that words are formed on top and below that you can associate with opposites.

Word Sudoku

Complete the grid so that each row, each column and each 3 x 3 frame contains the nine letters from the black box below. The hidden nine-letter word is in the diagonal from top left to bottom right.

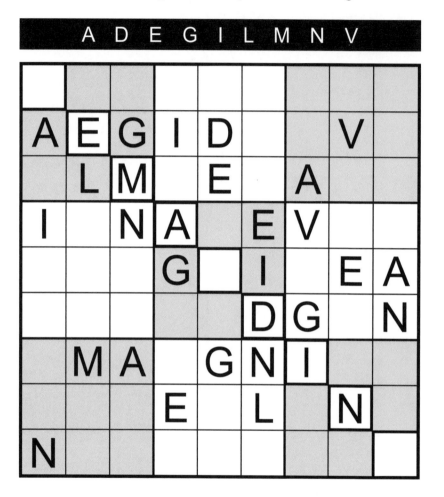

A D E G I L M N V

do you KNOW?

What's the largest Scandinavian country?

_____

_____

SANDWICH

What three-letter word belongs between the word on the left and the word on the right, so that the first and second word, and the second and third word, each form a common compound word or phrase?

CREW _ _ _ THROATS

CROSSWORD **The Space Race**

ACROSS

1 *Call Me* _____
6 _____ fide
10 One of the five Ws
14 Early game console
15 Run _____
16 Copter prefix
17 Great Lakes mnemonic
18 See 37 Across
20 Rascal
21 Shortly
23 Cropped up
24 Pottery oven
25 Banana brand
27 Licorice liqueur
30 The Jackson _____
31 Cycle or athlon
34 ET or Yoda
35 Metal joining pin
36 Owns
37 Launch site on Space Coast, with 18 Across
38 Apollo _____ Module, first launched in 1968
39 First walker on the moon, with 55 Across
40 Summer in Toulouse
41 Type of numeral
42 Paris river
43 Elected rep. (abbr.)
44 Type of organic compound
45 Rose drawback
46 Drug addict
47 Person, place or thing
48 Magnitude
51 "You _____ seen nothing yet"
52 Hush sound
55 See 39 Across
58 Conical structure
60 Song
61 Promise
62 Former first lady Bush
63 Leave
64 Native of the UK
65 _____ & Young

DOWN

1 Dolphinfish (with repeated word)
2 Nuclear fission can split one
3 Moist
4 "_____ we there yet?"
5 NASA's _____ control
6 *Apollo 13*'s Kevin
7 Neighbor of Yemen
8 Fiction prefix
9 Initials for an alias
10 See 10 Across
11 Superman or Spider-Man
12 Regrettably
13 Flooring option
19 Car parker
22 Classic
24 Leg joint
25 Sofa
26 Finished
27 Walks impatiently
28 Gladden
29 Grow to peak perfection
30 College exam
31 Beat them at _____ own game
32 *The Office* actor Wilson
33 Keys
35 Gossip
38 Solitary
39 Gas for a sign
41 Button in bowling
42 Space _____, reusable vehicle retired in 2011
45 2,000 pounds
46 Bothered
47 Elie Wiesel book
48 Fill
49 Heart
50 Present or potent prefix
51 Contra
52 Wove
53 Word on a towel
54 Miami team
56 Steal
57 Paddle
59 It has a drum

Sport Maze

Draw the shortest way from the ball to the goal. You can only move along vertical and horizontal lines, not along diagonal lines. The figure on each square indicates the number of squares the ball must be moved in the same direction. You can change direction at each stop.

2	4	4	2	3	3
2	1	2	3	3	3
5	4	1	2	2	5
1	4	3	●	3	5
2	2	2	4	2	1
1	2	2	2	2	1

do you **KNOW**?

Who composed
Porgy and Bess?

_____

_____

UNCANNY TURN

Rearrange the letters of the phrase below to form a cognate anagram, one which is related or connected in meaning to the original phrase. The answer can be one or more words.

CARE IS NOTED

42

Futoshiki

Fill in the 5 x 5 grid with the numbers from 1 to 5 once per row and column, while following the greater than/lesser than symbols shown. There is only one valid solution that can be reached through logic and clear thinking alone!

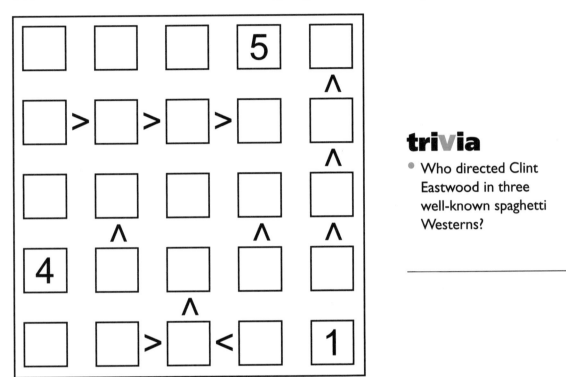

trivia

- Who directed Clint Eastwood in three well-known spaghetti Westerns?

CONNECT TWO

An oxymoron is a combination of seemingly contradictory or incongruous words, such as "science fiction" (science means "knowledge or study dealing with facts or truth" while fiction means "an imagined or invented creation"). Connect the words with meanings that oppose each other and make oxymorons.

WORK	LABOR
MUTUALLY	CHOICE
FREE	PARTY
ONLY	EXCLUSIVE

Sudoku

Fill in the grid so that each row, each column and each 3 x 3 frame contains every number from 1 to 9.

5					9	2		
		4		2				1
	7		4				3	8
		8	2	5				9
	3						4	
2				4	3	8		
8	6				7		2	
3				8		1		
		1	6					3

do you **KNOW**?

Who painted
"The Scream"?

_____

_____

FRIENDS

What do the following words have in common?

GRAPH MORPH SYLLABLE PHONIC GALA

CROSSWORD Flower Parts

ACROSS

1 Table insert
5 Language that gives us "kiwi"
10 Barracks VIPs
14 Trademarked tangelo
15 Barkin in *Drop Dead Gorgeous*
16 Catcall
17 BUD
19 "Super Trouper" group
20 Taylor of silent films
21 Toper
23 Floral necklace
24 Canadian First Nations people
25 Possessing wisdom
29 Virtuoso
32 Is contiguous with
33 Mine entrances
35 Kiss of peace
36 SpongeBob's pet snail
37 Hubris
38 Sheet of stamps
39 A lot of fluff?
40 Quartet member
41 Berry of Motown
42 Driver's Ed driver
44 Highland terrier
46 Consequently
47 He coached Rudy in *Rudy*
48 Discredit a witness
51 Former
55 Olympic swimmer Torres
56 ROOTS
58 Utah city
59 Colombian plain
60 Former Orioles manager Weaver
61 Minstrel songs
62 "Honky Cat" singer John
63 Dagger in *The Mikado*

DOWN

1 Olympic sled
2 Prima-donna problems
3 Quite considerable
4 Loyalty
5 Camelot wizard
6 Shepard's ___ of the Mind
7 Bullfight cheer
8 Flat payment
9 Point to
10 Has an effect on
11 STEM
12 "Oh, ___ in England ...": Browning
13 Magi guide
18 Runs for it
22 POTUS part: Abbr.
25 Savants
26 Toward the stern
27 STALK
28 Mystic's card
29 Phrygian king of lore
30 Rhodes of talk radio
31 Daisy type
34 *Rugrats* infant
37 Queen of spades/jack of diamonds meld
38 Idaho veggies
40 Brightest star in the Harp
41 Bridge expert Charles
43 *Field of ___* (1989)
45 *A river runs through it*
48 Word with screen or teen
49 Rooney in *The Girl with the Dragon Tattoo*
50 Campus building
51 Wine prefix
52 Catcher Rodriguez
53 A ___ formality
54 *Glamour* rival
57 Midback muscle, briefly

Word Pyramid

Each word in the pyramid has the letters of the word above it, plus a new letter.

E

(1) extraterrestrial
(2) consume
(3) cooperative unit
(4) boiling water
(5) good conductors of electricity
(6) talismans
(7) imitate

do you **KNOW** ?

What is the capital
of Belize?

_____

_____

TRIVIAL PURSUIT 1957

Do you want fries with that?
A whopping 4.3 million babies were born in 1957—the biggest year of the
U.S. baby boom. No wonder busy moms included fast food on the menu.

TEST YOUR FAST-FOOD IQ BELOW.

1 Burger King introduced the fast-food industry's first gimmick burger in 1957. Name it.

_____

2 Housewives in 1957 could serve a "home-cooked" dinner without turning on the stove, thanks to the new Bucket Meal. Which restaurant sold it?

_____

3 Brazier-cooked burgers and hot dogs joined Dilly Bars and banana splits at this chain in 1957.

_____

4 McDonald's boasted 40 locations (and $4.4 million in sales) in 1957. About how many of its restaurants operate today?

_____

5 _Fast Food_ magazine declared Billy Ingram to be the "granddaddy of the hamburger" in 1957. Name the slider-serving chain he founded in 1921.

_____

6 Sonic Drive-In (known as Top Hat in 1957) revolutionized ordering with this technology. What was it?

_____

7 The birthplace of Chick-fil-A (aka the Dwarf House, founded in 1946) is in which state?

_____

TEST YOUR RECALL

On July 6, 1957, John Lennon met Paul McCartney by chance and later invited him to join his band. What was the name of that band?

_____

Themeless

ACROSS

1 Thompson in *Howards End*
5 Implement
9 Baltic seaport
13 Boromir portrayer Sean
14 Sculpted work
15 Hawkish deity
16 Canada Dry, for one
19 African language
20 Shmi Skywalker's son
21 Links area
22 Singer Cassidy
23 Most expensive
25 Dry region of Canada
28 Match the bet
29 Grammy winner Celine
30 Mink relative
34 Period following Passover
36 Speedy horses
39 Harvard rival
40 Jennifer in *Selena*
42 Dolt
44 Cover
45 Dry white wine
49 Sportsman's mount
52 Oka River tributary
53 Butterfield in *Hugo*
54 "The Bells" poet
55 Drool
59 *The Heart Is a Lonely Hunter* novelist
62 Like omelets
63 Spanish appetizers
64 1999 Ron Howard film
65 Stalk in a duck blind
66 King's *Faithful* coauthor
67 Ooze

DOWN

1 Recedes
2 Cat call
3 ___ Hari
4 "O Canada" is one
5 Collette in *Little Miss Sunshine*
6 Part of WHO
7 Silver-screen awards
8 Canadian coin
9 Hip-hop
10 Angered
11 Hereditary factors
12 Until this moment
14 Menu fish
17 Fit to be tied
18 Prefix for brewery
23 Kind of soccer kick
24 Tiny, to tiny tots
25 Disney clownfish
26 Retain
27 Buzzing bug
28 Our star
31 Anklebones
32 Fiorucci of fashion
33 Canadian flag color
35 Taken-back item
37 Mire
38 Excess
41 Nada
43 Alpine region
46 "From ___ Starry Night": Whitman
47 Kind of band
48 *Anne of Green ___*: Montgomery
49 Harness horse
50 Ornamental orange
51 Sizable
55 Read a barcode
56 Eliot's *Adam ___*
57 Art Deco artist
58 "Please respond"
60 Bristow of *Alias*
61 Number-cruncher

St. Paddy's

All the words are hidden vertically, horizontally or diagonally—
in both directions.

```
S U S V Y B R G V B R B G R F N J L K
W T D S J F P S A C V U U R E T T E S
Z K L W I J O G H Y H O N A U S M H W
P O V I D K I X S G A S C P L K S E A
U O U B K J G M A E E P A I C U R R C
F V A N A D Q L N K O T P O T D O I O
B L L L B T E L A D R T R U T L N N R
L I I R I L V N B I T M A R U T E O N
Y H U M L F S H C L A R Y T S A T C E
C X D I E X A K X H X J T A O N V W D
O X H S G R M R S V F Q F D E P W Z B
L S R P O R I G O X F L X E E H O C E
L S L D L O A C N L E P R Z U P B F E
E Z A O D E J V K B W G B C L F N N F
E V W I L H F N I L B U D X W R I P L
N X L I E N U A H C E R P E L K A F I
D N C U D A N W P R W Y P R A H R D J
U L G Y Q X Q X B V Q S I F U Y U R I
O B L A R N E Y E G D N M V K O X J J
```

- BELFAST
- ERIN
- KILTS
- RAINBOW
- BLARNEY
- GAELIC
- KISS
- SETTER
- CELTIC
- GOLD
- LEPRECHAUN
- SHAMROCK
- COLLEEN
- GREEN
- LIMERICK
- SHILLELAGH
- CORNED BEEF
- HARP
- PATRICK
- SNAKES
- DUBLIN
- JIG
- POTATOES
- TENORS

Spot the Amoeba

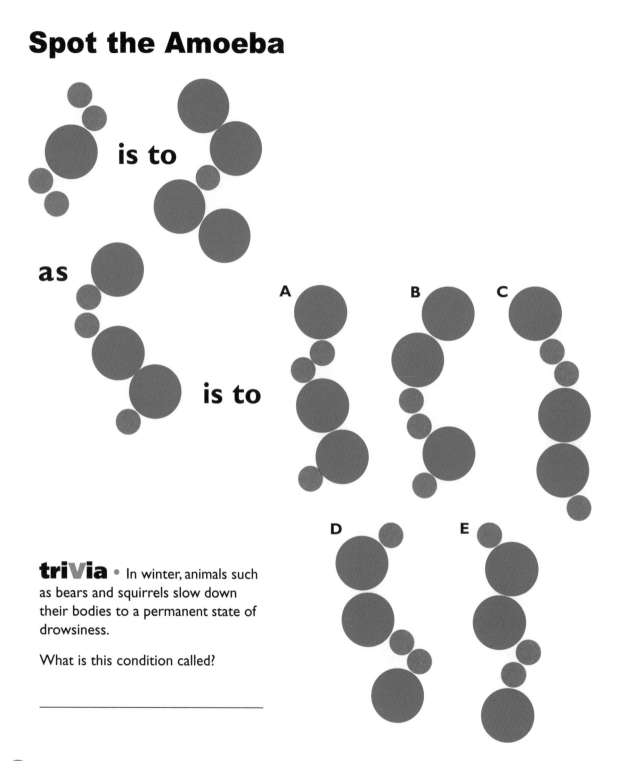

is to

as

is to

A

B

C

D

E

triVia • In winter, animals such as bears and squirrels slow down their bodies to a permanent state of drowsiness.

What is this condition called?

_____

CROSSWORD # Meryl Streep

ACROSS

1 *Star Wars* princess
5 Farther down
10 Cigar ender
14 Sparkling wine
15 Algerian citizen
16 Pillowcase
17 1978 Meryl Streep film (with *The*)
19 Polo of *Meet the Parents*
20 Old Italian currency
21 Checkout slip
23 Wading areas
26 Look like a satyr
27 Said "1, 2, 3 ..."
29 Triple Crown race
32 Puts in one's chips
33 Settle down
35 Michelle Obama, ___ Robinson
36 *Gentlemen Prefer Blondes* author
37 Dog genus
38 Nolo contendere, e.g.
39 Jack Russell's remark
40 Navajo abode
41 Starring roles
42 Whys and wherefores
44 Diner cooking surface
46 Helvetica, e.g.
47 Toed the mark
48 Sally in *Cars*
51 Not yours
52 Requiring irrigation
53 2002 Meryl Streep film
58 Gene sites
59 Hawkins of Dogpatch
60 Site of Shah Jahan's tomb
61 Put film in
62 Joyce Kilmer poem
63 Chicago district

DOWN

1 Boy
2 180° from WNW
3 Adherent
4 Flight paths
5 Paris stock exchange
6 Coastal eagle
7 Back muscle, briefly
8 Nonesuch
9 Like some headphones
10 Hold in honor
11 2011 Meryl Streep film
12 Turf protector
13 Give off rays
18 Saber handles
22 Boston NBAer
23 Graduated
24 Novelist de Balzac
25 1985 Meryl Streep film
28 Uses a grapnel
29 Sound of a bounce
30 Phonograph part
31 Backcombed
34 Homer's "___ Lee Shore"
37 TV adjustment
38 Place for a bust
40 Sharpen
41 The Scales
43 Tawdry
45 Ways to go
48 Ring up
49 Suffix for buck
50 Sixth Jewish month
51 1960s Ronny Howard role
54 Citrus drink
55 "___ to Extremes": Billy Joel
56 Spanish gold
57 Snooze

Binairo

Complete the grid with zeros and ones until there are 6 zeros and 6 ones in every row and every column. No more than two of the same number can be next to or under each other. Rows or columns with exactly the same content are not allowed. There is only one valid solution.

O											
										I	
			O				O				
		O	O			O					
I					O					O	O
	I		O								
		I		I			O				
	I			O			I			I	I
					I					I	
						O					O
	O	O			O						I

ONE LETTER LESS OR MORE

The word on the right side contains the letters of the word on the left side plus or minus the letter in the middle. One letter is already in the right place.

G E M S T O N E -O- **G** ☐ ☐ ☐ ☐

Hourglass

Starting in the middle, each word in the top half has the letters of the word below it, plus a new letter, and each word in the bottom half has the letters of the word above it, plus a new letter.

(1) cuddling
(2) gliding over a mountain slope
(3) male monarchs
(4) submerge
(5) twirl
(6) European country
(7) keyboards
(8) strong emotion

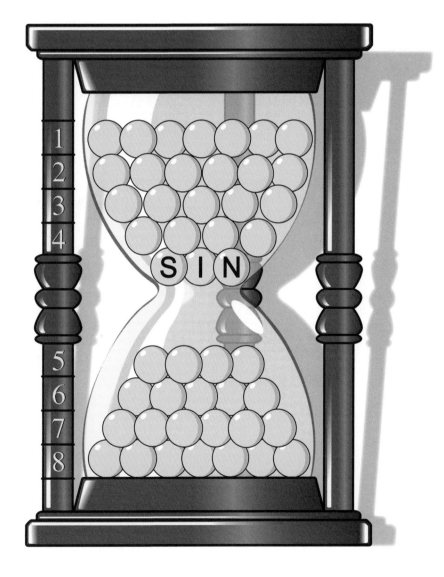

Planetarium 1

ACROSS

1 Egg on
5 Turns hard
9 Indian silk center
14 Homely fruit?
15 Parisian papa
16 Facial cosmetic
17 "___, poor Milan!": Prospero
18 Detrained, e.g.
19 Trainees learn these
20 Ford Escape cousins
23 Calligrapher's need
24 Swear to
25 How Theda Bara acted
29 1972 David Bowie hit
32 Be on cloud nine
33 "Heat Wave" singer Waters
35 "To Autumn," e.g.
36 Annoy greatly
37 All-encompassing
38 Fresh thought
39 Dracula, on occasion
40 Dueling sword
41 Showed obeisance
42 Shoes without laces
44 Frozen spikes
46 Shed feathers
47 "___ a perfumed sea": Poe
48 1948 Ava Gardner film
56 Diameter halves
57 Slack off
58 Flight prefix
59 Jazz groups
60 Poker stake
61 Swedish car
62 Meager
63 Full of good advice
64 Fanning in *Super 8*

DOWN

1 Marianas island
2 Amorous glance
3 Winged
4 Matthew or James
5 They fly in arguments
6 Long and slippery
7 Light haircut
8 Bee bristle
9 Landing
10 At an earlier date
11 Heidi Klum, for one
12 Antiquing "cheater"
13 Clutter
21 Infantry group
22 Gave a "G" or an "R" to
25 Action words
26 Located along a central line
27 Like the iPad
28 Chervil and mint
29 Lewis with Lamb Chop
30 "Set Fire to the Rain" singer
31 ___-foot oil
34 An area of Italy
37 Swazi, e.g.
38 Boost
40 Recital perfomer
41 Ukrainian city
43 Witch's brew
45 Arabica or robusta
48 Table scraps
49 Traffic cop
50 Crab feature
51 Hagar's daughter
52 Mister Ed's lunch
53 Elise in *Hustle & Flow*
54 Eurasian range
55 Beverage with a lizard logo

Sudoku

Fill in the grid so that each row, each column and each 3 x 3 frame contains every number from 1 to 9.

7			3		6	4		
		9					2	
1					2			3
	2		1	5		8		
		7				3		
		8		7	4		1	
8			7					4
	6					5		
		4	6		9			1

do you KNOW?

What was Duke Ellington's first name?

_____

_____

Cage the Animals

Draw lines to completely divide up the grid into small squares with exactly one animal per square. The squares should not overlap.

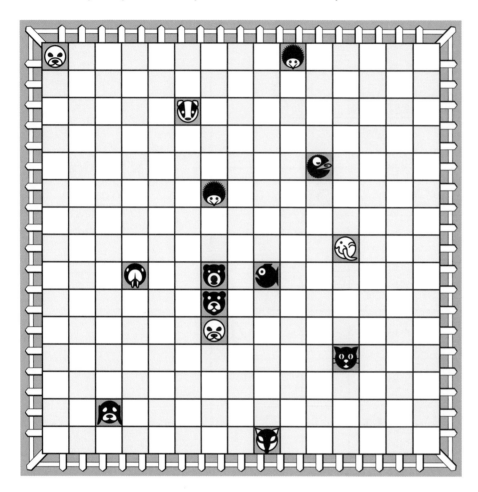

do you **KNOW** ?

What was Mickey Mouse's original name?

_____

_____

LETTERBLOCKS

Move the letterblocks around so that words are formed on top and below that you can associate with rivers. In some blocks, the letter from the top row has been switched with the letter from the bottom row.

CROSSWORD Planetarium 2

ACROSS

1 Charity
5 Blue partner
9 Bathroom floor item
14 Pertaining to the flock
15 "Cotton candy" trumpeter
16 Tannin source
17 Prologue follower
18 NBA All-Star team
19 Any port in a storm
20 1978 Faye Dunaway film
23 Treadmill site, perhaps
24 Pumping object
25 Blow away
29 Michigan State mascot
32 Gets top billing
33 Munched
35 Kerfuffle
36 Hacks
37 ___ Montgomery Ward
38 "___ a Woman": Ray Charles
39 Feel bad
40 PC storage medium
41 Bird similar to a loon
42 "Love Me Tender" singer
44 Pats on the back
46 Short-runway plane
47 Either-___
48 Mozart work in C major
56 Cain's eldest
57 "___ nice place to visit ..."
58 Tart plum
59 Feed a fire
60 Posture
61 Bart Simpson's teacher
62 Blair and Bennett
63 Barks up the wrong tree
64 Hebrew instrument

DOWN

1 Cupid's wings
2 Having a delicate open pattern
3 Plant parasite
4 Salon tool
5 1996 Robert De Niro film
6 Qom coin
7 Major in astronomy?
8 Senate rebuke
9 Like most of Mali
10 Ruckus
11 Edges
12 Desirous look
13 Coastal birds
21 *Mr. Holland's* ___ (1996)
22 Mature
25 Paul Williams' org.
26 Word with case or way
27 1/16 cup
28 Sweetie
29 Savoy dance
30 InDesign company
31 Study aids
34 Venezuelan river
37 "Rolling in the Deep" singer
38 Dún Laoghaire's waters
40 Threads
41 1982 Robin Williams role
43 Like a thief's fingers?
45 New Testament book
48 Bit of funny business
49 Golden rule word
50 Hoar
51 Swish a spoon in
52 Flanders river
53 Reo's creator
54 Forbiddance
55 Time between birthdays

Keep Going

Start on a blank square of your choice and connect as many blank squares as possible with one single continuous line. You can only connect squares along vertical and horizontal lines, not along diagonal lines. You must continue the connecting line up until the next obstacle, i.e., the rim of the box, a black square or a square that has already been used. You can change direction at any obstacle you meet. Each square can only be used once. The number of blank squares that will be left unused is marked in the upper square. There is more than one solution. We only show one solution.

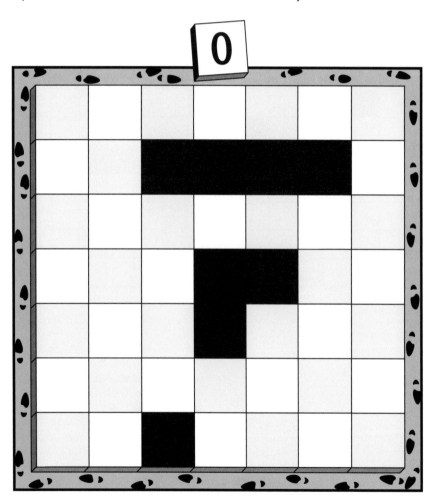

delete ONE

Delete one letter from
GREAT ON VISITS
and find one who is.

WEATHER CHART Sunny

Where will the sun shine? With the knowledge that each arrow points to a place where a symbol should be, can you locate the sunny spots? The symbols cannot be next to each other vertically, horizontally or diagonally. A symbol cannot be placed on top of an arrow. We show one symbol.

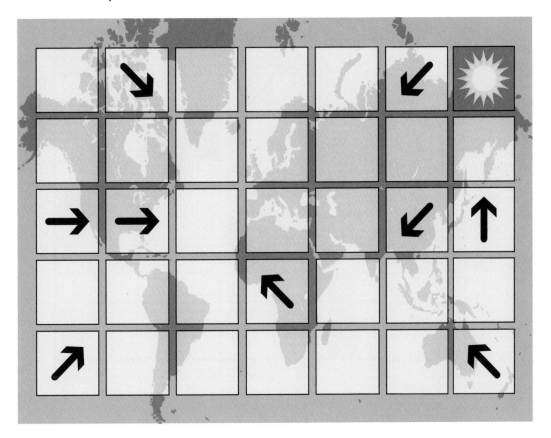

BLOCK ANAGRAM

Form the words that are described in the brackets with the letters above the grid. Extra letters are already in the right place.

PERSIAN (Oscar Best Foreign Language Film 2012)

A			A		T		O	

'70s Hits

ACROSS

1 Oleo squares
5 Darfur's land
10 In the clear for a pass
14 Large land mass
15 Trailer, for one
16 Take the bus
17 "Stayin' Alive" group
19 *Picnic* playwright
20 Apartment balcony
21 Pulled an oar
23 Declare firmly
24 Liesl von Trapp's love
25 ___-do-well
27 Curiosity piece
30 Copier brand
33 *Boléro* composer
35 40-decibel unit
36 Suffix for sheep
37 ___ Aviv
38 Supporter's vote
39 Middle marks
41 ___ four (teacake)
43 Sandler in *Jack and Jill*
44 Zoo bosses
46 Disraeli's nobility
48 Verdi heroine
49 Melancholy
53 Member of the lumpenproletariat
56 Tearoom urn
57 "___ Want to Do": Sugarland
58 "So Far Away" singer
60 "___ Around": Beach Boys
61 Act theatrically
62 Prefix for skeleton
63 Laddie's love
64 Floor samples
65 Breather

DOWN

1 "Too Many Tears" singer LaBelle
2 Grayish
3 Cake layers
4 Audrey Hepburn film
5 Ghost
6 Egg on
7 Nanny goat
8 City near Des Moines
9 Nasal opening
10 1970 World Series winners
11 "Another Brick in the Wall" group
12 Ford SUV
13 "When I ___ You": Sayer
18 Take the pressure off
22 Good name for a thief
26 Scores
27 Contradict
28 ___-Day vitamins
29 Play mates?
30 Rocker Jagger
31 "Of course!"
32 "Hotel California" group
34 Track doc
40 Hard stuff
41 Strutted about
42 Enchilada cousins
43 *Today* weatherman
45 Child-care author LeShan
47 "Tosca" setting
50 Kind of like ewe
51 White ___ Missile Range
52 Grain fungus
53 Colorado ski resort
54 Sea lettuce
55 Change from wild to mild
56 ___ speak (as it were)
59 Gypsy boy

WORD SEARCH Railways

All the words are hidden vertically, horizontally or diagonally—in both directions. The letters that remain unused form a sentence from left to right.

```
R N U M B E R A I L D W A E Y
N S S M E T S T R I K E W L E
I C E J A T I R E D E V L B E
A L R C U E S C O C O A L A P
R S E O U N T Y K D I N O T Y
T W I N S R C S S E E N C E G
S I L D L S I T S F T A O M N
S T D U E R I T I E F D M I A
E C I C E C E N Y O C A O T T
R H E T P T O G G I N T T H E
P B S O E E N R N T G I I S C
X N E R R I N T R E I N V O O
E G L O L F E A T I S H E E N
N I N P E R C T E E D S N T T
H C U E C K N T U R Y O A A A
S O A I M I N I N G T E R P C
C C T H N I Q C I F F A R T T
U Y E T I C K E T O F F I C E
```

- COAL
- CONDUCTOR
- CONTACT
- COUPLING
- CROSSING
- DELAY
- DIESEL
- EXPRESS TRAIN
- INTERCITY
- JUNCTION
- LOCOMOTIVE
- NUMBER
- PASSENGER
- SECTION
- SECURITY
- SIDE-CORRIDOR
- SLEEPER
- STAFF SYSTEM
- STEAM
- STRIKE
- SWITCH
- TICKET
- TICKET OFFICE
- TIMETABLE
- TRACK
- TRAFFIC

Sport Maze

Draw the shortest way from the ball to the goal. You can only move along vertical and horizontal lines, not along diagonal lines. The figure on each square indicates the number of squares the ball must be moved in the same direction. You can change direction at each stop.

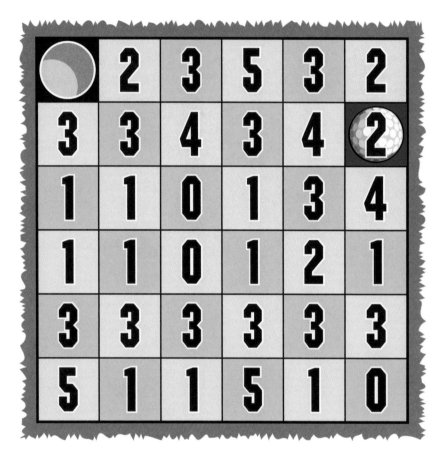

do you KNOW?

Where did Sweeney Todd have his barber shop?

_____

_____

UNCANNY TURN

Rearrange the letters of the phrase below to form a cognate anagram, one which is related or connected in meaning to the original phrase. The answer can be one or more words.

STRONGER AS SINS

Word Sudoku

Complete the grid so that each row, each column and each 3 x 3 frame contains the nine letters from the black box below. The hidden nine-letter word is in the diagonal from top left to bottom right.

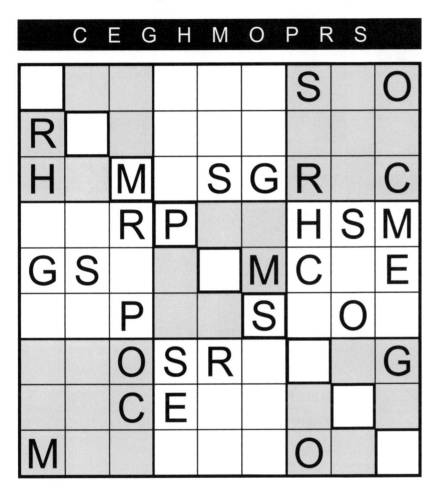

C E G H M O P R S

						S		O
R								
H		M		S	G	R		C
		R	P			H	S	M
G	S				M	C		E
		P			S		O	
		O	S	R				G
		C	E					
M						O		

SANDWICH

What five-letter word belongs between the word on the left and the word on the right, so that the first and second word, and the second and third word, each form a common compound word or phrase?

S L I P _ _ _ _ _ L I N E

Inspiring Women

ACROSS

1 Physicist and Nobel Prize winner Marie
6 Measuring abbrev. in a recipe
9 Container for beans or soup
12 Stage whisper
13 Mens ___, "guilty mind" in criminal law
14 Environmental prefix
15 Put pen to ___
16 Aviation pioneer Amelia
18 Assistants
20 Computer operator
21 Deaf-blind activist Helen
24 Overweight
25 Long-legged wading bird
26 Popular restaurant for breakfast (abbrev.)
29 Initials for an agenda
30 Prevent
31 Cotton gin inventor Whitney
34 Singer Horne
35 Makeup brand
36 Russian rulers
40 Mother ___ of Calcutta
42 Air prefix, as in "___sphere"
43 Secret or literary ___
45 Actress and humanitarian Audrey
47 Capital of Bangladesh
51 Iron ___
52 Little green veggie
53 Opposite of inner
54 Final
55 Used a chair
56 Diarist Anne

DOWN

1 Baseball ___
2 Canada's neighbor (abbrev.)
3 Tear
4 Standards of perfection
5 Creepy
6 Willow or oak
7 Sail the seven ___
8 Average in golf
9 Stop
10 Units of measurement on a farm
11 ___ Dame
17 Center of activity
19 Operate a car
21 First aid ___
22 ___ and flow
23 Cover
24 Choose
27 Female chicken
28 Give a speech
30 Charity for the ice bucket challenge (abbrev.)
31 Adam's counterpart
32 ___ Angeles
33 Steven Curtis Chapman song "See You ___ Little While" (2 words)
35 King ___ of Camelot
36 California-Nevada lake
37 Strict
38 Full of nervous energy
39 Steal
41 "The ___ ___ the Innocence," song by Don Henley (2 words)
43 Zone
44 Little pesky fly
46 Delivery service (abbrev.)
48 One ___ time (2 words)
49 Barbie's boyfriend
50 Noah's boat

Q&A

A question-and-answer session featuring the letters *q* and *a*—
may leave you in a quagmire. So if you're stumped by our q's, don't fear,
answers are in the back of the book.

. . . .

1. qua ('kwah) *prep.*—A: from top to bottom. B: beforehand. C: as, in the capacity of.

2. quay ('key) *n.*—A: wharf. B: game played with mallets. C: fox hunted by hounds.

3. quaff ('kwahf) *v.*—A: swing and miss. B: drink deeply. C: sing Christmas carols.

4. quasi ('kway- or 'kwah-zi) *adj.*—A: from a foreign country. B: having some resemblance. C: feeling seasick.

5. quahog ('co- or 'kwahhog) *n.*—A: edible clam. B: half penny. C: motorcycle sidecar.

6. quantum ('kwahn-tum) *n.*—A: type of comet. B: specified amount. C: Australian marsupial.

7. quaver ('kway-ver) *v.*—A: change your vote. B: sink down low. C: sound tremulous.

8. quinoa ('keen-wah or 'kee-no-eh) *n.*—A: grain from the Andes. B: beehive shape. C: chewable resin gum.

9. quondam ('kwahn-dem) *adj.*—A: enormous. B: former. C: backward or upside down.

10. quetzal (ket-'sall) *n.*—A: bow-shaped pasta. B: tropical bird. C: mica used in mirrors.

11. quatrain ('kwah-train) *n.*—A: end-of-semester test. B: underground railroad. C: four-line verse.

12. quiniela ('kwin-ye-la) *n.*—A: type of bet. B: porcupine's bristle. C: cheesy Mexican dish.

13. quotidian (kwoh-'ti-dee-en) *adj.*—A: janitorial. B: occurring every day. C: showing off one's knowledge.

14. quacksalver ('kwak-sal-ver) *n.*—A: ointment. B: glue. C: fraud or phony doctor.

15. quinquennial (kwin-'kwen-nee-el) *adj.*—A: of thigh muscles. B: flowing freely. C: occurring every five years.

Sudoku X

Fill in the grid so that each row, each column and each 3 x 3 frame contains every number from 1 to 9. The two main diagonals of the grid also contain every number from 1 to 9.

			6					
		2	3				8	
				2		3		
4	3						2	
		5	4	9		7		
8	1			3	2	4	9	
	2	4	8	7	9			
	7	8				2		
	9	3		6		5		

do you **KNOW**?

Which artist painted "American Gothic"?

_____

_____

LETTER LINE

Put a letter in each of the squares below to make a word which is "PART OF CLOTHING." The number clues refer to other words that can be made from the whole.

6 5 1 9 10 UPRIGHT; 1 5 5 4 7 DINER SEATING; 1 9 2 10 CAN BE A FEELING; 4 2 1 10 CONTAINER; 2 6 1 8 9 3 OPEN

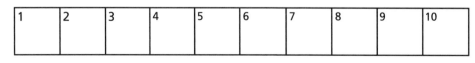

1	2	3	4	5	6	7	8	9	10

CROSSWORD Shaker Stuff

ACROSS

1 Office worker, at times
5 Robin Cook novel
9 Scottish musician
14 Riding the waves
15 UAE neighbor
16 Fred Astaire's sister
17 "Shoop" group
19 Conical residence
20 Endure
21 Slightly injured
23 "___ the first cock crow": Shak.
24 Sacred ceremony
25 Hold down
29 Swiss resort
32 Outward images
33 Salma in *Grown Ups*
35 Broadway's *Five Guys Named* ___
36 Hannibal's hurdles
37 Greek slave
38 Jack's tumbling partner
39 Savvy
40 Golfer Baddeley
41 Three-card ___
42 Sweet girl of song
44 More sugary
46 San ___ (Riviera resort)
47 Globe
48 Beethoven opera
51 Gets to Kennedy
55 Light on one's feet
56 Vodka-grapefruit juice drinks
58 Roadwork markers
59 Sound of relief
60 Joie de vivre
61 Copse members
62 "___ Without Rain": Enya
63 Romero and Rorem

DOWN

1 Cold War news agency
2 "Hairy man" in Genesis
3 *Alice* diner
4 Dressmaking guides
5 Knockoffs
6 Telltale sign
7 Travel guide
8 Teal genus
9 Swayze in *Dirty Dancing*
10 Come up with something
11 Patty of "Peanuts"
12 Robert at Appomattox
13 Bassoonist's purchase
18 Nostrils
22 Vinegar bottle
25 Brando's birthplace
26 In heaps
27 L.A. college
28 Hite of sex research
29 French cathedral city
30 Nick in *Warrior*
31 Conger catcher
34 Santo Domingo greeting
37 Vietnam city
38 47th U.S. Vice President
40 Without purpose
41 Festive
43 Sobieski in *The Wicker Man*
45 Deserving
48 Not fancy
49 Aeronautics pioneer Sikorsky
50 Tasmania's highest peak
51 One-celled plant
52 Lemming relative
53 "By Jove!"
54 Nine-digit IDs
57 Assistance

Kakuro

Each number in a black area is the sum of the numbers that you have to enter in the next empty boxes. The empty boxes that make up the sum are called a run. The sum of the across run is written above the diagonal in the black area and the sum of the down run is written below the diagonal in the black area. Runs can only contain the numbers 1 through 9 and each number in a run can only be used once. The gray boxes only contain odd numbers and the white only even numbers.

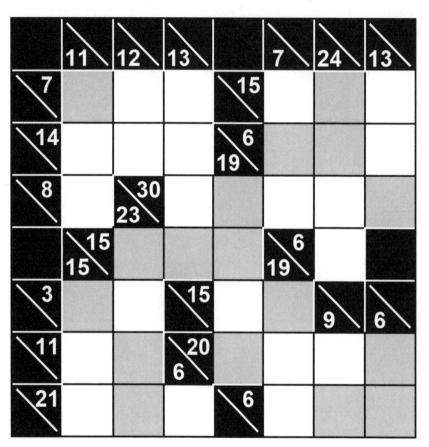

do you KNOW

Which sport includes pikes and twists?

_____

_____

FRIENDS

What do the following words have in common?

STREET WATER MOON SNOW TOWN CITY

Spot the Differences

Find the nine differences in the image on the bottom right.

Who is
Gladstone Gander's
cousin?

_____

_____

trivia

• Name of the lion befriended by
the children in C. S. Lewis's series
of Narnia stories

_____

CROSSWORD George Clooney

ACROSS

1 Persian monarch
5 Rocky rival Apollo
10 Order
14 Door feature, perhaps
15 Imposing swarm
16 Fabled loser
17 Nick and Nora's pet
18 Out on the waves
19 Big-budget film
20 Where George was Matt King
23 Tennis do-over
24 "Achy Breaky Heart" singer: Init.
25 Earned an Olympic podium spot
29 Bush Supreme Court pick
33 Molecular constituent
34 Blunt or Deschanel
36 "___-hunting we will go ..."
37 Where George was Billy Tyne
41 High hill
42 Alicia Keys hit
43 Banana stalk
44 Perfume
46 Picture puzzles
49 "Disgusting!"
50 Jollity
51 Where George was Mike Morris
59 Feudal estate
60 Ocarina-shaped
61 Lunar sea
62 Stocking shade
63 Derived from wine
64 Dietary supplement
65 Winter air
66 To-be, in politics
67 Bar-tacks

DOWN

1 Soon-forgotten quarrel
2 Corned-beef ___
3 Poker throw-in
4 Miner's light
5 Uncorrupted
6 College military org.
7 Highland language
8 Eve's birthplace
9 It's a lock
10 Question regarding origin
11 More than engaged
12 Purple bloom
13 Sleuth, slangily
21 Slitherer in the water
22 Beefy fast-food chain
25 Dull finish
26 Societal standards
27 They walk the walk
28 Creator of Crusoe
29 Kitchen gadget
30 Origins
31 Magi number
32 Emma in *Supernova*
35 *A Few Good* ___ (1992)
38 World-weary feeling
39 Pigeon
40 Scary waves
45 A lot to see
47 Result
48 Loafer
51 Native Costa Rican
52 Roll response
53 Dastardly doings
54 Compos mentis
55 Of the ear
56 Like the spotted owl
57 Brag
58 *Chicken Run* prisoners
59 Quagmire

BRAINSNACK® Resistance

Which resistor (A or B) is missing here?

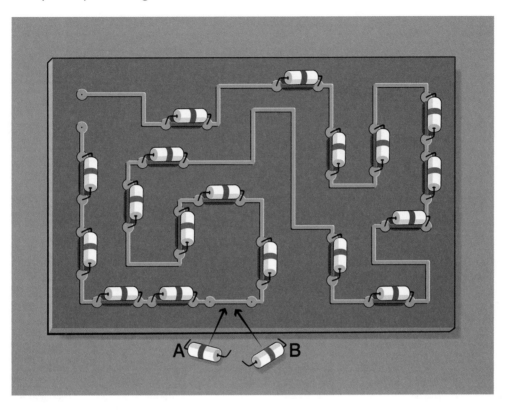

QUICK WORD SEARCH

Find the CANINE terms listed below in the grid.

```
I  P  P  P  O  M  Y  N  S  P  Q  F  P  V  Y
G  U  Z  W  K  R  X  C  U  I  O  R  W  A  F
W  G  O  J  R  O  F  P  M  O  T  R  T  A  L
X  H  C  B  O  X  E  R  W  W  P  S  U  O  G
C  F  B  A  R  K  R  I  G  J  V  L  G  N  Q
```

BOXER CHOW POM PUG PUP WAG SIT STAY WOOF BARK

One Among Many

You'll see what looks like several identical items. Only one item in the each bunch is different from the others. Find and circle that item.

1

triVia • The ears of an African elephant can be over 3 ft. wide.

Apart from improving the elephant's hearing, what other purpose do they serve?

_____

2

3

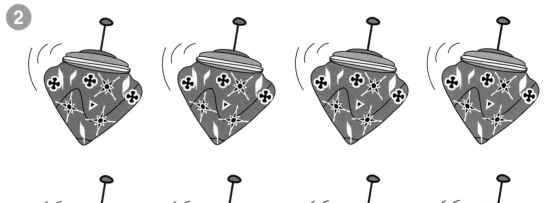

Fun in the Sun

All the words are hidden vertically, horizontally or diagonally—
in both directions.

A	Y	E	K	S	A	Z	V	O	I	R	O	Y	W	T	O	B	N	Q
N	K	L	S	E	A	V	H	R	D	O	Y	B	R	X	O	G	H	B
A	J	C	B	N	T	W	I	D	L	V	O	U	F	A	P	O	O	L
Y	W	I	O	R	O	U	X	W	D	Z	N	U	R	E	Z	Z	L	J
Y	B	S	F	N	L	R	E	G	L	K	V	D	O	C	D	U	J	T
T	Y	P	W	E	E	C	K	N	S	I	W	N	W	A	G	W	A	N
O	Z	O	A	E	M	I	M	E	O	A	F	H	M	A	S	F	R	D
W	R	P	V	R	O	F	S	N	L	I	W	E	E	D	Z	O	S	R
E	G	K	E	C	N	T	T	K	P	V	T	S	G	Q	M	J	L	Z
L	I	F	S	S	A	Y	F	R	U	S	I	A	U	U	C	K	S	I
G	N	K	E	N	D	C	E	P	E	W	T	M	C	R	A	J	A	V
J	I	A	X	U	E	R	H	S	O	M	B	L	A	A	F	R	N	Q
Q	K	Y	X	S	O	S	S	A	V	B	M	Y	S	E	V	V	D	A
Y	I	A	Y	H	A	A	V	V	S	B	A	I	D	G	L	J	Z	W
P	B	K	S	L	L	C	P	X	B	C	L	I	W	R	C	K	K	M
R	B	A	P	G	X	B	U	Z	H	F	P	B	V	S	Q	P	Q	O
D	E	S	N	W	P	F	L	T	A	Y	D	Z	C	Y	H	B	V	I
S	J	U	N	R	J	F	C	K	F	G	O	G	G	L	E	S	Q	O
S	S	B	E	A	C	H	N	E	E	B	S	I	R	F	C	O	S	C

- GOGGLES
- SURF
- SNORKEL
- TRUNKS
- BEACH
- POPSICLE
- POOL
- SAND
- VACATION
- TOWEL
- SUNSCREEN
- LIFEGUARD
- SEAGULL
- SUNGLASSES
- WAVES
- SWIMMER
- BIKINI
- YACHT
- LEMONADE
- BOARDWALK
- SEASHORE
- SPLASH
- FRISBEE
- KAYAK

BRAINSNACK® Go Fly

Which kite (1–6) does not belong?

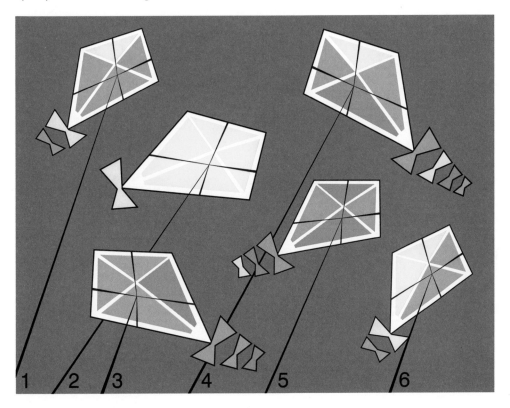

QUICK CROSSWORD

Place the words listed below in the crossword grid.

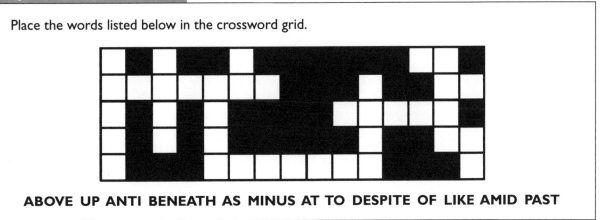

ABOVE UP ANTI BENEATH AS MINUS AT TO DESPITE OF LIKE AMID PAST

Next in Line

Study the sequence below and figure out which image should come next.

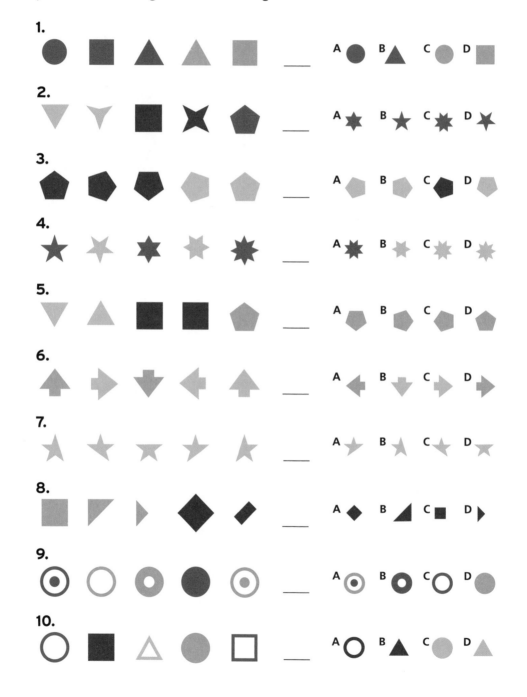

Sudoku

Fill in the grid so that each row, each column and each 3 x 3 frame contains every number from 1 to 9.

		4			3	5		
	8	1					4	3
	5		4	8				
			2	6			1	7
4				3				2
1	3			7	9			
				4	6		2	
7	2					4	8	
		9	8			6		

do you KNOW?

Who wrote
"My love is like a red,
red rose"?

_____

_____

BRAINSNACK® Gridlock

Which number should replace the question mark?

QUICK WORD SEARCH

Find the TENNIS terms listed below in the grid.

```
G Y L B A Q A T M E Y N F X B
K A W O S U T L I V F O R T Y
A H M T V C M O X T M R T L T
C W U E H E I B E H T S K E Z
E O U Q I G W S D O Q R N T P
```

LOVE MIXED NET OUT SET ACE FORTY GAME LET LOB

CROSSWORD '00s Hits

ACROSS

1 Land in a depression
5 Jeweler's glass
10 Joyous
14 Waxed cheese
15 DuPont acrylic fiber
16 Lacoste founder, _____Lacoste
17 "You're Beautiful" singer
19 Geraldine Chaplin's mom
20 *The Devil's Dictionary* author Bierce
21 Killed by submergence
23 Make believe
24 Italian summer resort
25 Crept up on
29 Sports page listings
32 Stick fast
33 Brother of Romulus
35 Father of François
36 Black cuckoo
37 Slow pitch
38 Wheaton of *Star Trek: TNG*
39 Bridal shower
41 Botanical shelter
43 Seven Dwarfs' workplace
44 Christmas tree trimming
46 Formidable foe
48 *GoldenEye* villain Trevelyan
49 Have some catching up to do
50 Some native Canadians
53 Do the voice-over
57 Two-___ (ballroom dance)
58 "Party in the U.S.A." singer
60 Hula hoops and yo-yos
61 Parisian school
62 Displays
63 Building projection
64 Bard of old
65 Geese that rarely swim

DOWN

1 "___ Vu": Warwick
2 Rock star Ant
3 Moussaka meat
4 Gemstone
5 Maine delicacy
6 Heraldic border
7 Curved Eskimo knife
8 Pollywog's home
9 Plats du jour
10 Like Peter Pan in *Hook*
11 "Bleeding Love" singer
12 Bancroft or Murray
13 The Grateful ___
18 Anklet
22 Put-___ (spoofs)
25 Lamb Chop's friend Lewis
26 Mixologist's mixer
27 "No One" singer
28 Site of an oracle of Apollo
29 Blades in *Predator 2*
30 "If I Had a Hammer" singer Lopez
31 Monica of tennis
34 Trim a fairway
40 High-level cover-up?
41 Turns into
42 Passed the baton
43 *Sleepless in Seattle* star
45 Moon craft, for short
47 Mr. Chagall
50 "Cómo ___ usted?"
51 Street sign
52 Ailing
53 Paramour of England's Charles II
54 Indy-winner Luyendyk
55 Move
56 Latin 101 infinitive
59 Mauna ___

TRIVIA QUIZ Cool Cats

Cats may be our most popular pet with over 600 million estimated
to be in homes all over the world.
How well do you know your favorite felines?

1. What feature does a Manx cat lack?
   a. Vocal cords
   b. A tail
   c. Fur
   d. Whiskers

2. Which member of the big cat family is the world's fastest animal on land?
   a. Cheetah
   b. Leopard
   c. Panther
   d. Lion

3. Which is the largest of the big cats?
   a. Tiger
   b. Lion
   c. Jaguar
   d. Wildcat

4. Which of the big cats can be found in both cold and warm climates?
   a. Cougar
   b. Tiger
   c. Leopard
   d. Snow leopard

5. Which spotted cat, found in the lowland areas from Texas to northern Argentina, has short, smooth fur patterned with black-edged spots?
   a. Manx
   b. Mountain lion
   c. Ocelot
   d. Cheetah

6. What is distinctive about the Sphynx cat?
   a. Its hairlessness
   b. Its almond-shaped eyes
   c. Its especially long incisors
   d. Its ability to understand Egyptian

7. Which big cat is unique in not being able to fully retract its claws?
   a. Cheetah
   b. Lion
   c. Tiger
   d. Cougar

8. What breed of domestic cat can be fully colored blue, brown, chocolate, lilac, red, or tortoiseshell?
   a. Persian
   b. Burmese
   c. Abyssinian
   d. Siamese

9. Which modern breed of domestic cat is considered to be closest to the cats of ancient Egypt?
   a. Abyssinian
   b. Siamese
   c. Burmese
   d. Rex

10. Which of the following is not a wild species of cat in Europe?
    a. Lynx
    b. Wildcat
    c. Manx
    d. Tabby

Keep Going

Start on a blank square of your choice and connect as many blank squares as possible with one single continuous line. You can only connect squares along vertical and horizontal lines, not along diagonal lines. You must continue the connecting line up until the next obstacle, i.e., the rim of the box, a black square or a square that has already been used. You can change direction at any obstacle you meet. Each square can only be used once. The number of blank squares that will be left unused is marked in the upper square. There is more than one solution. We only show one solution.

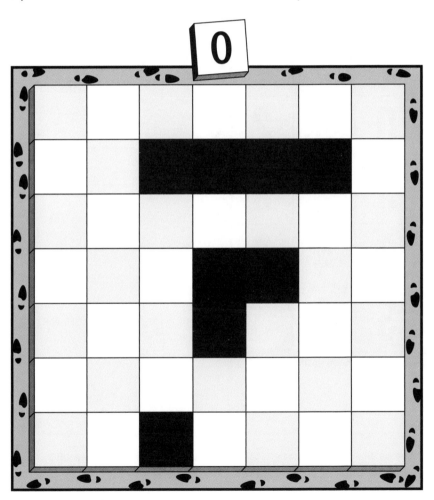

delete ONE

Delete one letter
from
PIONEER
and find another
first word.

Sport Maze

Draw the shortest way from the ball to the goal. You can only move along vertical and horizontal lines, not along diagonal lines. The figure on each square indicates the number of squares the ball must be moved in the same direction. You can change direction at each stop.

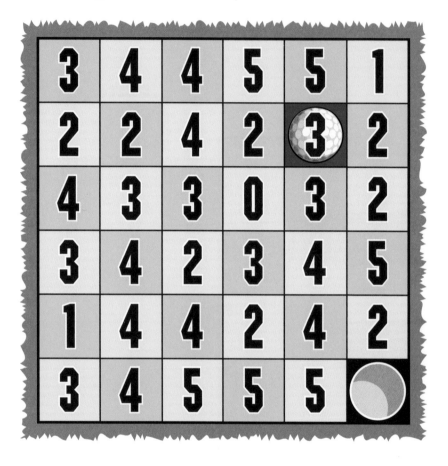

do you KNOW?

Who wrote
Lolita?

_____

_____

UNCANNY TURN

Rearrange the letters of the phrase below to form a cognate anagram, one which is related or connected in meaning to the original phrase. The answer can be one or more words.

A SORE POINT

CROSSWORD Sticks and Stones

ACROSS

1 Three Stooges blow
5 Squash rebound
10 Electric GM car
14 Trevi Fountain request
15 With mouth wide open
16 Dunkable cookie
17 "An apple ___ keeps ..."
18 Schnozz-related
19 Praise for toreadors
20 STICKS
23 *ER* setting
24 Ark unit
25 Drop
29 Pressurized spray
33 Cantina pot
34 Capital near the Gulf of Tonkin
36 *The Aviator* airline
37 STONES
41 Probable lifetime
42 Santa Clara chip maker
43 Laine of jazz
44 Absolute rulers
46 Rolle and Williams
49 Irish sea god
50 Lao-tzu's principle
51 "Sticks and stones ___ ..."
60 Tricky move
61 Group of TV experts
62 Franco in *Camelot*
63 River of Hesse
64 Peace goddess
65 Good's counterpart
66 Grunge
67 "Monopoly" cards
68 Leaf collector

DOWN

1 Quid pro quo
2 Italian resort island
3 Quickly, in memos
4 Bodily
5 Mexican island resort
6 "I've got ___ she's Big Foot Sal ..."
7 Level to the ground, in London
8 Colorful fish
9 Small reed organ
10 Witchcraft
11 Architectural fillet
12 Salacious glance
13 Pitch
21 Cold cube
22 Gruesome
25 Robert of *The 39 Steps*
26 Thomas Gray work
27 More foxy
28 "___ all, folks!"
29 Lizard
30 Snatched
31 Team bigwig
32 Populous African city
35 1952 hit "Botch-___"
38 Eatery in *The Sting*
39 Sporty Dodge
40 Grand Banks vessel
45 Alligator in *Pogo*
47 Does a salon job
48 Keyboard key
51 "A horse is a horse" horse
52 Bavarian car company
53 River to the North Sea
54 River rising in the Bernese Alps
55 Shinbone end
56 Darn with thread
57 Gulf of Finland feeder
58 Composer Satie
59 A flatfish

Futoshiki

Fill in the 5 x 5 grid with the numbers from 1 to 5 once per row and column, while following the greater than/lesser than symbols shown. There is only one valid solution that can be reached through logic and clear thinking alone!

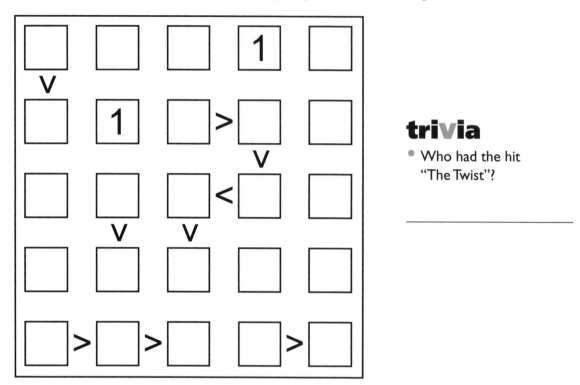

trivia

• Who had the hit "The Twist"?

_____

CONNECT TWO

An oxymoron is a combination of seemingly contradictory or incongruous words, such as "science fiction" (science means "knowledge or study dealing with facts or truth" while fiction means "an imagined or invented creation"). Connect the words with meanings that oppose each other and make oxymorons.

ALMOST	ROUTINE
STUNTED	SHOW
TALK	READY
UNUSUAL	GROWTH

Word Sudoku

Complete the grid so that each row, each column and each 3 x 3 frame contains the nine letters from the black box below. The hidden nine-letter word is in the diagonal from top left to bottom right.

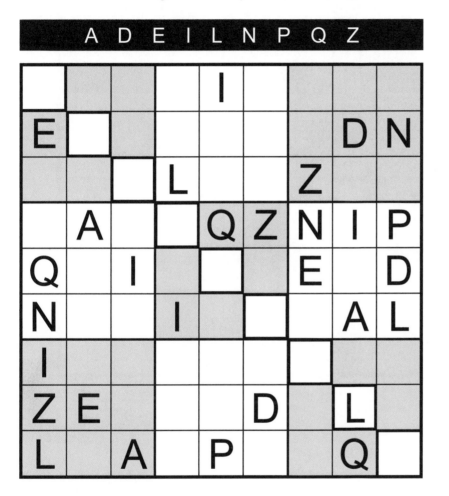

A D E I L N P Q Z

				I				
E							D	N
		L				Z		
	A			Q	Z	N	I	P
Q		I				E		D
N			I				A	L
I								
Z	E				D		L	
L		A		P			Q	

do you KNOW?

Who killed Polonius?

_____

_____

SANDWICH

What four-letter word belongs between the word on the left and the word on the right, so that the first and second word, and the second and third word, each form a common compound word or phrase?

CROSS _ _ _ _ RUNNER

Stormy Weather

ACROSS

1 Serb, e.g.
5 Hard to deal with
10 Store safely
14 Prefix for "scope"
15 Bellybutton type
16 Cronyn in *Lifeboat*
17 Goes to a restaurant
18 Asian river and range
19 Lombardy Castle city
20 1990 A-ha hit
23 Mother's hermana
24 Cutup
25 Starbucks worker
29 Expert with a joystick
33 Once more, in Dogpatch
34 One may be seen on a model
36 Before, to Keats
37 1952 Debbie Reynolds film
41 Game stew meat
42 What Grafton's "N" stands for
43 Under sail
44 Purifies, in a way
46 Zinc-carbon battery
49 Shania Twain hit
50 "A mouse!"
51 2000 Enya album
60 Make espresso
61 High times
62 River through the Czech Republic
63 Theda of silent films
64 Pre-meal recitation
65 Terrible twos responses
66 Words on some cigars
67 Sometimes they battle
68 Primer

DOWN

1 Many authors write on it
2 *All in the Family* producer
3 Dilettantish
4 Calling on
5 Snickers ingredient
6 Ear: Prefix
7 Shaw in *Fried Green Tomatoes*
8 Pinball term
9 Rabbinical seminary
10 Native of Himalayan slopes
11 Fish in a casserole
12 Futuristic magazine
13 Gradually withdraw (from)
21 Birthplace of Constantine the Great
22 Hirsch in *The Emperor's Club*
25 Working (out of)
26 Twinkle-toed
27 Places for curlers
28 "So long, Sancho!"
29 Feigned
30 Pester
31 Window for plants
32 Near the kidneys
35 Some dashes
38 Acquired relative
39 Whisper sweet ____
40 Greedy landlord's income
45 "Nevertheless ..."
47 Utilizes a hand-me-down
48 Eventually
51 "Fernando" group
52 Humdrum
53 Designed to minimize wind resistance
54 Put a rip in
55 Paul is dead, e.g.
56 It's enough, according to some
57 Emollient ingredient
58 Mountain goat
59 Wren's dwelling

WORD SEARCH Journalism

All the words are hidden vertically, horizontally or diagonally—in both directions. The letters that remain unused form a sentence from left to right.

```
T E L E V I S I O N S A E R J
S P E E D O U R N L A Z T A N
W O B D L I Y C A V I R P D M
E L I S I T O N I R O C M I U
B I L E S T D S P P A G E O L
L T A N O E O R S C O O P S O
O I W H R E E R E R S T H P C
G C P E Q Z Y C S U E M R S T
I S O N T S O A O W W E N H O
R E G I O N T B S E S D E R W
L H L A O S J T I S T I W E D
A U W M E E R V R H E A S U E
P E Y N C A R E S W E N P T S
T R O T I E L E W H E N A E A
O H I N T E R N E T W H P R I
P V I N A N O I T A S N E S B
E N I S N O I S S E F O R P Y
G A E N S C A N D A L D H O W
```

- BIASED
- COLUMN
- ECONOMY
- EDITORS
- ESSAY
- HONEST
- INTERNET
- INTERVIEW
- LAPTOP
- LIBEL
- MEDIA
- NEWS
- NEWSPAPER
- OBJECTIVE
- PHOTO
- POLITICS
- PRESS RELEASE
- PRIVACY
- PROFESSION
- PULITZER PRIZE
- RADIO
- REGION
- REUTERS
- SCANDAL
- SCOOP
- SENSATION
- SLANDER
- SPEED
- SPORT
- TELEVISION
- TRAINING
- WEBLOG

Sudoku Twin

Fill in the grid so that each row, each column and each 3 x 3 frame contains every number from 1 to 9. A sudoku twin is two connected 9 x 9 sudokus.

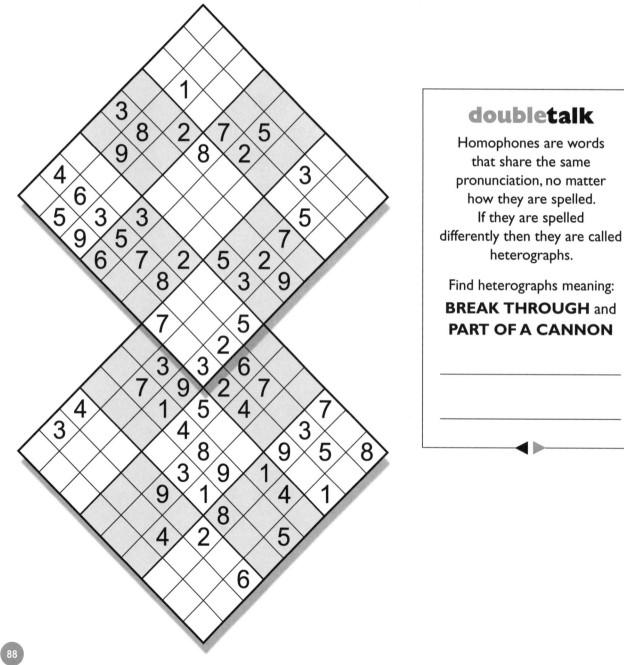

CROSSWORD In the Backyard

ACROSS

1 Wander down a gravel ___ in the backyard
5 *Finding* ___
9 Monkees song, "___ Believer" (2 words)
12 Inkling
13 Skating rink shape
14 "My country, ___ of thee..."
15 Sports group
16 Spot for feathered friends to frolic in the backyard
18 Shopping center
20 Hubbub
21 Go against
24 Woodland deities
25 ___ and field
26 Jogged
27 Tick ___
28 Cooking vessel
29 Tool or potting ___ in the backyard
33 Small drop
34 Native of Havana
35 Flavorful Italian herb
39 Mrs. in Madrid
40 Popular mineral water
41 Trudge
42 Home for Fido in the backyard
44 Small bit
48 Lute kin, in brief
49 Defrost
50 Once more
51 Apiece
52 Salamanders
53 Solitary

DOWN

1 Throw another log into the fire ___ in the backyard
2 Fruit drink
3 Steeped beverage
4 Swaying spot for a nap in the backyard
5 Upstanding
6 Nefarious
7 Blemish
8 *The* ___ *and the Sea* (2 words)
9 Home for Rome
10 Wood joint
11 Campfire leftovers
17 Wager
19 Request
21 Hall of Famer Mel
22 Not an amateur
23 Special interest group that raises money (acronym)
24 Used a chair
26 Steal
28 Buddy
29 Clock in the backyard
30 Cable channel
31 Play it by ___
32 Gene-carrying substance
33 Indicate
34 Business president (abbrev.)
35 Exasperated (2 words)
36 Elicit
37 Country covered by the Sahara
38 Slangy "no"
39 Turns sideways
41 Early college test (abbrev.)
43 Abbreviation on early TVs
45 Artist Yoko
46 "Perfect" number
47 Reverence

Building Blocks

Where (A–E) do building blocks 1, 2 and 3 belong?

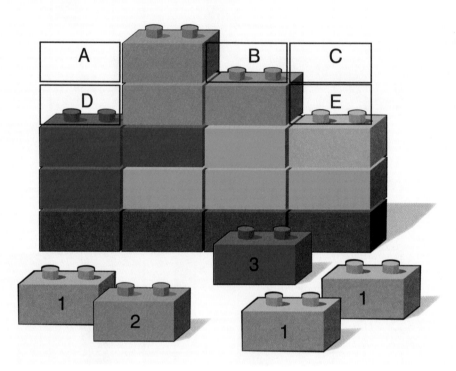

QUICK CROSSWORD

Place the NEWSPAPER terms listed below in the crossword grid.

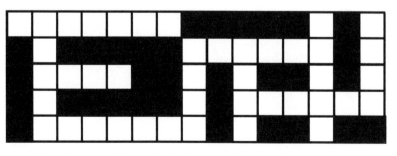

FEATURE COLUMN TEXT EXTRA INDEX FONT ADVERT APOLOGY COPY LEAD

Binairo

Complete the grid with zeros and ones until there are 6 zeros and 6 ones in every row and every column. No more than two of the same number can be next to or under each other. Rows or columns with exactly the same content are not allowed. There is only one valid solution.

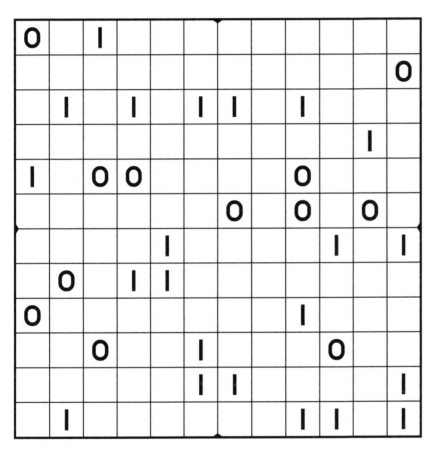

delete ONE

Delete one letter from **HOSPITAL TOGAS** and find someone who might wear one.

ONE LETTER LESS OR MORE

The word on the right side contains the letters of the word on the left side plus or minus the letter in the middle. One letter is already in the right place.

| B | A | R | N | D | O | O | R | -R | | | B | | | | |

Hoofers

ACROSS

1 Sew with an egg
5 Snopes subject
9 Cossack's weapon
14 Canal to Oneida Lake
15 Mr. Saarinen
16 Shy of a treaty
17 *Sugar Babies* dancer
19 Exorcised
20 FBI head?
21 Mighty mount
23 "Seventh ___": Johnny Rivers
24 Correct a key problem?
27 Mattress coils
31 Artisans in clay
32 Thereby
33 Like some seals
35 Like ___ out of hell
36 Emblem of sovereignty
37 Impertinence
38 MTA stop
39 Installs carpeting
41 "___ porridge hot …"
43 Pickled root
44 Edmonton football team
46 Hardly mild
48 Liam who voiced Aslan
49 Lupine lair
50 Piece for the piano
52 Ricocheted
56 Monica of tennis
58 *Singin' in the Rain* dancer
60 Crystal-gazers
61 Pâté de foie ___
62 4-point H, e.g.
63 Unlike filibusters
64 Pre-college exams
65 *The Wind in the Willows* hero

DOWN

1 Heedless
2 *The Temple of Dullness* composer
3 Orange zest source
4 Ness vis-à-vis Capone
5 Jumble
6 Team booster
7 Three, in Roma
8 ___ d'oeuvres
9 Concourse
10 Short operatic piece
11 *Broadway Melody of 1938* dancer
12 Prefix for sphere
13 One whistling at athletes
18 Rustable metal
22 Stomped
25 Jabbers on
26 Waugh's Brideshead, e.g.
27 Purloined
28 Expression
29 *42nd Street* dancer
30 Gross receipts
31 Gatorade parent
34 Sea inlet
40 *Hannah and Her ___* (1986)
41 Swimming hole
42 Lasting forever
43 "Just in Time" singer Tony
45 Creamy dessert
47 Boat wood
51 Clutch in a coop
52 Black fly
53 Ad writer's honor
54 Jazz giant Fitzgerald
55 Colored artificially
56 Rapid transport of yore
57 Wide shoe width
59 NOW objective, once

BRAINSNACK® Intersection

Which intersection (1–9) is missing a red circle?

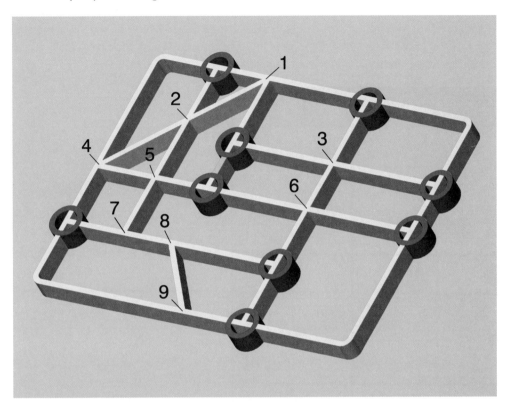

Horoscope

Fill in the grid so that every row, every column and every frame of six boxes contains six different symbols: health, work, money, happiness, family and love. Look at the row or column that corresponds with your sign of the zodiac and find out which of the six symbols are important for you today. The symbols appear in increasing order of importance (1–6). It's up to you to translate the meaning of each symbol to your specific situation.

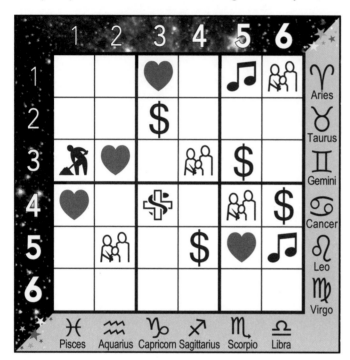

do you **KNOW**

Who had the
1979 hit
"Let's Go"?

_____

_____

END GAME

The words you are seeking all have the letters END in them in the position indicated.
When you have found all of the answers with help from the clues on the right, one column will reveal the END GAME word and give you an emotional feeling.

__	__	__	**E**	**N**	**D**	__	__	__	Rising toward the zenith
__	__	__	__	__	**E**	**N**	**D**	__	Gradual volume increase
__	__	__	__	**E**	**N**	**D**	__	__	Drink dispenser
E	**N**	**D**	__	__	__	__	__	__	Eleven sides and angles

CROSSWORD Hard Stuff

ACROSS

1 College mil. program
5 Letter after rho
10 Like two peas in ___
14 Con ___ (spiritedly)
15 Diet guru Jenny
16 Tackle box item
17 "Holy Smoke" band
19 Federal law officer
20 Hustler in *The Hustler*
21 *Beatles for Sale* song
23 Rickles zinger
26 Femme's husband
27 Venomous snake
29 Makes conscious (of)
32 Molding style
33 Novarro of silent films
35 *The Morning Watch* novelist
36 "As if, laddie!"
37 Male swan
38 "___ had better days"
39 Steve Harvey column "Only ___"
41 Union Pacific stop
43 Derby projection
44 Wranglers
46 1979 Janis Joplin biopic
48 *Laugh-In* giggler
49 Came down
50 Outstanding, as a performance
53 Goalie's glove
54 Mars: Comb. form
55 Superman's sobriquet
60 Ceramics oven
61 Not merely sluggish
62 Impose a tax on
63 ___ dixit (no proof needed)
64 Subtly mean
65 Exuberance

DOWN

1 Stat for a Dodger
2 Bruin Hall-of-Famer
3 Nadal's uncle
4 Prove wrong
5 Disperse
6 Six-petaled flower
7 Type of fly
8 Way of carrying oneself
9 Additional name
10 Batna's country
11 Bodybuilding film of 1977
12 Said aloud
13 Make a counterstatement
18 Promenade
22 Bighorn male
23 Double-edged
24 1998 Olympics site
25 1989 Rolling Stones album
28 Track events
29 Auto plant worker
30 Think up
31 Appeared
34 Disheveled hair
40 Large sea snail
41 Vigorous
42 Prudent with one's resources
43 Liable to crack
45 Minerva's symbol
47 Din-din
50 Hector Hugh Munro's pen name
51 Fall cause
52 Frog genus
53 Publisher Zuckerman
56 Bottom-line figure
57 Wiggling fish
58 Mendes in *The Women*
59 Indy racer St. James

TRIVIAL PURSUIT 1962

A MAN NAMED JED

Well, doggies! *The Beverly Hillbillies* debuted in 1962 and shot to the
top of the Nielsen ratings after only three weeks.
We bet you can still sing the theme song. What else do you remember about the clan?

1 Name the show's theme song and three synonyms used in the song to describe oil.

_____

2 The song ends with what invitation?

_____

3 What did the Clampetts call the swimming pool?

_____

4 What did Elly May affectionately call her pets?

_____

5 What was Jethro's last name and how was he related to Jed?

_____

6 What was Granny's relationship to Jed?

_____

7 What was the name of Jed's cranky banker?

_____

8 What was the name of the banker's stuffy secretary?

_____

9 Who owned Duke and what kind of dog was he?

_____

10 What was Granny's most popular stew?

_____

11 Where was the Clampett family originally from?

_____

12 What did the family call the billiards table?

_____

13 What type of truck did the Clampetts drive?

_____

14 What was Granny's first name?

_____

BRAINSNACK® City Gates

We enter the city at point A. With which point (1–10) on the floor plan does point A correspond?

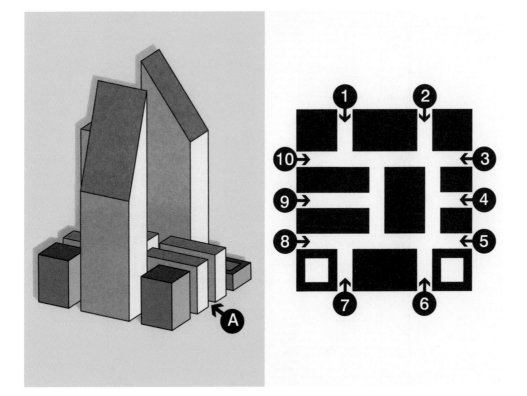

QUICK CROSSWORD

Place the SPORTS terms listed below in the crossword grid.

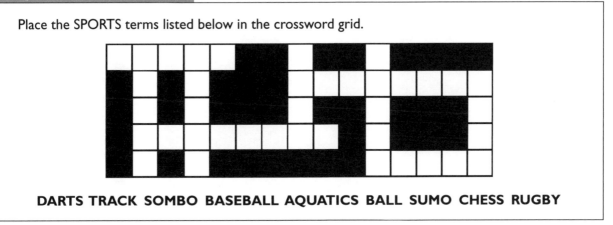

DARTS TRACK SOMBO BASEBALL AQUATICS BALL SUMO CHESS RUGBY

Metallica

ACROSS

1 Author Silverstein
5 Swift humor
10 "Anything ___ do?"
14 City in Romania
15 Vergara of *Modern Family*
16 Parcel (out)
17 "Photograph" band
19 Duelist's blade
20 Record keepers
21 Broke loose
23 Kind of profit or loss
24 SUV
25 Emily Dickinson's home
29 Clemente of baseball
33 Palm off
34 "___ On, Harvest Moon"
36 Goblin
37 Stocking stuffers
38 Doll sounds
39 Pierre's papa
40 "Xanadu" group
41 Gypsy's deck
42 Uninviting, to vegans
43 Little devils
45 Tom in *Brokedown Palace*
47 Not up to snuff
48 Saturn model
49 Skunk
53 Kibbutz resident
57 Thomas ___ Edison
58 Oddjob's boss
60 *Glengarry ___ Ross* (1992)
61 Division signs
62 R&B singer Braxton
63 Rabbit ___ antenna
64 *The Balcony* playwright
65 Mach 1 breakers

DOWN

1 Moral lapses
2 ___-fellow-well-met
3 Suffix for opal
4 Semblance
5 Cruise stopovers
6 Pulls a heist on
7 Birds ___ feather
8 Riviera resort
9 Long-haired mammals
10 Engage in brainstorming
11 North American viper
12 Windward's opposite
13 Prerequisite
18 Tennis legend Chris
22 Sugar form
25 In search of
26 Money (sl.)
27 Lone Ranger's cry
28 Pre-1917 Russian rulers
29 Gaucho's lasso
30 Switch positions
31 Austrian cake
32 Toes the line
35 Med. care provider
38 Prefix for practice
39 Tapered ship flags
41 After-bath powder
42 Language related to Hawaiian
44 Vacuums
46 Square peg in a round hole
49 Senator's gofer
50 Widemouthed jug
51 Bug-eyed
52 Fit ___ tied
53 Between gigs
54 Swelled heads
55 Mardi Gras follower
56 Rainbow goddess
59 Lesser of "Seinfeld"

WORD SEARCH **Belgian Beers**

All the words are hidden vertically, horizontally or diagonally—in both directions. The letters that remain unused form a sentence from left to right.

```
J L T C A M B R I N U S R J A
U E R P B R I G A N D P I A E
P G O S T B E E R B I S B C U
I E K L L E U Q S L R A K O V
L U C N I K P A H R J A L B E
E R O E W E E D B U Y A B I L
R B B T R N A G L P V P L N L
E O I S T S O I G I M O E S E
I O C N K S U L R U R O V F B
B A E H T S A O L V R H U E O
L E F F E T L R A I D B D E R
E I F F S F O L F T T H E C I
M S E I L T O D E U G N I E T
M E R F R I C R C H I M A Y I
O C O A M N G S T O F T H C E
H S L T M A R E D S O U S R I
C T F O B S N A M E D N I L S
E R V A G R I S E T T E N C E
```

- AFFLIGEM
- BARBAR
- BELLEVUE
- BOCKOR
- BRIGAND
- BRUEGEL
- BRUGGE
- CAMBRINUS
- CANTILLON
- CHIMAY
- CRISTAL
- DEUGNIET
- DUVEL
- FLOREFFE
- FLORIVAL
- GRISETTE
- HAPKIN
- HOMMELBIER
- JACOBINS
- JULIUS
- JUPILER
- KARLSQUELL
- LEFFE
- LIEFMANS
- LINDEMANS
- MAREDSOUS
- ORVAL
- ROCHEFORT

Sudoku

Fill in the grid so that each row, each column and each 3 x 3 frame contains every number from 1 to 9.

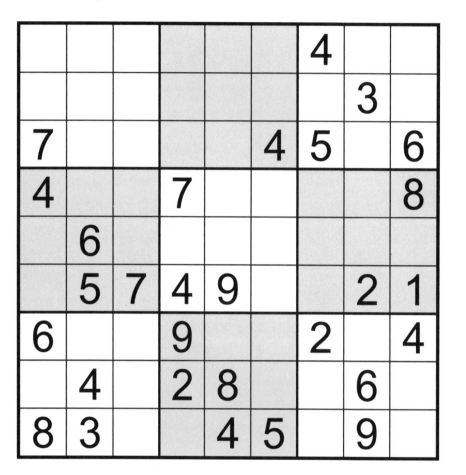

do you **KNOW**

Which writer inspired the Huguenots?

_____

_____

TRIANAGRAM

Three-word groups of anagrams are also called triplets or trianagrams.
Complete the group:

R A S H ES _ _ _ _ _ _   _ _ _ _ _ _

Map File

Can you match the listed countries and regions with the outlines shown below? Some are definitely more difficult than others: None is drawn to scale and north is not always at the top.

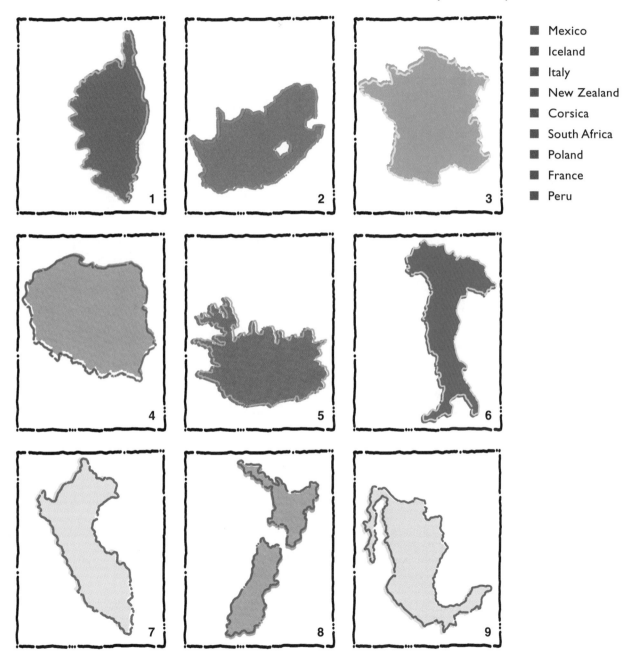

■ Mexico
■ Iceland
■ Italy
■ New Zealand
■ Corsica
■ South Africa
■ Poland
■ France
■ Peru

Historic Aircraft

ACROSS

1 Whiskey serving
5 Eye-fooling design
10 Word muttered after a mulligan
14 Rachel's sister
15 Hyland of *Modern Family*
16 *Pinocchio* goldfish
17 Capt. Kirk's craft
19 Cheese from Holland
20 Make, as dinner
21 Fit to imbibe
23 Angry address
24 Viking letter
25 Forks over
27 "Everybody's Talkin' " singer
30 Muscle
33 Prepare to be knighted
35 ___-mo replay
36 Abu Dhabi VIP
37 Innocent ones
38 Old Thailand
39 Anderson Cooper's network
40 Something to toss
41 Pet annoyance
42 "New York, New York" singer
44 Give the once-over to
46 Do a pressing job
47 Palette holder
51 Varnish
54 Truancy
55 Domicile
56 NASA's second Space Shuttle
58 Put ___ act
59 Auto dealer transaction
60 List made to help decision-making
61 Chippendale chair feature
62 Group cultural values
63 Sermon ending?

DOWN

1 Rested
2 First Bourbon king
3 Cowboy cinema
4 1994 Michael Keaton film
5 Sea hawk
6 Trim with a knife
7 *Exodus* hero
8 Blacksmith's file
9 Conjectures
10 Vast quantities
11 Amelia Earhart's plane
12 Tintinnabulate
13 "___ Kind of Wonderful": Grand Funk
18 Speed reader?
22 Rock group Jethro ___
26 Lilia in *Lilies of the Field*
27 Musts
28 Patron saint of Norway
29 Alaskan seaport
30 Winter boots
31 American hotel chain
32 Wiley Post's plane
34 Blake Griffin's org.
37 Nautical hanger-on
38 It follows a guilty verdict
40 Quick-rising plane
41 Analyze in detail
43 Garfield's girlfriend
45 Sends by telegraph
48 Mint bar
49 Whiff
50 Short and sweet
51 "Scat!"
52 Author Maxine ___ Kingston
53 "Country Gentleman" Atkins
54 To boot
57 Comment to a dentist

Sport Maze

Draw the shortest way from the ball to the goal. You can only move along vertical and horizontal lines, not along diagonal lines. The figure on each square indicates the number of squares the ball must be moved in the same direction. You can change direction at each stop.

2	1	1	4	3	2
2	1	1	1	2	2
4	3	2	1	2	2
2	3	1	3	4	3
3	2	2	4	4	1
1	5	1	1		3

do you KNOW?

Who wrote
Out of Africa?

_____

_____

UNCANNY TURN

Rearrange the letters of the phrase below to form a cognate anagram, one which is related or connected in meaning to the original phrase. The answer can be one or more words.

TO A POT

Keep Going

Start on a blank square of your choice and connect as many blank squares as possible with one single continuous line. You can only connect squares along vertical and horizontal lines, not along diagonal lines. You must continue the connecting line up until the next obstacle, i.e., the rim of the box, a black square or a square that has already been used. You can change direction at any obstacle you meet. Each square can only be used once. The number of blank squares that will be left unused is marked in the upper square. There is more than one solution. We only show one solution.

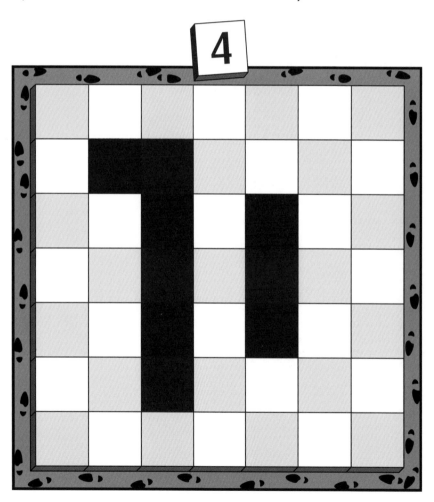

CROSSWORD Get Set for Back to School

ACROSS

1 Give a nickname
4 Level
8 Gab
12 Judge of the '90s
13 Actor dog of the '30s
14 Tribe in NE Arizona
15 Way to carry school supplies
17 Prayer ending
18 Western starring Alan Ladd
19 Comfort
21 Norse god
24 Geeks
27 Has to
30 Frog's kin
32 Olive or peanut product
33 Circle section
34 Silly, like a show
35 *Cat ___ Hot Tin Roof* (2 words)
36 Oof
37 Expression of pity
38 LA problem
39 Onion relatives
41 Erase
43 Bucks' mates
45 Promises
49 Water, in Mexico
51 School picture, or class ___
54 Shopping center
55 Prepare for publishing
56 ___-de-France
57 Not guilty, for one
58 Example
59 Near the bottom

DOWN

1 Call ___
2 Nevada's neighbor
3 ___ Raton, FL
4 Recorded
5 "A dream ___ wish your heart makes" (2 words)
6 And so forth (abbrev.)
7 Lawn care need
8 Run after
9 Class assignment for the new school year
10 Zoo favorite
11 Popular metal
16 One nautical mile per hour
20 Comedian Samberg
22 Slanted typeface (abbrev.)
23 Desert dweller
25 Flintstones' pet
26 Mining waste
27 Attack like a bear
28 Desire
29 List of courses for new school year
31 Church section
34 It could be upper or lower
38 Burn
40 Australian mammal
42 Powerball, for example
44 Raced
46 A skink's is detachable
47 Hawaiian city
48 Thick soup
49 Electric guitar need
50 Female
52 "___ to Joy"
53 Edge

Floor Plan

Which floor plan (1-3) doesn't correspond with the maze shown?

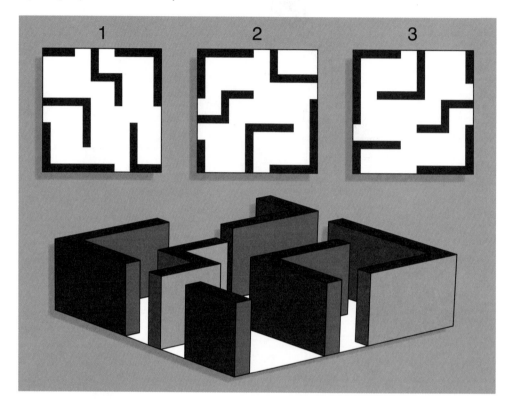

QUICK CROSSWORD

Place the CITIES listed below in the crossword grid.

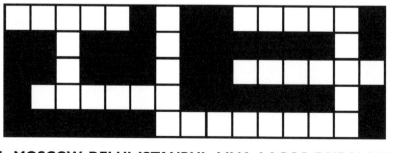

SEOUL MOSCOW DELHI ISTANBUL LIMA LAGOS DUBAI MALAGA

Word Pyramid

Each word in the pyramid has the letters of the word above it, plus a new letter.

O

(1) depart
(2) self
(3) box in a theater
(4) sphere
(5) baffle
(6) person who maintains a weblog
(7) Plays STNG bartender

do you KNOW?

What river flows
through Rome?

_____

_____

O
1
2
3
4
5
6
7

Word Sudoku

Complete the grid so that each row, each column and each 3 x 3 frame contains the nine letters from the black box below. The hidden nine-letter word is in the diagonal from top left to bottom right.

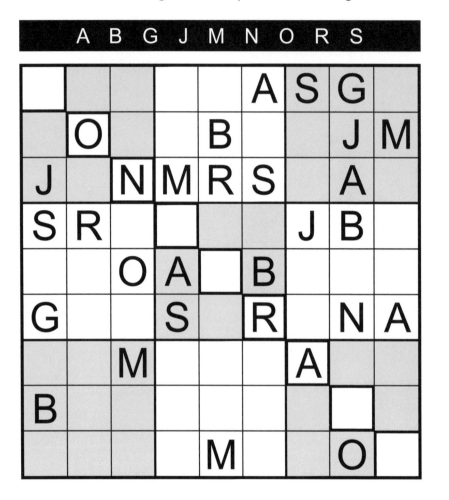

A B G J M N O R S

					A	S	G	
	O			B			J	M
J	N	M	R	S		A		
S	R				J	B		
	O	A		B				
G		S		R		N	A	
	M			A				
B								
			M			O		

SANDWICH

What five-letter word belongs between the word on the left and the word on the right, so that the first and second word, and the second and third word, each form a common compound word or phrase?

H O B B Y _ _ _ _ _ H A I R

BRAINSNACK® Flower Power

What is the shortest road from the bee to the flower? Answer like this: 1–6–7–8–14–18–19–20.

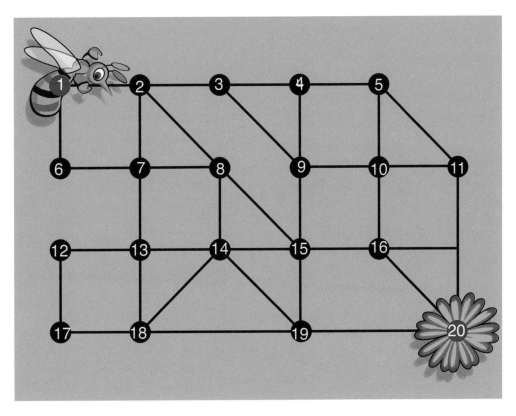

QUICK CROSSWORD

Place the FEATHERY terms listed below in the crossword grid.

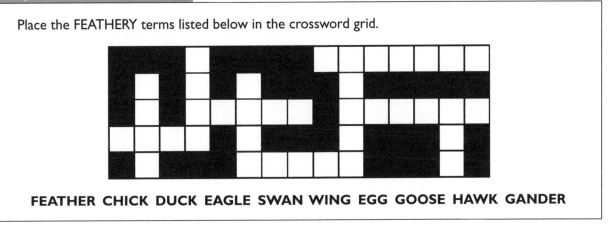

FEATHER CHICK DUCK EAGLE SWAN WING EGG GOOSE HAWK GANDER

Weather

You can't change the weather—but you can at least talk about it sensibly and intelligently. Here's a flurry of useful terms you can try sprinkling into your everyday chitchat.

• •

1. **inclement** (in-'kle-ment) *adj.*—
A: comfortably warm. B: severe.
C: ever-changing.

2. **temperate** ('tem-pret) *adj.*—
A: marked by moderation. B: steamy.
C: frigid.

3. **aridity** (uh-'ri-de-tee) *n.*—
A: harshness. B: blazing sunshine.
C: drought.

4. **nimbus** ('nim-bus) *n.*—
A: frostbite. B: rain cloud. C: weather vane.

5. **doldrums** ('dohl-drumz) *n.*—
A: sounds of booming thunder.
B: stagnation or listlessness.
C: weather map lines.

6. **inundate** ('ih-nen-dayt) *v.*—
A: overheat or melt. B: form icicles.
C: flood.

7. **abate** (uh-'bayt) *v.*—A: decrease in force, as rain. B: increase, as wind.
C: pile up, as snow.

8. **convection** (kun-'vek-shen) *n.*—
A: cyclonic movement. B: hot air rising. C: meeting of weatherpersons.

9. **striated** ('striy-ay-ted) *adj.*—
A: jagged, as hail. B: banded, as clouds.
C: patchy, as fog.

10. **hoary** ('hor-ee) *adj.*—A: hazy.
B: white with frost or age. C: lightly sprinkling.

11. **leeward** ('lee-werd) *adj.*—
A: by the shore. B: out of balance.
C: not facing the wind.

12. **graupel** ('grauw-pel) *n.*—
A: snow pellets. B: mudslide.
C: warm-water current.

13. **insolation** (in-soh-'lay-shen) *n.*—
A: sunstroke. B: shade. C: winter clothing.

14. **permafrost** ('per-muh-frost) *n.*—
A: dusting of powdery snow.
B: stalled front. C: frozen subsoil.

15. **prognosticate** (prahg-'nahs-ti-kayt) *v.*—A: forecast. B: chill.
C: take shelter.

CROSSWORD At the Track

ACROSS
1 Distribute hands
5 Roast host
10 Hushed "Hey you!"
14 Hence
15 Like lager
16 *Barnyard* bull
17 Passport datum
19 Evening, in Milan
20 Eryngo
21 Of any kind
23 "New Age" singer Tori
24 Lively baroque dance
25 Fish hawk
28 See 27 Down
31 Reserved
32 Pledge a tenth
33 Lobster coral
34 Source of poi
35 Polyphonic composition
36 Mattress size
37 Sundial hour
38 Sources of milk
39 Place for a watch
40 Beautiful escort, slangily
42 Ella in *Tall in the Saddle*
43 Tries to persuade
44 Michener story, e.g.
45 Affectedly clever
47 Zingers
51 Feverish fit
52 Westminster grand prize
54 Made a case
55 Fed the kitty
56 Opie of Mother Goose fame
57 Palette globs
58 Magnetic flux unit
59 Crescent moon tip

DOWN
1 Coming-out girls
2 Lake in HOMES
3 Taj Mahal site
4 Ladies' man
5 Take on
6 Shopping centers
7 Pot composition
8 Misc. ending
9 Optometrist's concern
10 Charlatan
11 "The Crocodile Hunter"
12 Part of a horse's pedigree
13 Royal Russian, once
18 Returned to headquarters
22 Vaulted arch
24 Microsoft founder
25 Port in the Punic Wars
26 Way up
27 Puzzle theme (with 28-A)
28 Good at repartee
29 Boom, vroom, zoom, etc.
30 Mannerly chaps
32 Relatives of frogs
35 Armored truck item
36 Period of the first dinosaurs
38 One-liners
39 Family car, informally
41 Doctrines
42 Where the river runs fast
44 Construction spots
45 Guitar adjunct
46 Unattractive citrus?
47 Queue after Q
48 Biblical "you"
49 Long stretch
50 Barter
53 Bambi's aunt

Happy Anniversary

All the words are hidden vertically, horizontally or diagonally—
in both directions.

Y R E T T O P D H Q L W N L A C E W Y

K E X Z V X W I E R O I H E W P S O S

P R F W G M K O D A T L O O W E J O Z

W I A W Q U B R O N Z E N H P I B D O

N H L G L P K P R R E C P P E U S I O

N P W B Q C P V M R O M M T A Y T R D

E P A K W S B E U T E J T N R O Q O U

N A W Q A U W T T E G T A I L W H N N

I S L A P O I O Q F D A V V I M O P E

L X R I U N N X V U M S T G X X G Q A

J S D H R V O Z M U A D Q N U O V R Y

K T O U J R F K N N A F D C L I E T Y

Q J F W E D H I I Q W R A D L V N A G

P C N P M B M H Q R Y D D W L T H B O

X V A R V U C V Z E R L P I G K D C L

I P G X L X P R J D O O S Y P H V R E

Q D I A M O N D A A V O D A U Z I K E

J H J O U S I N M J I T N F F R S F T

M Y A E A X L D L A R E M E C E U M S

- ALUMINUM
- BRONZE
- CHINA
- COTTON
- DIAMOND
- EMERALD
- FURNITURE
- GOLD
- IRON
- IVORY
- JADE
- LACE
- LINEN
- OAK
- OPAL
- PAPER
- PEARL
- POTTERY
- SAPPHIRE
- SILVER
- STEEL
- TIN
- WOOD
- WOOL

Sudoku

Fill in the grid so that each row, each column and each 3 x 3 frame contains every number from 1 to 9.

5	2			1		6		7
	6		7			8		
9		8	3	2		4		
3	1				9	2		
	5		1			3	8	9
	4			6	3		7	
				3		9		
					4			3
						1	4	

do you KNOW?

Who wrote
De Profundis
while in jail?

_____

_____

TRIANAGRAM

Three-word groups of anagrams are also called triplets or trianagrams.
Complete the group:

W R I T H E _ _ _ _ _ _   _ _ _ _ _ _

CROSSWORD **Fashion Fads**

ACROSS

1 After time and landing (pl.)
6 Decorative stitch
11 Fashion fad: _____ pants
14 *Carmen*, e.g.
15 Greek market
16 *A Chorus Line* song
17 Cared for the Tin Man
18 '70s fashion fad: Knee-high footwear (hyph., 2 words)
20 _____ Aviv
21 They act
23 Dick and Jane's dog
24 Haze
25 Monkey from *Aladdin*
27 Guilt
30 Quote
32 Org. for welfare of minors
35 '70s hairstyles
36 Inborn
37 Early internet service provider (abbr.)
38 _____ *of the Titans*
39 Sphere
40 Judy Garland's daughter _____ Luft
42 Dine
43 Green hue
45 _____ and Decker
46 Ave.
47 Ireland, to the Irish
48 Facial hair
49 Employ
50 After KP or heavy
51 Org.
54 West _____ Prep
56 Between the kays and ems
59 Fashion fad: 1960s revealing look
62 "I've Got a Crush _____" (2 words)
64 French friend
65 Principle
66 _____ Gras
67 Fashion fad: _____ huggers
68 Foe
69 Ghost costume

DOWN

1 Fashion fad: _____ suit
2 Ron Howard role
3 Dudley Do-Right's girlfriend Fenwick
4 Before
5 '50s fashion fad: Oxford footwear (2 words)
6 Doctor's messenger
7 Famous assistant
8 Wheel gears
9 Spanish gold
10 Type of cola
11 Hula-_____
12 Aware
13 Exam
19 Buckeyes' school
22 Away
24 Ringling _____
25 _____ glance (2 words)
26 '70s fashion fad similar to boot cut
27 *Speed* _____, cartoon
28 Note between D and E (2 words)
29 Prep cheese
30 Decorate a pumpkin
31 "Let _____" (2 words)
32 Gemstone weight
33 Explorer _____ de Leon
34 Quench
36 French black
41 Oil of _____
44 Fib
48 Squirt _____
49 Single, prefix
50 Song
51 Housemaid
52 _____ Valley, CA
53 Cut
54 Evergreen
55 Utah city
56 Brontë book *Jane* _____
57 Mineral vein
58 Fashion fad: Leisure _____
60 Sault _____ Marie
61 Baseball's Griffey Jr.
63 Slangy denial

BRAINSNACK® Losing Marbles

Which marble (1–6) should replace the question mark?

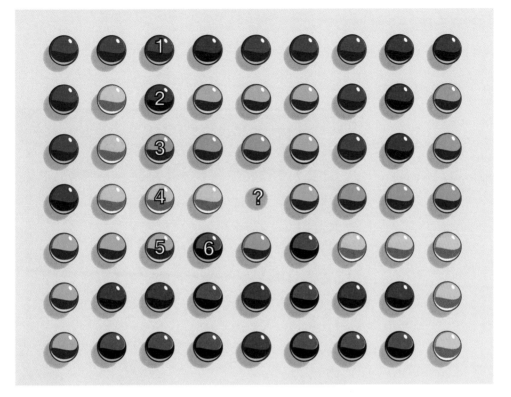

QUICK CROSSWORD

Place the COUNTRIES listed below in the crossword grid.

SPAIN JAPAN ETHIOPIA CHINA PAKISTAN NORWAY PERU USA

Hourglass

Starting in the middle, each word in the top half has the letters of the word below it, plus a new letter, and each word in the bottom half has the letters of the word above it, plus a new letter.

(1) narrow band of rubber
(2) palace
(3) take without permission
(4) story
(5) dislike intensely
(6) 3rd planet from the sun
(7) ribbon
(8) supply water to a person

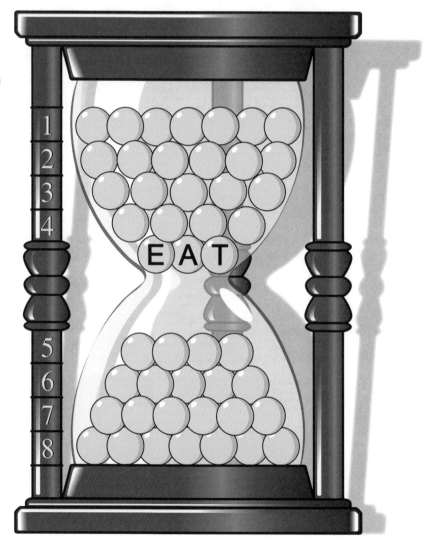

CROSSWORD **High Spirits**

ACROSS

1 Melville whaler
5 Die
10 Spice Girls hit
14 *Avatar* humanoids
15 Pews divider
16 Facetious "I see"
17 Donald L. Coburn play
19 Film unit
20 Heroin, on the street
21 Wardrobe
23 Chops finely
26 *Star Trek* navigator
27 Ones providing arms?
29 Thorny problem
32 Oodles
33 ___ Bell (Anne Brontë)
35 Author LeShan and others
36 Soak flax
37 Weed out
38 Winning candidates
39 Faction within a faith
41 Truffles et al.
43 Wife of a rajah
44 Joseph's second son
46 Concert bonuses
48 Comedienne Roseanne
49 1981 royal wedding figure
50 Mocks or knocks
53 Judi Dench, for one
54 Stratford-___-Avon
55 Colorful Kentucky turkey
60 Wee bit
61 Heavens: Comb. form
62 "Big Yellow ___": Joni Mitchell
63 Motrin target
64 Eva in *Gigi*
65 Main part of a word

DOWN

1 Pismire
2 "Pfft! Right!"
3 "Greetings, Caesar!"
4 Pooh bah
5 Multi-deck game
6 Diana of *The Avengers*
7 Mama bear in Marbella
8 ___ mater
9 Constrains
10 Hilshire Farm parent
11 2011 Johnny Depp film
12 Hosea, in the Douay Bible
13 Trend determiner
18 NHL penalty killer
22 Afghan coin
23 Funeral car
24 In slumberland
25 Barley soup
28 Rugby action
29 Avoid artfully
30 Staffed
31 Home of St. Francis
34 A base metal
40 Recent hire
41 Pyromaniac
42 About to deliver
43 Chipmunk and squirrel, e.g.
45 Suffix for drunk
47 Hunting wear, for short
50 ___ *Key*: Stephen King
51 Of historic dimensions
52 Common rail
53 Bond baddie with a base on Crab Key
56 Birmingham college
57 Nick in *Chicken Run*
58 Program file extension
59 Barely lit

WEATHER CHART Sunny

Where will the sun shine? With the knowledge that each arrow points to a place where a symbol should be, can you locate the sunny spots? The symbols cannot be next to each other vertically, horizontally or diagonally. A symbol cannot be placed on top of an arrow. We show one symbol.

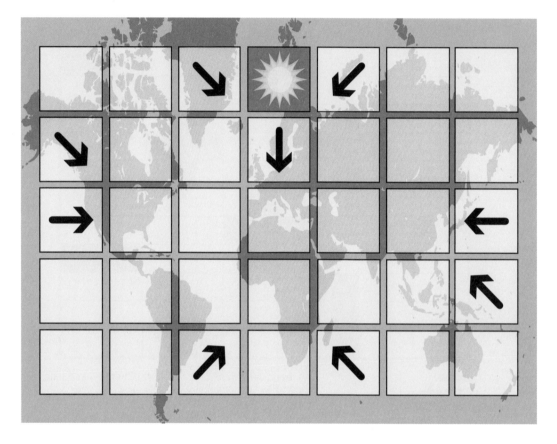

BLOCK ANAGRAM

Form the words that are described in the brackets with the letters above the grid. An extra letter is already in the right place.

INTACT (Only film to receive 14 Oscar nominations and won 11)

Sudoku X

Fill in the grid so that each row, each column and each 3 x 3 frame contains every number from 1 to 9. The two main diagonals of the grid also contain every number from 1 to 9.

	6				8		1	3
1								
					7			
		1	8					2
5		8	6			9		
				9			3	8
4		6			1		9	7
2		9	3					1

do you KNOW?

Which Richard starred in *Pretty Woman?*

_____

_____

Spot the Differences

Find the nine differences in the image on the bottom right.

120

CROSSWORD · In Memoriam 1

ACROSS

1 Saharan country
5 Tumbler
10 Thunderstruck
14 Mass assent
15 Jaipur royal
16 ___ of passage
17 "Thrilla in Manila" boxer
19 Penny-___
20 Wife, slangily
21 Cheap tire
23 Second purchase
24 Puckerman on *Glee*
25 Badlands rise
27 Drawing from 29 Down
30 They might have kinks
33 Swap
35 Thurman in *Bee Movie*
36 Formicary dwellers
37 Still in contention
38 Plays for a sap
39 Cold cubes
40 Burner
41 Regarding
42 Exposes
44 Fa followers
46 Film director Petri
47 Manatee
51 Balearic island
54 "Smells Like Teen Spirit" group
55 Askew
56 Former *60 Minutes* wit
58 Too good ___ true
59 Some sculptures
60 Hold back
61 *Touched by an Angel* angel
62 Lessens the discomfort of
63 New Haven school

DOWN

1 Captain's superior
2 Soap plant
3 Yorkshire city
4 Burning
5 Report card info
6 Slothful
7 "Reckoning" singer DiFranco
8 Clairvoyant
9 Suitor's song
10 Ark's landfall
11 Amy who sang "Rehab"
12 Blues singer James
13 Brave act
18 Chesty sounds
22 Ran full tilt
26 Much-burdened Titan
27 ___ *and Ale*: Maugham
28 Foreshadowing
29 Boss Tweed's lampooner
30 Kind of trigger
31 At a previous time
32 Apple cofounder
34 Glasses part
37 Earmark
38 Distasteful
40 Worth a C
41 Last Oldsmobile model
43 Ties a running knot?
45 Tut's underworld god
48 City in Crete
49 *Investor's Business Daily* founder
50 Knight of *Seinfeld*
51 Dillon or Drudge
52 Salve ingredient
53 Celebes beast
54 Wall Street tetragram
57 Spock and Seuss

Sport Maze

Draw the shortest way from the ball to the goal. You can only move along vertical and horizontal lines, not along diagonal lines. The figure on each square indicates the number of squares the ball must be moved in the same direction. You can change direction at each stop.

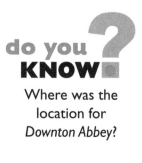

UNCANNY TURN

Rearrange the letters of the phrase below to form a cognate anagram, one which is related or connected in meaning to the original phrase. The answer can be one or more words.

EARN PART

WORD SEARCH Hobbies

All the words are hidden vertically, horizontally or diagonally—in both directions. The letters that remain unused form a sentence from left to right.

```
S H O B R A S S B A N D B B G
R S P H O T O G R A P H I E N
A T R A I N S P O T T I N G I
C B S E A R E A K P B U R M K
S A E R W U R I O H C R O O L
Y K R U E O T N O D Y R E D A
M E T T O A L T C H I U T E W
O B A A B T O F P G F I E L D
N R E R N T E A A N A R H T E
O E H E S T R M Y I R N C R E
R A T T C G I R O N T T O A L
T D A I I E S P E S D R I B
S C U L P T S P Q D E E C N M
A A L I T D L U W R H L O S A
D A R O K A I E M A C C T H G
C R P E N L Y A D G R Y R E D
O N A T T E F O R O O C P L E
K R O W H C T A P A M S U R E
```

- ASTRONOMY
- BAKE BREAD
- BATIK
- BIRDS
- BRASS BAND
- BREED
- CALLIGRAPHY
- CARS
- CHOIR
- COOK
- CROCHET
- CYCLE
- DRAW
- FLOWERS
- GAMBLE
- GARDENING
- LITERATURE
- MODEL
- MODEL TRAINS
- MUSIC
- ORCHESTRA
- ORIGAMI
- PAINT
- PATCHWORK
- PHOTOGRAPH
- PLANT
- POTTERY
- QUILT
- SCULPT
- THEATRE
- TRAIN SPOTTING
- WALKING

In Memoriam 2

ACROSS

1 On ___ with (equal to)
5 Coins in a $5 roll
10 Humane org.
14 Lake Tahoe neighbor
15 Massey in *Rosalie*
16 2004 Usher hit
17 2011 Indy 500 winner
19 Town WSW of Caen
20 South American wildcats
21 Like Wayne Manor
23 Flea market deal
24 Eisner's Disney successor
25 Flanders and Kelly
27 Damaging
30 Tosses in the cards
33 Insect stage
35 Rarebit ingredient
36 Cow-horned goddess
37 Court employee
38 *Licence to Kill* director
39 Pince-___ glasses
40 Articulate
41 ___ Alaska
42 Finer points
44 Con game
46 "Rule, Britannia!" composer
47 Concert venues
51 Florida race place
54 Irreverent
55 Parisian diva Medeiros
56 Dodger nicknamed "The Silver Fox"
58 Some may be inflated
59 *Marcovaldo* author Calvino
60 Perform with the choir
61 Hair line
62 Elder statesman
63 More than dislike

DOWN

1 Fervor
2 Flower child's farewell
3 Murray and Hathaway
4 Gena in *The Notebook*
5 Reduced, in a way
6 Misfortunes
7 New-wave
8 Eve's grandson
9 Capital of Chile
10 Methodology
11 *Columbo* star
12 Don't raise
13 Salty salute
18 Alibi flaws
22 Word form for "field"
26 Building locations
27 *Philadelphia* Oscar winner
28 Beekeeper of film
29 Do a bank job
30 Come upon
31 Douay Bible book
32 *Cleopatra* star
34 "Give ___ break!"
37 Wonderful
38 Marlin, for one
40 Chinese prefix
41 Frankenstein, for one
43 2011 B&W film (with *The*)
45 Scout Kit
48 *Birthday Girl* heroine
49 Apropos of
50 Worsted fabric
51 Profound
52 Kelp is one
53 Aries or Taurus, e.g.
54 Soccer's "Black Pearl"
57 Michael Corleone's wife

Number Cluster

Cubes showing numbers have been placed on the grid below, with some spaces left empty. Can you complete the grid by creating runs of the same number and of the same length as the number? So, where a cube with number 5 has been included on the grid, you need to create a run of five number 5's, including the cube already shown. The run can be horizontal, vertical, or both horizontal and vertical.

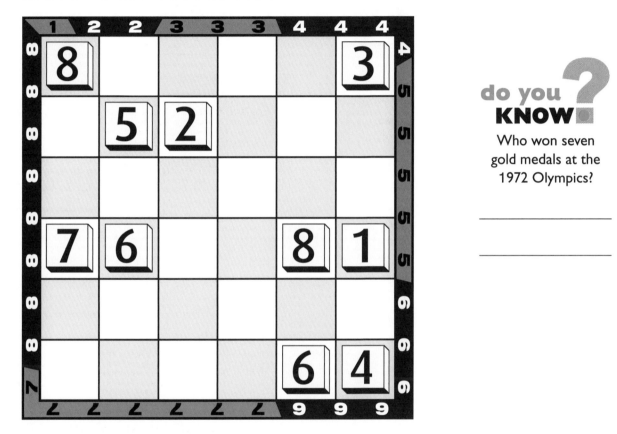

do you KNOW?

Who won seven gold medals at the 1972 Olympics?

_____

_____

DOODLE PUZZLE

A doodle puzzle is a combination of images, letters and/ or numbers that represent a word or a concept. If you cannot solve a doodle puzzle, do not look at the answer right away. Think hard—and outside the box.

Great Ships

Get ready to set sail with these seaworthy questions!

1. What name is given to the powered water buses on the canals in Venice?

   _____

2. What was the name of the oil tanker that sank off the coast of Brittany in 1978?

   _____

3. What is the name of the cruise ship that German forces sank off the coast of Ireland in 1915?

   _____

4. In what river did more than 1,500 former Union POWs die in the explosion of the steamship *Sultana* in 1865?

   _____

5. What was the name of the ship that ultimately rescued 705 people from the sinking *Titanic*?

   _____

6. What slammed into the starboard side of the *Andrea Doria* just after 11 p.m. on the night of July 25, 1956?

   _____

7. Before it became known as one of the world's most luxurious ocean liners, what was the *Queen Mary* used to transport in World War II?

   _____

8. What was the name of the ship Christopher Jones commanded when it set sail from Southampton, England, on September 16, 1620?

   _____

9. This clipper broke records regularly between 1885 and 1895 on the Australia-England route.

   _____

10. This giant liner was supposed to have been called *Queen Victoria*, but had to be renamed due to a misunderstanding.

   _____

11. Built in 1957, this Soviet icebreaker was also the first nuclear-powered surface ship.

   _____

12. *Titanic*'s sister ship, which also sank tragically and mysteriously during World War I, was called by this name.

   _____

13. Laid down in 1914, this was the first aircraft carrier.

   _____

14. Which was the fastest-ever clipper ship on the China tea route?

   _____

Kakuro

Each number in a black area is the sum of the numbers that you have to enter in the next empty boxes. The empty boxes that make up the sum are called a run. The sum of the across run is written above the diagonal in the black area and the sum of the down run is written below the diagonal. Runs can only contain the numbers 1 through 9 and each number in a run can only be used once. The gray boxes only contain odd numbers and the white only even numbers.

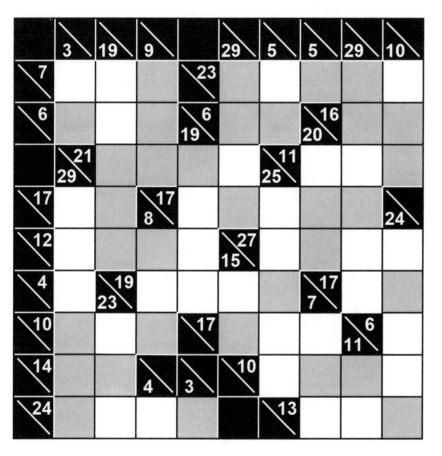

do you **KNOW**?

Who won the
Tour de France
in 1986?

_____

_____

Keep Going

Start on a blank square of your choice and connect as many blank squares as possible with one single continuous line. You can only connect squares along vertical and horizontal lines, not along diagonal lines. You must continue the connecting line up until the next obstacle, i.e., the rim of the box, a black square or a square that has already been used. You can change direction at any obstacle you meet. Each square can only be used once. The number of blank squares that will be left unused is marked in the upper square. There is more than one solution. We only show one solution.

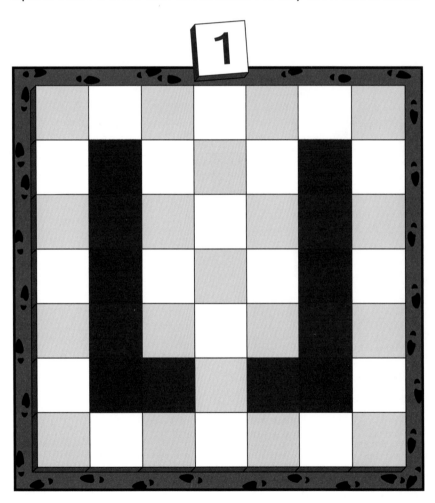

delete **ONE**

Delete one letter from
CARES IF NOTED
and do not cause inconvenience or hurt to others.

CROSSWORD   A Short Distance

ACROSS

1 Crushed grain
5 Blood fluid
10 Word with fried or crazy
14 Confederate
15 Birdie beater
16 Capt. Picard's counselor
17 Play hooky
19 Cheese coat
20 "The Lusty Month of May" musical
21 Pleasant distractions
23 "Do ___ say!"
24 Garage stock
25 ___ in the Dark (1964)
29 Paul Revere's light
33 Deuces
34 Like stuntmen
37 ___ alai
38 A short distance
41 Alley ___ (basketball pass)
42 Margin
43 Lucky Jim author
44 Booze
46 "The ___ Cried": Lou Christie
47 Bread of India
48 Judge Judy's org.
50 Jungle female
54 "Leaping ___!"
59 "I'll get this one"
60 Took French leave
62 Type of history or vaccine
63 Specialized market
64 Prefix with graphic
65 Apple-pie order
66 "Slammin' Sammy" of golf
67 Drop a dime on

DOWN

1 A gender: Abbr.
2 ___-Seltzer
3 Slender
4 Big buildup
5 Texas river
6 Christine of Chicago Hope
7 In the past
8 Wild plum
9 Gibson and Tillis
10 Narrow waterway
11 Track-and-field event
12 Skye of River's Edge
13 Relieves (of)
18 Part of a venetian blind
22 "1-2-3-kick" dance
25 A Musketeer
26 Plunge suddenly
27 On the warpath
28 Spy org. of WWII
29 Filmmaker Wertmuller
30 Murray of tennis
31 Harold in Ghostbusters
32 Yorkshire pub game
34 South Beach ___
35 King Kong's subjects?
36 Like new recruits
39 Kevin in The Pink Panther
40 Crested blue bird
45 Very seldom
46 Look steadily
48 Dog in Up
49 Two-footed
50 Blow one's horn
51 Cross letters
52 Payroll IDs: Abbr.
53 Peel
55 Mine entrance
56 Took the bus
57 Where seconds are important
58 Short-runway plane
61 Winter road hazard

Fictional Ships

ACROSS

1 Really bad show
5 Feather or wing
10 Ontario tribe
14 Epithet of Athena
15 Cantilevered window
16 Inferno
17 *Pirates of the Caribbean* ghost ship
19 Some prosecutors, briefly
20 New York team
21 Sheepskin ___
23 Muckraker Nellie
24 Oscar winner Guinness
25 Wheedled
29 Like macramé
32 Misery
33 Jerk the knee
35 "___ Carousel": Hollies
36 *A ___ of Two Cities*
37 *Beauty and the Beast* heroine
38 Lean against
39 Caesar's 950
40 *Golden Hind* captain
41 "John ___ Tractor": Judds
42 Hick
44 Used a teaspoon
46 *Green Mansions* girl
47 *Ab ___* (from the beginning)
48 1942 Abbott and Costello comedy
51 Horse barns
55 Opera singer Haugland
56 *Treasure Island* ship
58 FBI agents
59 Flynn in *The Sea Hawk*
60 Genesis murderer
61 Headset, to hams
62 Takes a break
63 Unseen catch

DOWN

1 Justin Bieber hit
2 Paella pot
3 Statistical number
4 Fortitude
5 Cartoon sailor
6 Fits of rage
7 Long in *Boiler Room*
8 Geekazoid
9 Coalition
10 Alpine abode
11 Submarine of film
12 Jack in *The Comancheros*
13 Mexican model Benitez
18 Gene in *Anchors Aweigh*
22 Piece of property
25 Hidden downside
26 Colorful lizard
27 *Peter Pan* ship
28 Consternation
29 Curly cabbages
30 Caseharden
31 Took out
34 Large deer
37 Brief break
38 Dance exercise
40 "Get Back" singer Lovato
41 Couch
43 Alluring women
45 Wrecks a car
48 Road anger
49 "___ Lonesome Hobo": Dylan
50 Yorkshire river
51 Munsters' pet dragon
52 Part of S&L
53 Literary pen name
54 Performed at a karaoke bar
57 AARP members: Abbr.

MIND MAZE # Number Maze

Starting at the top left, number 8, complete the sum so that the total at the end of the equation is zero. You may not pass two numbers in a row, or two symbols in a row, and you may not travel along the same path more than once (although your path may cross).

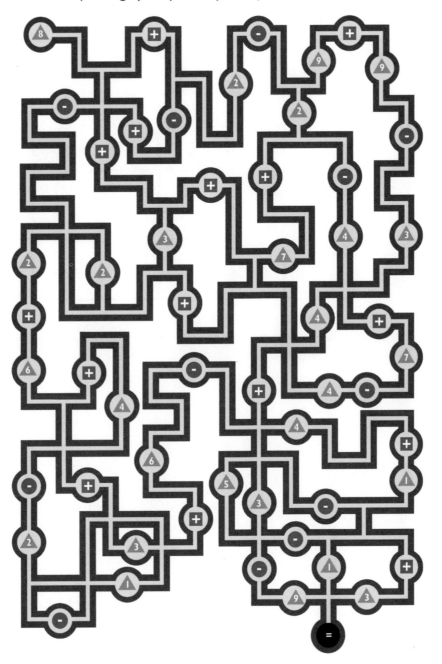

BRAINSNACK® Missing Art

Which rectangles (A–I) in this unfinished work of art still have to be colored in?

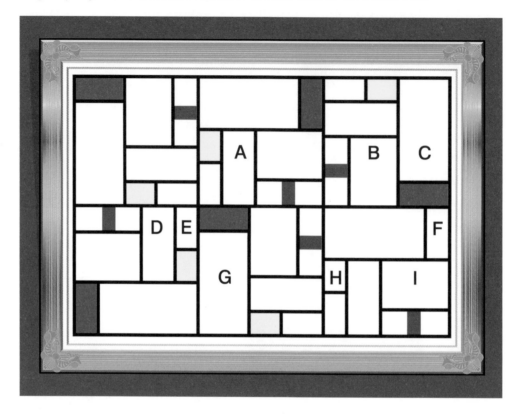

QUICK WORD SEARCH

Find the FRUIT terms listed below in the grid.

P X L I M E O O R A N G E G E
E N M E M J I F I G Z D Z C P
A I T U G R A P E W I I Q Q P
R A L B E R R Y Z J D Y S I H
D P A K I W I M B P P D H M J

BERRY DATE FIG GRAPE HIP KIWI LIME ORANGE PEAR PLUM

WORD SEARCH Tea

All the words are hidden vertically, horizontally or diagonally—in both directions. The letters that remain unused form a sentence from left to right.

```
M W H E N T H E S T E E P L E
A S N G E L E A R L G R E Y I
S O S B D H H A B N G A V C E
S B A L I F T B O E V E H L R
A I C A S N U L R E W A A I O
R O O C N B O A S A M P L P R
E O O K I O U B T O S I M T U
D R K S A O L E M A Q O I O K
W B I T T E R I N U O N N N O
O A G T N R L G O W H I T E Y
P T R D U E A R A N I H C H G
N E E M O A I I N O L Y E C A
U T E H M C L E N Y D R R I N
G E N I E F F A C E B K V E R
S O F T W O O D Y S R S T R O
N G E T N I M R E P P E P T E
R A V O M A S A W I T H L O T
S O F M I L K A N D S U G A R
```

- ASSAM
- BITTER
- BLACK
- BLEND
- BUBBLE
- CAFFEINE
- CEYLON
- CHAMOMILE
- CHINA
- COOK
- EARL GREY
- GREEN
- GUNPOWDER
- GYOKURO
- HERBS
- ICE TEA
- LAPSANG
- LEAVES
- LIPTON
- LIQUORICE
- MINT
- MOUNTAINSIDE
- OOLONG
- PEPPERMINT
- RITUAL
- ROOIBOS
- SAMOVAR
- SOFTWOOD
- STEEP
- STRAINER
- TOUAREG
- WARM
- WATER
- WHITE

Sudoku

Fill in the grid so that each row, each column and each 3 x 3 frame
contains every number from 1 to 9.

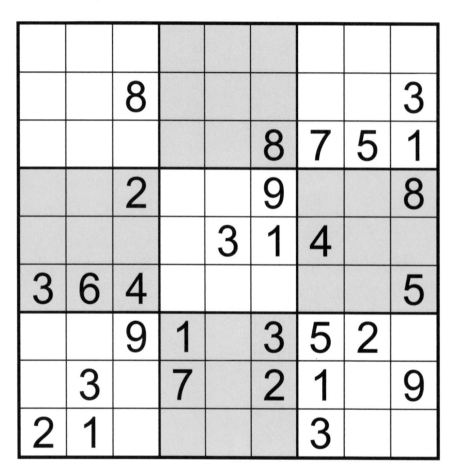

TRIANAGRAM

Three-word groups of anagrams are also called triplets or trianagrams.
Complete the group:

REMAIN _ _ _ _ _ _   _ _ _ _ _ _

CROSSWORD # Smorgasbord

ACROSS

1 Joad and Kettle
4 Braying beasts
9 West Point freshman
13 Uraeus figure
14 Prickly pear
16 Trickle out
17 Madder, e.g.
18 Don McLean hit
20 Front-rank
22 One, in Paris
23 Makes a pass at
24 "Don't miss it!"
26 "The Glory of St. Dominic" painter
27 Toast alternative
32 Young herring
34 Sailor's reply
35 Ice sheet
36 Luau staple
37 Happy souls
41 Taco Bell parent
42 Flair
44 Commotion
45 Dispatch boat
47 Egg McMuffin meat
51 Browns up
52 Parts of email addresses
55 ___ hatter (nuts)
58 Rudder locale
59 Spring event
60 St. Paddy's Day drink
63 Chill the bubbly
64 Belg. neighbor
65 2006 Olympics site
66 Grad school test
67 Where Samson toppled the temple
68 Fishing holes
69 With it

DOWN

1 "My good woman"
2 Shakespeare's ___ Like It
3 Like The Faerie Queene stanzas
4 Here, in Havana
5 Poet Coleridge
6 Act opener
7 French 101 verb
8 ___ generis
9 Pope
10 Takes a bough
11 Pinza of South Pacific
12 "It's ___ a hard day's night ..."
15 Cabalist
19 Indigenous Japanese
21 Sicilian volcano
25 RCMP ranks
26 "Seven Seas of ___": Queen
28 Sitting room
29 Soaring
30 Debtor's slips
31 Verne submariner
32 On ___ (not contracted)
33 Negri in Madame Bovary
38 It gets top billing
39 Lupino and Wells
40 Alveoli
43 Stage actress Richardson
46 Basketball brand
48 Short race
49 Bay of Greenland
50 Take care of
53 Mother-of-pearl
54 Tidy up
55 Yao of basketball
56 Locale
57 Lamebrain
58 Bushy hairstyle
61 Alley of Moo
62 Dawn deity

Futoshiki

Fill in the 5 x 5 grid with the numbers from 1 to 5 once per row and column, while following the greater than/lesser than symbols shown. There is only one valid solution that can be reached through logic and clear thinking alone!

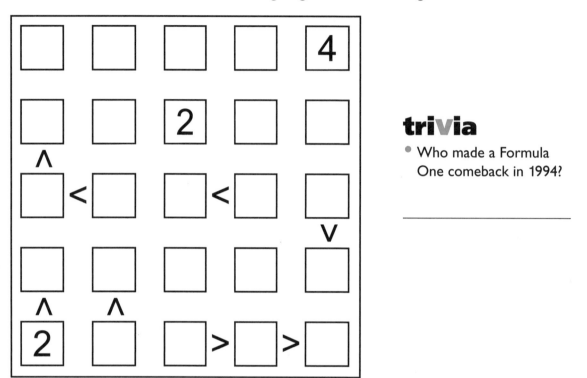

triVia

- Who made a Formula One comeback in 1994?

_____

Word Sudoku

Complete the grid so that each row, each column and each 3 x 3 frame contains the nine letters from the black box below. The hidden nine-letter word is in the diagonal from top left to bottom right.

A B D E L N P Q S

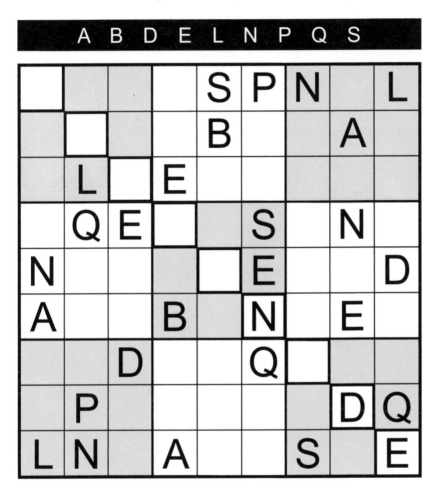

do you KNOW?

Who wrote
As I Lay Dying?

_____

_____

SANDWICH

What four-letter word belongs between the word on the left and the word on the right, so that the first and second word, and the second and third word, each form a common compound word or phrase?

PIT _ _ _ _ FRAME

Sunny

Where will the sun shine? With the knowledge that each arrow points to a place where a symbol should be, can you locate the sunny spots? The symbols cannot be next to each other vertically, horizontally or diagonally. A symbol cannot be placed on top of an arrow. We show one symbol.

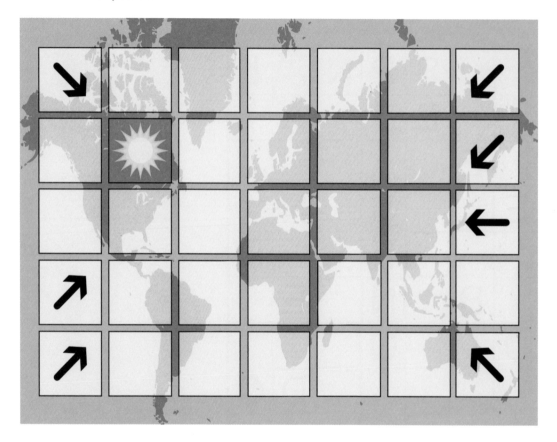

BLOCK ANAGRAM

Form the words that are described in the brackets with the letters above the grid. Extra letters are already in the right place.

SALOON CHICK (Actor with most Oscar nominations)

J					N							

CROSSWORD AKA 1

ACROSS

1 "Hairy man" in Genesis 27:11
5 *Shrek* princess
10 Hoe target
14 Demands payment
15 Cherbourg ciao
16 Garret of *Deadwood*
17 Jerome Silberman aka ___
19 Roil
20 "Flower of my heart" in song
21 Twist
23 Nurse a grudge
24 Chicken feed
25 Go ___ (leave the band)
27 Colorful, crested bird
30 Talk back
33 An Ivy Leaguer
35 *Shark Tale* dragon fish
36 Female turkey
37 In addition
38 "Walk on By" lyricist David
39 Aphrodite's son
41 Gaucho's rope
43 Old dagger
44 Back country
46 Returned to the perch
48 Vanilla beans
49 Sci-fi film set on Pandora
53 Giant tree of California
56 "I, Too, Sing ___": Langston Hughes
57 Particle
58 Richard Starkey aka ___
60 Hardly petite
61 Took a crack at
62 U.S./Canada border lake
63 Aries or Taurus
64 Fool's lack
65 Root beer brand

DOWN

1 Writer Burroughs
2 Glove leather
3 Queen ___ lace
4 Dysfunctional
5 In a whisper
6 Doing nothing
7 Suffix for planet
8 Have to have
9 Outer ear
10 Extravagant one
11 Reginald Dwight aka ___
12 Riyadh royal
13 Blowgun ammo
18 A.A. candidate
22 ___'wester (waterproof hat)
26 Warren in *The Wild Bunch*
27 Flora and fauna
28 Insect wings
29 Where Clinton studied law
30 C&W singer Wooley
31 Houston hockey player
32 Calvin Broadus, Jr. aka ___
34 Mauna ___
40 Snow sculptures
41 Getaways
42 Dessert request
43 Commenced
45 Bachelor's last words
47 Burl in *Summer Magic*
50 Coronation wear
51 Foul-smelling
52 Prime-rib orders
53 Cheering section noises
54 Lady's small case
55 Desperate, as a warning
56 Who-knows-how-long
59 *Collages* novelist Anaïs

Several significant movies came out in 1974, including works by filmmakers at or approaching the height of their creative powers. Perhaps the best example is Francis Ford Coppola, who had two films nominated for Best Picture, including the winner, *The Godfather: Part II*. Can you name these other influential movies from that banner year?

1 Coppola wrote and directed this thriller featuring Gene Hackman and a haunting score by David Shire, who was Coppola's brother-in-law.

_____

2 This black-and-white satire starred Gene Wilder, who was nominated with Mel Brooks for an adapted screenplay Oscar.

_____

3 Another Mel Brooks satire featured Cleavon Little as the sheriff of Rock Ridge.

_____

4 This mystery was director Roman Polanski's tribute to old-style detective stories.

_____

5 Steven Spielberg made his feature film debut with this Goldie Hawn comedy-drama.

_____

6 Martin Scorsese directed this film, for which Ellen Burstyn won the Best Actress Oscar.

_____

7 Jack Clayton directed Robert Redford in this romantic drama.

_____

TEST YOUR RECALL

People magazine debuted on March 4. What actress from the Great Gatsby was featured on the cover?

_____

BRAINSNACK® Spot It

How many spots should replace the question mark on the domino?

QUICK WORD SEARCH

Find the PARTY terms listed below in the grid.

```
W W Z C A N A P E S P I L L R
K I Q U C O C K T A I L T U O
P E N G H D G L A S S O U P D
J G U E S T D E S S E R T R L
N A P K I N A H V D I N N E R
```

DINNER SOUP GUEST COCKTAIL NAPKIN SPILL CANAPES DESSERT WINE GLASS

Friends from the Start

ACROSS

1 It's home to Castro
5 Storehouse
10 Cyberspace nuisance
14 Astronaut Shepard
15 Brazilian port city
16 Headless cabbage
17 Mom or Dad, e.g.
19 Skating star Kulik
20 Dense fog
21 Having turned
23 Solecize
24 Hägar the Horrible's daughter
25 Drained fully
29 1988 Winter Olympics host
32 *Giant* setting
33 Big name in heating
35 Water tester
36 *Spamalot* creator Eric
37 Throw out a tenant
38 Kunis in *Black Swan*
39 Machinery wheel
40 Leaning
41 Not a spendthrift
42 "OK"
44 Induce a "wow!"
46 Morales the actor
47 Berne river
48 Superficial
51 Newspaper story
55 Nothing at all
56 Casket carrier
58 The raven, to Poe
59 Perfect 10
60 Chuck Barris game show prop
61 Minstrel poet
62 Condor nest
63 *Ghostbusters* car

DOWN

1 *Li'l Abner* cartoonist
2 Wings
3 Ramon's room
4 Licorice liqueur
5 Abide
6 Infield cover
7 From ___ Z
8 Grier and Shriver
9 Horton, who Heard a Who
10 Biathlon event
11 Soothing
12 "Shall Caesar send ___?": Shak.
13 Arizona-Nevada lake
18 Waterwheel
22 Jabba's slave dancer
25 Durance of *Smallville*
26 Citation
27 One who takes a hands-on approach
28 Ship's crane
29 Arizona plants
30 Play parts
31 Quite a spell
34 Wire measure
37 Addis Ababa locale
38 Nuptials
40 "I've Got ___ in Kalamazoo"
41 Glut
43 What no man is?
45 Sculpting material
48 High muck-a-muck
49 Syrian city
50 Walk in water
51 Half a handball game
52 *Peter Pan* reptile
53 Palm Sunday's season
54 Thus
57 Celtic sea god

Balls

Which ball (1–4) should replace the question mark?

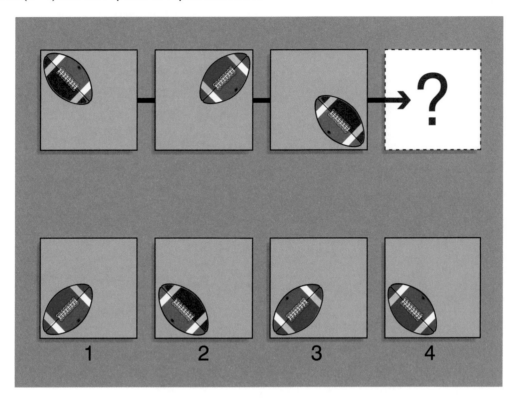

QUICK WORD SEARCH

Find the WEATHER terms listed below in the grid.

```
E E C V W J R A I N S X L I B
W Z M O S I W L A F O G G Y J
U I N H U R R I C A N E V A L
B S N V N L E H I B F L O O D
C U B D W P Z U D R O U G H T
```

RAIN SNOW HURRICANE FLOOD DROUGHT FOGGY SUN WIND

Sport Maze

Draw the shortest way from the ball to the goal. You can only move along vertical and horizontal lines, not along diagonal lines. The figure on each square indicates the number of squares the ball must be moved in the same direction. You can change direction at each stop.

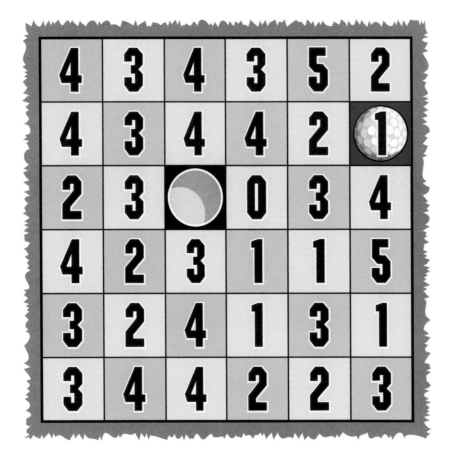

UNCANNY TURN

Rearrange the letters of the phrase below to form a cognate anagram, one which is related or connected in meaning to the original phrase. The answer can be one or more words.

AT TIMES I PONDER

CROSSWORD # Friends to the End

ACROSS

1 Oscar-winning Scorsese film
5 Switch
9 Caught a few z's
14 Concluded
15 The elder Dumas
16 Cone-shaped tent
17 Kind of bond
19 Well-coordinated
20 Gracefully refined
21 Sherwood and Black
23 Swift vehicle?
24 Iron galvanizer
25 Short message
27 Approve of
30 Leaf of the calyx of a flower
33 Cast carrier
35 Khmer Rouge leader Pot
36 Lovelock
37 Put into words
38 Prioritize
39 Vince's agent on *Entourage*
40 Rub the wrong way
41 Commission sources
42 Maugham's *Of Human ___*
44 Interstate hauler
46 Closing notes
47 Mata Hari was one
51 Take to the cleaners
54 High-pitched flute
55 Pontifical
56 Dark gem from Australia
58 5½-point type
59 Force from office
60 *Thomas and Sally* composer
61 Graf tennis rival
62 Noncoms
63 Shavers

DOWN

1 Great Lakes mnemonic
2 Soft palate part
3 *The Balcony* playwright
4 Innovative
5 Compact piano
6 "Jesus ___": John 11:35
7 Heavenly altar
8 Lucre
9 Rubberneck's activity
10 Map table
11 Protestant Church
12 Trading post item
13 Tiger's pegs
18 Comedienne Burnett
22 Stratosphere layer
26 Floral Lauder perfume
27 Refers to
28 Not a lick
29 Horned buglers
30 Picket-line crosser
31 Capital of Spain?
32 Headmaster
34 Head
37 George of *Blume in Love*
38 Columbo's trademark
40 Business ends of defibrillators
41 Thwack
43 Be charitable
45 Bulls
48 Dried coconut meat
49 Gnu's cousin
50 Positions or functions
51 Vichy and Ems
52 Salary
53 Bard's black
54 Part of UTEP
57 Violinist Jean-___ Ponty

Many Thanks

All the words are hidden vertically, horizontally or diagonally—
in both directions.

```
P L Y M O U T H F F O O T B A L L S Z
L Y G N T K B B N M V X N P B I G S J
A I S T S G Y B W M V F N W I R R K N
T Z S Y E P N O V E M B E R P P A V D
T J L V V K X X O Q Y A M S X D C Y M
E Q A G R Z F R B F N E S D F F E B F
R B I U A W W A Y A D I L O H G G P M
J L P R H I E E S U W L S S P N D A H
O E O L O I K I T E V K R C I G Y R R
P S C P Z R R I T K I E S R X F D A E
I S U O U H T G M W V R E U L O G D V
L I N T B A B O N O T H R O Z N T E T
G N R Q R S D C T I T W W E I R E S T
R G O G L E L F F A F E S V B R W S G
I S C Z E W E H G F R F R Q U N A G C
M D B R C L H W H G E A U F U E A Q K
S M F H J L U E F X C N A T F A Y R F
I E X Z E I P N I K P M U P S G S D C
F X I G E G O C J U F S B C C Q B H J
```

- BLESSINGS
- FREEDOM
- LEFTOVERS
- PLYMOUTH
- CARVING
- GATHERING
- MAYFLOWER
- PUMPKIN PIE
- CORNUCOPIA
- GRACE
- NOVEMBER
- SQUASH
- CRANBERRIES
- GRATITUDE
- PARADES
- STUFFING
- FEAST
- HARVEST
- PILGRIMS
- TURKEY
- FOOTBALL
- HOLIDAY
- PLATTER
- YAMS

Sudoku

Fill in the grid so that each row, each column and each 3 x 3 frame contains every number from 1 to 9.

		1	9	7		5	8	
	7				1	9	4	3
	9	5				6	2	1
	2			4	7		5	
7	5					8		
			2					
6				5				9
			7		4			
		2	1					

do you KNOW

Who recorded the studio album *Graceland* in 1986?

_____

_____

TRIANAGRAM

Three-word groups of anagrams are also called triplets or trianagrams.
Complete the group:

STAIN _ _ _ _ _   _ _ _ _ _

AKA 2

ACROSS

1 Heaping Pelion upon ____
5 Toss out
10 Hammer-wielding god
14 *The First Wives* ____ (1996)
15 São ____, Brazil
16 Prefix for graph
17 Anna Mae Bullock aka ____
19 Smudge
20 Praise to the skies
21 Alley X's
23 Exile
24 Justice Ginsburg
25 ____-do-well
27 Understands
30 Put below
33 Pass on, as information
35 "____ in Calico": Crosby
36 Singer Lorain
37 Bud
38 Heavenly altar
39 *Rent* heroine
41 Tricked
43 Tenth Commandment sin
44 Jeff in *True Grit*
46 Laura of the big screen
48 Deal with
49 Nabokov heroine
53 Didn't sink
56 Goes out of business?
57 Hot items
58 Steven Demetre Georgiou aka ____
60 Concerning, in legalese
61 Valuable find
62 German duck
63 Even-steven
64 Footprints
65 Straw home

DOWN

1 Quartet x two
2 Water-park feature
3 Crack of dawn
4 Ornamental shell
5 Speak explosively in anger
6 Solicitude
7 Kennel feature
8 Heady drinks
9 Play on stage
10 *Bewitched* daughter
11 Terry Gene Bollea aka ____
12 Great Plains tribe
13 Becomes compost
18 Allowance for weight
22 Wagon trail
26 Brother of Romulus
27 Went to bat against
28 Fab
29 Vanquish a vampire
30 Suckling sheep
31 Gulf States bigwig
32 Demetria Gene Guynes aka ____
34 Once around at Indy
40 Used one's imagination
41 Uses radar
42 X's out
43 Jazz up
45 Dig, so to speak
47 Unthinking repetition
50 Papas in *Zorba the Greek*
51 Bivouac shelters
52 It's black on the balance sheet
53 Fly like a hummingbird
54 Anderson of *The Mullets*
55 Small pointed missile
56 Send one's regrets
59 Pump part

BRAIN FITNESS # Seating Plan

Kate and Larry are getting married. It's your job to help them design a seating plan for the table at which their relatives will sit—but there are a few restrictions. See if you can figure out who should sit where.

PEOPLE TO SEAT:

- Kate's Aunt Alice and Uncle Bob *(married couple)*
- Larry's Cousin Carl
- Kate's Cousin Dave
- Larry's Aunt Ella and Uncle Frank *(married couple)*
- Kate's Uncle George
- Larry's Aunt Harriet
- Kate's Cousin Ida
- Larry's Uncle Jack

SEATING RESTRICTIONS
(in order of importance)

1. All of Kate's relatives sit together, and all of Larry's relatives sit together

2. Married couples must sit together

3. Cousin Dave plays in a rock band and wants to sit as close to the band as possible

4. You're trying to get Cousin Carl to date Cousin Ida, so seat them together

5. Uncle Frank isn't talking to Uncle Jack, so they can't sit next to each other

6. Uncle George owes money to Cousin Dave, so he wants to sit as far from Dave as possible

7. Uncle Bob hasn't seen Uncle George for 20 years, and they have a lot to catch up on

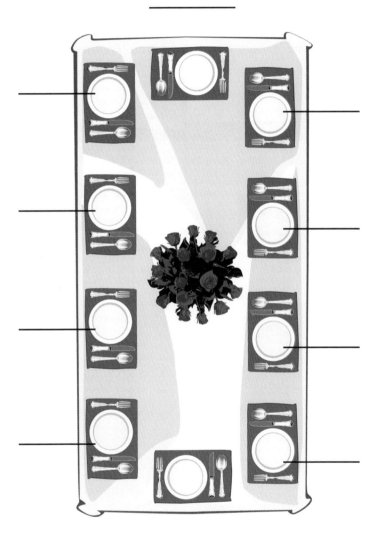

Keep Going

Start on a blank square of your choice and connect as many blank squares as possible with one single continuous line. You can only connect squares along vertical and horizontal lines, not along diagonal lines. You must continue the connecting line up until the next obstacle, i.e., the rim of the box, a black square or a square that has already been used. You can change direction at any obstacle you meet. Each square can only be used once. The number of blank squares that will be left unused is marked in the upper square. There is more than one solution. We only show one solution.

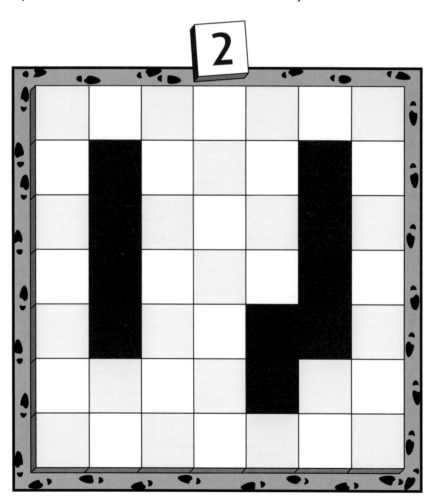

CROSSWORD Before and After

ACROSS
1 *There's Something About ____* (1998)
5 *Beauty and the Beast* teapot
10 "I almost forgot ..."
14 Away from the wind, on a yacht
15 "Sail on, ____ of State!": Longfellow
16 Utensil
17 Game show gal/First Family home
20 Finalize
21 Border collie
22 Powerful person
24 Childcare writer LeShan
25 Horse of a certain color
28 Alien ships
30 Splinter
35 Rainbow goddess
37 A few, to Francisco
39 *Absolutely Fabulous* role
40 Tenacious D member/ Thanksgiving follower
43 Ninja Turtles cohort April
44 Deanna of *Star Trek: TNG*
45 Córdoban cat
46 Shark on the links
48 Bern river
50 *Funeral in Berlin* author Deighton
51 Put-down, in the hood
53 Meadows
55 Hypothetical
60 Strive toward an end
64 "Godfather of Soul"/ freshwater fish
66 Parroted
67 Paul in *Stateside*
68 2012 UFC champion José
69 Actor Auberjonois
70 Paradises
71 Harry Potter, for one

DOWN
1 Dallas hoopsters
2 Wings, in old Rome
3 "Will I?" Broadway musical
4 1983 Streisand film
5 Mighty
6 Kyrgyzstan city
7 "____ Boy": Beatles
8 Church pledge
9 Passes a limit
10 Seated on
11 Vibrant
12 Not good, but not bad
13 Mr. Cassini
18 Baseball brothers
19 Medicine man
23 *The 39 Steps* star
25 Mustard with a kick
26 Heavens: Comb. form
27 Sweeter
29 Pelvic bones
31 Beatnik's "Got it!"
32 *1876* author
33 Mother's kin
34 Textile type
36 Read cursorily
38 "To your health!"
41 Schick Quattro foursome
42 Stinging insects
47 "Jack Be ____"
49 90 degrees from north
52 Begot
54 Herringlike fish
55 Cracked, as a door
56 Dracula's wear
57 Grace ender
58 "____ Dinah": Frankie Avalon
59 Johnny-____-lately
61 Captive of Hercules
62 Unmannered
63 Thames River town
65 White as a ghost

BRAINSNACK® Tiles

This sliding puzzle starts at A and ends at B.
Which order (1–4) was the puzzle done in? Answer like this: A2314B.

QUICK CROSSWORD

Place the words listed below in the crossword grid.

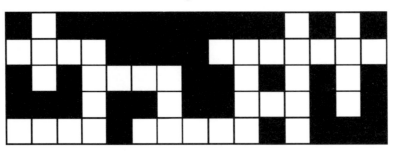

DEEP NEW AWAKE RED MARRIED BROWN BENT OPEN LOW DEAR POOR ABLE

Binairo

Complete the grid with zeros and ones until there are 5 zeros and 6 ones in every row and every column. No more than two of the same number can be next to or under each other. Rows or columns with exactly the same content are not allowed. There is only one valid solution.

	0	I		0						
			I							
		I	I		0		I		I	
0		I							I	
					0					
						I	I			
	0		0							
I		0			0		I		I	
			I	I					I	
								0		
		I	I		I				I	

delete ONE

Delete one letter from **INCA MATERIALS** and find where you might discover them.

ONE LETTER LESS OR MORE

The word on the right side contains the letters of the word on the left side plus or minus the letter in the middle. One letter is already in the right place.

F A N A T I C S -F [ ] [ ] **T** [ ] [ ] [ ]

Themeless

ACROSS

1 Raise, in poker
5 ___ the Conqueror (1988)
10 Gale sound
14 "___ penny ... hot cross buns"
15 Cantilevered window
16 Spread of a sort
17 *War Horse* director
20 Social set
21 Mooches
22 W.C.'s *My Little Chickadee* costar
23 *Oz* network
24 Redgrave in *Coriolanus*
28 Sauerkraut
32 Make uniform
33 Cold and unfeeling
35 Metro alternative
36 Caboose's place
37 Brown ermine
38 4:00 socials
39 Suffix with morph
40 Totally tired
41 Don't just want
42 More boisterous
44 Hot and dry
46 Corporate abbr.
47 Square root of XLIX
48 Breslin in *Little Miss Sunshine*
52 Supper serving
56 *Wanderlust* star
58 Hautboy
59 Defensive hockey action
60 Two of Caesar's last words
61 ___ It Like Beckham (2002)
62 Selected
63 Performs

DOWN

1 Autumn pear
2 "Do ___ others ..."
3 Get together
4 Crosswalk milieu
5 Shetlands, e.g.
6 Irish Gaelic
7 Stiff upper ___
8 Floral garlands
9 Hannibal's Alpine mount
10 Hang with
11 Tverdovsky of hockey
12 "The Way We ___"
13 Yule cracklers
18 Recorder button
19 Hotel waiting area
24 Nancy of *Baywatch*
25 Famous Texas mission
26 Japanese-American
27 Fall flower
28 Ulsters
29 "Fuzzy Wuzzy was ___ ..."
30 Kind of jelly
31 German steel city
34 Won ___ soup
37 Particular
38 Wandered
40 Gaza neighbor
41 Wiener topper
43 Inked
45 Get satisfaction for
48 Do ___ on (work over)
49 Lilith portrayer on *Cheers*
50 Part of the loop
51 Peace Nobelist Walesa
52 Conried or Brinker
53 "Take ___ the Limit": Eagles
54 Fridge posting
55 Maned antelopes
57 2011 animated film

TRIVIA QUIZ **Cookie Monster**

Test your cookie knowledge with the questions below.

1. A Belgian *spekuloos* is:
   a. A lens for a microscope
   b. A question
   c. A spicy hard gingerbread biscuit
   d. A chocolate cookie with frosting

2. In Britain, a digestive is:
   a. A tablet to settle your stomach
   b. A wholemeal cookie, sometimes dipped in chocolate
   c. A "breakfast biscuit" with barley in it
   d. A drink after dinner

3. The Italian word *biscotti* literally means:
   a. Cut in two
   b. Double-sugar
   c. Hard as baked clay
   d. Twice-baked

4. Dijon's baked specialty, *pain d'epices*, is:
   a. A spicy gingerbread
   b. A sweet white bread bought in slabs at the grocer's
   c. A black-pepper and chocolate cookie
   d. A chewy anise-flavored candy

5. America's word *cookie* is from:
   a. The African *koonky*, meaning snack
   b. The Dutch *koekje*, meaning little cake
   c. The German *kunkle*, meaning rest break
   d. The Irish Gaelic *comhke*, meaning sweet

6. Hermits are typically:
   a. A large spice cookie with raisins
   b. A small, hard ginger-flavored biscuit
   c. A long-keeping spicy cookie with no butter
   d. An eggless cookie with lots of ginger

7. Snickerdoodles are:
   a. A large, flat chocolate cookie without a lot of sugar
   b. Crisp wafers with a pink and brown layer
   c. A soft cinnamon-spiced cookie with a crackled surface
   d. Chewy cookies with chopped peanuts

8. Pfefferneüse, or "peppernuts," are a German cookie:
   a. That's dipped in chocolate
   b. That's flavored with lots of ground caraway
   c. That was created for traveling since it can be stored all winter long
   d. Spiced, baked in balls, and rolled in powdered sugar

9. The English word "marchpane" has been superseded by:
   a. Frangipane
   b. Eccles cakes
   c. Marzipan
   d. Crème fraiche

do you KNOW What do vanilla, cocoa and tofu have in common?

Number Cluster

Cubes showing numbers have been placed on the grid below, with some spaces left empty. Can you complete the grid by creating runs of the same number and of the same length as the number? So, where a cube with number 5 has been included on the grid, you need to create a run of five number 5's, including the cube already shown. The run can be horizontal, vertical, or both horizontal and vertical.

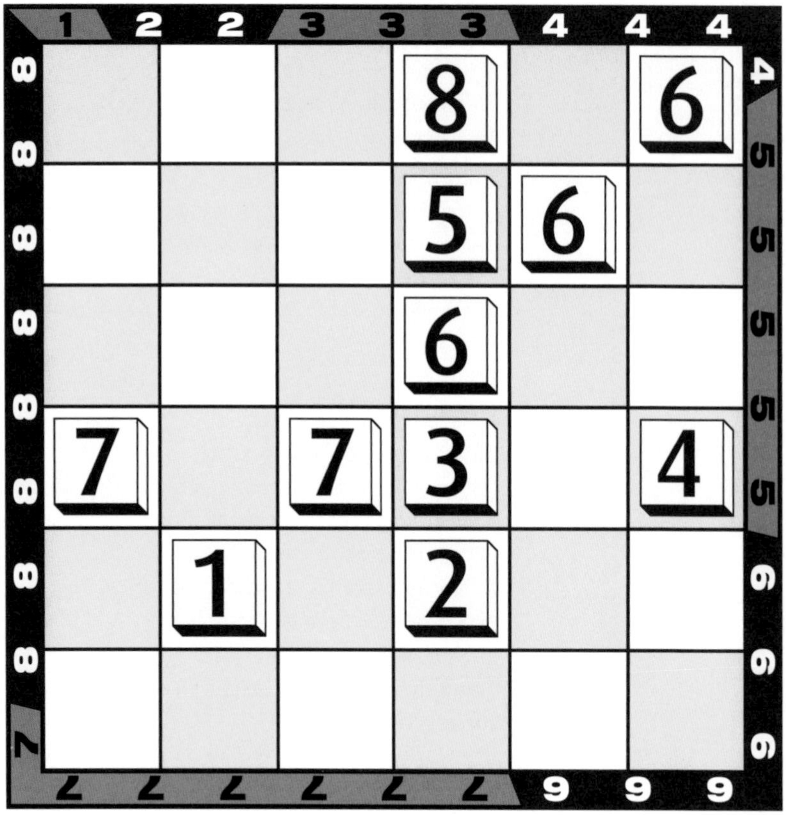

1 2 2 3 3 3 4 4 4
8 6
5 6
6
7 7 3 4
1 2
4 5 5 5 5 5 6 6 6
8 8 8 8 8 8 8 8 7
7 7 7 7 7 7 9 9 9

do you KNOW?

Which Ugandan general seized power in 1971?

____

____

DOODLE PUZZLE

A doodle puzzle is a combination of images, letters and/or numbers that represent a word or a concept. If you cannot solve a doodle puzzle, do not look at the answer right away. Think hard—and outside the box.

WORD SEARCH Garden

All the words are hidden vertically, horizontally or diagonally—in both directions. The letters that remain unused form a sentence from left to right.

```
A H E R B G A R D E N L L O P
T M E N T S C N R O M E I R N
G R E E N D A E I R F F U S E
P R E C N S P T E S O N R T T
A W S N R E A N N D E S H C T
T A A P E O E E O S S I N E E
I T F R C D P L U X U D I S M
O E C O R P R R N N Y M G N P
P R V A U O E A O G E G U I E
L F G E T N T I G T A T E H R
A A B A L D T S E E A G T N A
N L W A N A R A O D L T E L T
T L N N T I S O I P R T I N E
D A M I E N C B T N M A S O L
L G D C L I M B E R A O R A N
O E E K A R D E N N S A C N C
M L A W N M O W E R C D R O C
K G A R D E D R O U G H T N S
```

- BENCH
- CASTLE GARDEN
- CLIMBER
- COMPOST
- CREEPER
- CROP ROTATION
- DROUGHT
- FOUNTAIN
- GARDENER
- GREEN
- HERB GARDEN
- HUMUS
- INSECTS
- LAWN
- LAWN MOWER
- MEDITATION
- MOLD
- NETTLE
- ORGANIC
- OXYGEN
- PATIO PLANT
- POND
- PRUNE
- RAKE
- SAND
- TEMPERATE
- WATERFALL

CROSSWORD | In the Vanguard

ACROSS

1 Irish Spring, e.g.
5 Ignorance, to some
10 Send headlong
14 Word with happy or zero
15 Show of a scarce vowel
16 Cross a stream, say
17 Poet Pound
18 Cost ___ and a leg
19 Self-cleaning appliance
20 Certain cross-examination query
23 Like some lots and socks
24 1052, in a proclamation
25 *Monty Python's Flying Circus* producer
28 Go nuts
31 Mountaineer Hillary
35 Diamond Head locale
37 Austrian artist Schiele
39 Selection word
40 Feature of many autos
43 Hatchet man
44 Outermost of the Aleutian Islands
45 Goblet feature
46 Affording beautiful vistas
48 Jets with delta wings
50 Doubles in tennis?
51 Big ball
53 "A likely story!"
55 On the cutting edge
63 Fearsome tooth
64 Suitor
65 Assembly of competitors
66 Novel ending
67 Water wheel
68 "Do ___ others ..."
69 Another man's flower
70 Rudder's spot
71 Not long

DOWN

1 "Spaghetti" poet Silverstein
2 Move viscously
3 Enveloping atmosphere
4 Home of many Goyas
5 Just released
6 Country singer k.d.
7 Desert Storm arena
8 Syringe filler
9 Mother of Bacchus
10 Double-crossers
11 Saxophonist Coltrane
12 Thought: Comb. form
13 Sean in *Mystic River*
21 Passports et al.
22 Agreed (with)
25 Broadway hits, in slang
26 Containing element #56
27 Dusting, e.g.
29 Turkish lord
30 *Dead ___ Society* (1989)
32 Come together
33 David in *The Pink Panther*
34 Has an opinion
36 Not promised to
38 New Jersey cagers
41 Three-toned chord
42 Protestant sect
47 Rodeo distractions
49 Cul-de-___
52 Going on, to Sherlock
54 Organic soil material
55 Half a dozen, say
56 Despise
57 Grafted, in heraldry
58 Went like the wind
59 Next in line
60 Neighbor of Sparks, Nevada
61 Nix from the governor
62 Hugh Laurie's alma mater

158

Sudoku Twin

Fill in the grid so that each row, each column and each 3 x 3 frame contains every number from 1 to 9. A sudoku twin is two connected 9 x 9 sudokus.

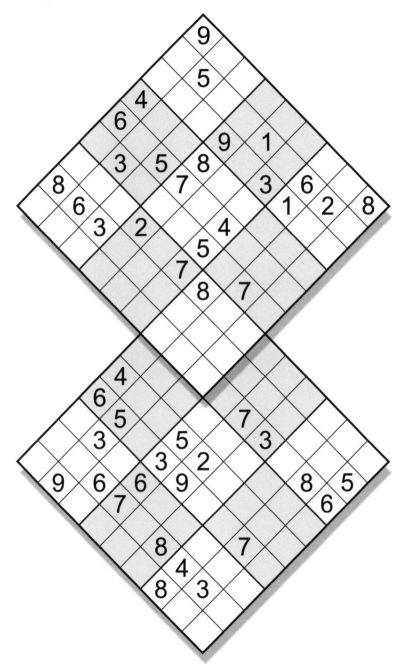

doubletalk

Homophones are words
that share the same pronunciation,
no matter
how they are spelled.
If they are spelled
differently then they are called
heterographs.

Find heterographs meaning:

TURN OVER AND OVER and
AN ASSUMED FUNCTION

_____

_____

Melting

All the ice cubes together form a cube of 3 x 3 ice cubes. There is one ice cube too many.
Which ice cube (1–9) needs to melt away?

QUICK WORD SEARCH

Find the CLOTHING terms listed below in the grid.

```
V  S  X  Y  T  C  R  D  F  M  S  F  E  R  R
E  Y  S  R  L  A  U  I  C  T  Z  K  H  F  U
S  O  I  U  R  P  F  C  A  P  E  W  O  U  D
T  H  D  G  I  C  F  P  T  H  O  V  S  R  Z
S  G  O  W  N  T  S  R  O  M  V  G  E  W  O
```

CAP FUR CAPE GOWN HOSE RUFF SHIRT SPATS SUIT VEST

Word Sudoku

Complete the grid so that each row, each column and each 3 x 3 frame contains the nine letters from the black box below. The hidden nine-letter word is in the diagonal from top left to bottom right.

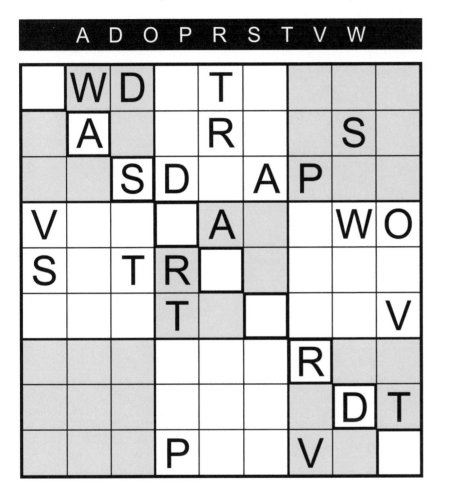

A	D	O	P	R	S	T	V	W
	W	D		T				
	A			R			S	
		S	D		A	P		
V				A			W	O
S		T	R					
			T					V
						R		
							D	T
			P			V		

do you KNOW?

Which nation is split by Cook Strait?

_____

_____

SANDWICH

What three-letter word belongs between the word on the left and the word on the right, so that the first and second word, and the second and third word, each form a common compound word or phrase?

STRAW _ _ _ BOX

161

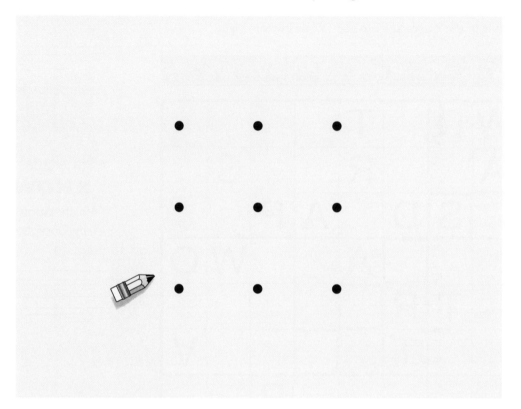

BRAINSNACK® # Concentration—Join the Dots

Connect the nine dots with one continuous line. You can only change direction three times.

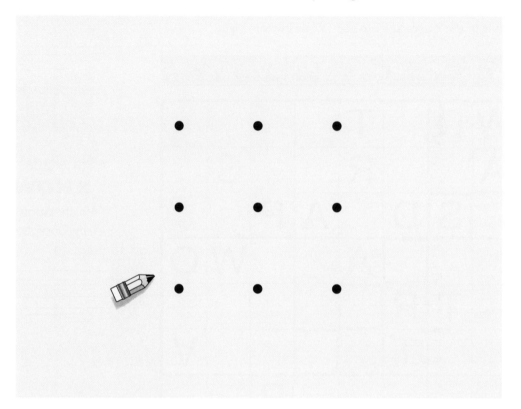

QUICK WORD SEARCH

Find the CARD terms listed below in the grid.

```
L M G S C S O W C L C J S R J
M N H A N D J Q K O W Q N G I
E V D B C G X A Z S P J A E N
R K I N G E Z Y C E H R P P A
K W H O C P L A Y K B E T C P
```

BRAG PLAY BET ACE JACK KING HAND LOSE NAP SNAP

CROSSWORD Night Lights

ACROSS
1 ___ *Male War Bride* (1949)
6 Prudent, as advice
10 Mrs. Garrett on *The Facts of Life*
14 Libyan coin
15 Outback birds
16 Place to park it
17 Tedium
18 Green Chevrolet
19 ___-nine-tails
20 1988 Richard Dreyfuss film
23 G ___ "George"
24 Convertiplane, in brief
25 Shar-___ dog
28 Eight: Comb. form
30 Chalk remover
34 Lanchester in *The Bishop's Wife*
36 Ethereal prefix
38 Keyboard piece
39 2002 sci-fi film
42 Rockne was one
43 *The Concrete Jungle* actress Talbot
44 Aarhus resident
45 Many rulers have 12
47 Kind of egg
49 Cole of song
50 "Flying Scotsman" Liddell
52 Where some sheep sleep
54 Downtown Disney theme restaurant
61 Splash Mountain, e.g.
62 Dice unit
63 Specialized talk
64 Biblical evictee
65 Of the ear
66 Iridescent stones
67 One of two English queens
68 Come together
69 Zellweger in *Miss Potter*

DOWN
1 As above, in footnotes
2 Lush
3 ___ Domini
4 Site to sweat it out
5 Musical passage
6 Booth Tarkington book
7 Youngest god
8 Chug-a-lugs
9 Many-acred residence
10 Stepped up
11 Rock's Grateful ___
12 Pact since WW2
13 Suffix for fabric
21 Chapel cleric
22 *Sky Music* composer
25 Joe in *The Good Shepherd*
26 "Your Song" singer John
27 Child taken to Moriah as a sacrifice
29 *The In-Laws* actor Alan
31 Gordon's wife on *Sesame Street*
32 *Absolutely Fabulous* character
33 Fix the blinking 12:00
35 Lex Luthor, to Superman
37 Mind
40 First word of many limericks
41 Studio prop
46 *The Office* is one
48 President for 16 months
51 Rodeo holding pen
53 Pick pockets
54 Victoria Park stroller
55 Rose in a *Music Man* song
56 Feast of Esther month
57 Theater award since 1956
58 *Faithful* coauthor Stewart
59 Gaze amorously
60 Medicine bottle notation

BRAINSNACK® Maximize

Which 3 different numbers are missing above the line to make the number below the line as big as possible?

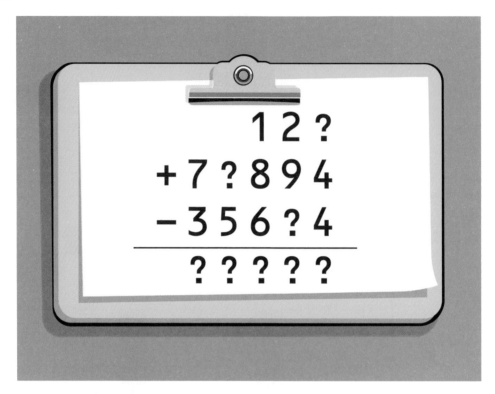

$$12?$$
$$+7?894$$
$$-356?4$$
$$?????$$

164

QUICK CROSSWORD

Place the words listed below in the crossword grid.

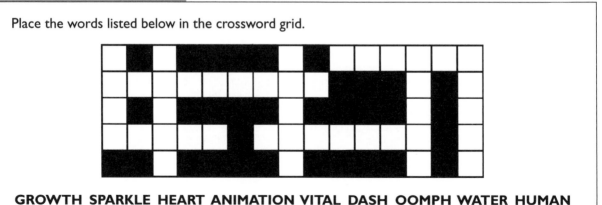

GROWTH SPARKLE HEART ANIMATION VITAL DASH OOMPH WATER HUMAN

Cooking Terms

Add some zest to your vocabulary with this feast of nutritious
words and phrases. If you can't stand the heat in
our kitchen, cool off with the answers in the back of the book.

. . . .

1. gustatory ('guh-stuh-tohr-ee)
adj.—A: full-bellied. B: relating to
taste. C: rich and flavorful.

2. au gratin (oh 'grah-tin) *adj.*—
A: cooked to medium rare. B: free of
charge. C: covered with cheese and
browned.

3. succulent ('suh-kyu-lent) *adj.*—
A: sun-dried. B: juicy. C: sipped with
a straw.

4. mesclun ('mess-klen) *n.*—A: mix
of greens. B: shellfish. C: Cajun dipping
sauce.

5. piquant ('pee-kent) *adj.*—A: in
season. B: in small amounts. C: spicy.

6. chiffonade (shih-fuh-'nayd) *n.*—
A: whipped margarine. B: shredded
herbs or veggies. C: lemon pudding.

7. toothsome ('tooth-sum) *adj.*—
A: chewy. B: delicious. C: hungry.

8. sous vide (soo 'veed) *adv.*—
A: without salt. B: on the side.
C: cooked in a pouch.

9. culinary ('kuh-lih-nehr-ee) *adj.*—
A: of the kitchen. B: buttery. C: cage-
free.

10. umami (ooh-'mah-mee) *n.*—
A: oven rack. B: chopsticks.
C: savory taste.

11. tempeh ('tem-pay) *n.*—A: part-
time chef. B: soy cake. C: fondue pot.

12. fricassee ('frih-kuh-see) *v.*—
A: cut and stew in gravy. B: deep-fry.
C: sauté with mushrooms.

13. oenophile ('ee-nuh-fiyl) *n.*—
A: wine lover. B: food critic.
C: egg fancier.

14. poach (pohch) *v.*—A: cook in
simmering liquid. B: fry in a small
amount of fat. C: heat slowly in a
covered pot.

15. fondant ('fahn-duhnt) *n.*—
A: food lover. B: cake icing. C: large
bib.

BRAINSNACK® # Dominator

The eight shapes and colors in the top row of the illustration below are combined in pairs with the stronger shape and/or color moving to the next row. This process is repeated until one shape and color are left. Can you see what they will be?

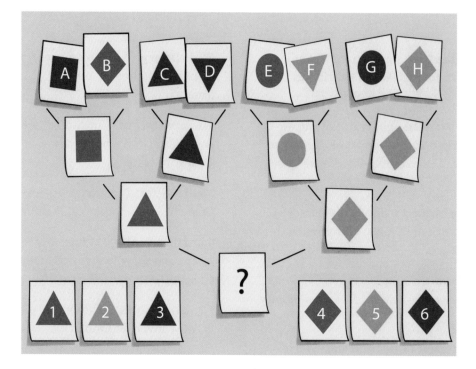

QUICK CROSSWORD

Place the MOVIE TITLES listed below in the crossword grid.

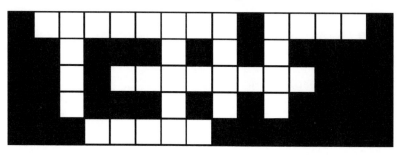

TRUEGRIT GIJOE PANDORUM PUSH RITE RANGO THOR PAUL

CROSSWORD   Stripes

ACROSS

1 Magician's hiding spot
5 Outspoken
10 Girder of a sort
14 Notion
15 Polynesian greeting
16 Many an opening event
17 Treats with stripes
19 Magnitogorsk river
20 Crafty one?
21 Ghastly
23 Come into
24 "Long Time ____": Dixie Chicks
25 Garb
29 "Get ready!"
32 Alpine pool
33 Feel without touching
35 Floored it
36 Pasta suffix
37 Bird in a cage, e.g.
38 Japan's largest lake
39 Henley's *The ____ Firecracker Contest*
41 Confuse
43 Nations in solidarity
44 Two-wheeled vehicle
46 Worst off
48 First capital of Japan
49 He opened the 1996 Olympics
50 Agape
53 They may be busts
57 Not yet risen
58 Ways with stripes
60 Small estuaries
61 High roost
62 "The proof ____ the pudding"
63 Adopted son of Claudius
64 Southern side dish
65 Wash. ball club

DOWN

1 About 1/6 inch
2 Nisan's antecedent
3 Good Friday's time
4 Amy in *Field of Dreams*
5 Moves out
6 *The Good Earth* heroine
7 Cheat
8 Cousin of "psst!"
9 Baked Italian dish
10 Spiny lizards
11 Sign with stripes
12 Apple spray of yore
13 Unhealthy rattle
18 Flanders river
22 Slip a ____ (err)
25 Molecule makeup
26 Lose one's cool
27 Clothes with stripes
28 Social outcast
29 Thwart in court
30 Aspiring singer's tapes
31 It's the law
34 Ship-shaped clock
40 Scoundrel
41 Legless chair
42 Graffiti beards
43 Largest European island
45 Glyceride lead-in
47 One of five Norwegian kings
50 Adventurer's tale
51 Anne Nichols hero
52 Opera or concert attachment
53 Like some skirts
54 Bear in the heavens
55 Cut film
56 Form data: Abbr.
59 Mystifier Geller

Cooking Techniques

All the words are hidden vertically, horizontally or diagonally—in both directions. The letters that remain unused form a sentence from left to right.

```
H T H E V E R P R E S E R V E
S B M U R C D A E R B U B T O
U C O A H O K G E I I S A A C
R O E C R L N L N P U R E U L
C E A X C I B D I N O T A I L
V O E R T M N C T A I E U R L
P B A L E I K A S M F A G A I
O E A S R L N T T A L M R L K
S S S K E T G G H E A D A T S
K A E W E A R Y U E S T T C S
C H A T R E I F T I O O I O T
O D C E U A L S N B S E N O N
T P V D E G L A Z E R H E K E
S O N K B L A N C H P A R E M
C O O K U N T I L D O N E R R
F M E N P A P I L L O T E Y E
S G R I N D Y R F P E E D E F
E U C E B R A B B R A I S E D
```

- ASSEMBLE
- AU GRATIN
- BAKE
- BARBECUE
- BIND
- BLANCH
- BRAISE
- BREADCRUMBS
- COOK UNTIL DONE
- COOKERY
- COVER
- CRUSH
- DEEP FRY
- DEGLAZE
- EN PAPILLOTE
- EXTINGUISH
- FERMENT
- FONDUE
- GRILL
- GRIND
- LARD
- LUAU
- MARINATE
- PICKLE
- POACH
- PRESERVE
- PURE
- ROAST
- SALTING
- SEAR
- SKILL
- SMOKE
- STEAM
- STOCK
- STRAIN

Sudoku

Fill in the grid so that each row, each column and each 3 x 3 frame contains every number from 1 to 9.

	2			8		7		
	3		9			6		
		2						3
			2				4	
7	9							
		7			1	9	8	
	1	4			7	5		2
			3	9				7

do you KNOW?

Whose library is in Yorba Linda, California?

_____

_____

TRIANAGRAM

Three-word groups of anagrams are also called triplets or trianagrams.
Complete the group:

E A R T H _ _ _ _ _   _ _ _ _ _

Spot the Differences

Find the nine differences in the image on the bottom right.

do you KNOW

In golf, what is an Eagle?

_____

_____

trivia

• The pyramids were burial chambers for kings and queens of which North African empire?

_____

CROSSWORD Tennis Talk

ACROSS
1 Mideast bigwig
5 Hydra, e.g.
10 Verve
14 Oasis fruit
15 Keep ___ to the ground
16 AOL triangle, e.g.
17 Jim Carrey title role
19 "___ so sorry"
20 Reminder
21 Make out
23 Classic Japanese drama
24 Caterpillar hair
25 Curly lock
29 Afraid
32 Plaintiff
33 Got hitched again
35 Jimi Hendrix hairstyle
36 Singer "King" Cole
37 *Batman* sound effect
38 Back in time
39 Spaces between
41 Like winter coats
43 Dessert choices
44 Exploited, slangily
46 Compunction
48 Olive in a Caesar salad?
49 Gazetteer feature
50 Has another opinion
53 Sets fire to
57 Et ___ (and others)
58 Venue for a moonlighting judge?
60 Keep them about you
61 Follow immediately
62 Nashville star McEntire
63 "Candy is dandy ..." poet
64 Absorbs books
65 Muscovite's refusal

DOWN
1 Round Dutch cheese
2 Nutmeg spice
3 Inventory unit
4 Crime motive
5 Mountain lion
6 Knowing about
7 Bucharest coin
8 Badminton spot
9 Gave a big hand to
10 Cathy's cartoon dog
11 Amour
12 Stress may be one
13 Norse goddess of fate
18 Chemical compound
22 Locale of Davy Jones' locker
25 Ladder steps
26 Violinist Stern
27 Earnings
28 At room temperature
29 Reduced in number
30 Presses
31 Baggy
34 Emerged victorious
40 Egocentric
41 Novitiate
42 Removes stripes
43 Movie munchie
45 Minute
47 Muralist Chagall
50 First light
51 Gold-medalist skater Kulik
52 Trig function
53 Dull noise
54 Donald Duck's nephew
55 Kathryn of *Law & Order: CI*
56 On the double!
59 U.S. procurement agcy.

MIND MAZE **Spy Relay**

A group of highly trained female operatives plan to steal some top-secret government papers. Each is sent a strip of photographs showing the route to take, with the instruction not to turn back. At the point where the routes cross, they hand the papers to the next in the chain. The last spy puts the papers in a secret hideout somewhere on her route. In order to find the top-secret papers, match the photographs to the routes and mark each one on the acetate sheet. The first three spies hand the papers from one to the other at the point where their paths cross. Now work out the order in which they pass the papers along the chain to discover the parcel's secret location.

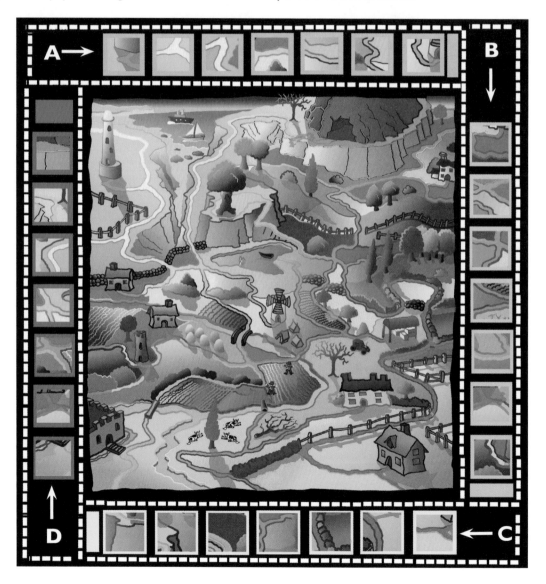

Futoshiki

Fill in the 5 x 5 grid with the numbers from 1 to 5 once per row and column, while following the greater than/lesser than symbols shown. There is only one valid solution that can be reached through logic and clear thinking alone!

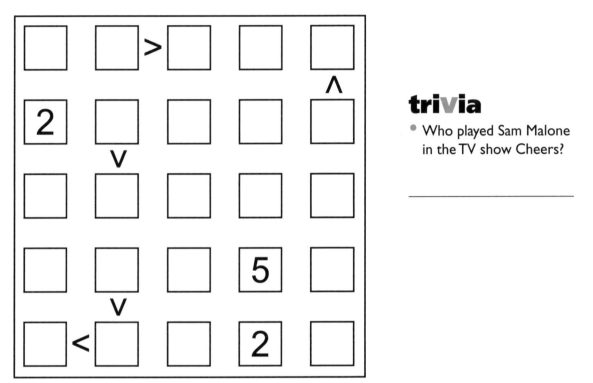

trivia

- Who played Sam Malone in the TV show Cheers?

_____

CONNECT TWO

An oxymoron is a combination of seemingly contradictory or incongruous words, such as "science fiction" (science means "knowledge or study dealing with facts or truth" while fiction means "an imagined or invented creation"). Connect the words with meanings that oppose each other and make oxymorons.

CLOSE	FANTASY
ZERO	LANDING
REAL	DISTANCE
CRASH	DEFICIT

Sport Maze

Draw the shortest way from the ball to the goal. You can only move along vertical and horizontal lines, not along diagonal lines. The figure on each square indicates the number of squares the ball must be moved in the same direction. You can change direction at each stop.

3	5	5	2	1	1
1	2	4	4	1	5
5	●	3	3	3	3
1	4	3	1	4	1
5	3	2	2	1	2
3	1	3	1	1	3

do you KNOW?

Who painted "The Last Supper"?

_____

_____

CROSSWORD Themeless

ACROSS

1 Soft stone used in making powder
5 Actor Chris of *Law & Order*
9 Famous killer whale
14 Cincinnati's state
15 Voice on an iPhone
16 Popular '80s band Hall & ____
17 Complaint about some wild meat
18 Cartoon character Fred who says "Yabba dabba doo!"
20 Man in charge of an abbey
22 Type of poem
23 Large Australian birds
24 Head, in French
27 Port on a computer
29 Follower
33 ____ *Valley PTA*
38 Type of scan (abbrev.)
39 Craze
41 Throng
42 Cartoon character Simpson who says "Ay caramba!"
44 "Five golden ____"
46 Cartoon character ____ Bear lives in Jellystone Park
47 ____ board (nail file)
49 Certain U.S. Navy members
51 Alien movie ____ *in Black*
52 Chemical element with atomic number 88
54 "And now, a word from our ____"
56 College in Cambridge (abbrev.)
58 Story about a hero
59 Certain savings accounts (abbrev.)
63 Word before a maiden name
65 Oscar-nominated actor Peter O'____
69 Cartoon moose and friend of Rocky the squirrel
73 All right
74 Country, home to the Taj Mahal
75 Fortune-teller
76 Soft white cheese
77 Data (abbrev.)
78 Paradise
79 Scotland ____

DOWN

1 Roman gown
2 Captain in literature
3 Arm or leg, for example
4 Cartoon character Wile E. ____
5 U.S. agency that supports research (abbrev.)
6 Word after olive or canola
7 Bigger than a duo
8 Mahatma Gandhi, for one
9 Distress signal (abbrev.)
10 Despise
11 Chemist's particle
12 List of offerings
13 Employs
19 Former *Entertainment Tonight* co-host John
21 Condition or semester
25 Rip
26 Town in Ireland or Texas
28 ____ humbug!
29 Fossilized plant resin
30 A type of play
31 Gave someone a job
32 Parts of a fork
34 Singer Orbison
35 Ad
36 Lawn tool
37 What a jockey needs
40 Mouth wide open
43 Prefix for "athlon"
45 Mess
48 Expression for delicious
50 Huff or tizzy
53 Compact car ____ Cooper
55 Hanna-Barbera cartoon character ____-Doo
57 Uptight
59 Wading bird
60 Smallest of the litter
61 MASH actor Alan
62 Thin opening
64 ____ out (got by)
66 Green veggie used in stews
67 Den
68 Stared at
70 Lived
71 Golfer Trevino
72 Sea bird

Riders

ACROSS

1 Tiebreaker result
5 Where Hawthorne wrote *The Scarlet Letter*
10 1944 ETO battleground
14 Where Bountiful is
15 Mariner's friend in *Waterworld*
16 "If ___ a Hammer"
17 Silver's rider
19 Aloha State bird
20 Serving no purpose
21 Flies the coop
23 502, in Roman numerals
24 "Thirty days ___ September ..."
25 Nougat nuts
29 Do the voice-over
32 Borrowed (with "on")
33 Support for an artist
35 Blue dye source
36 I topper
37 Marty McFly's friend
38 Jazz guitarist Farlow
39 Small newts
41 Torpedoes
43 Ripped
44 Project glowingly
46 P.T. Barnum, notably
48 *Young Frankenstein* girl
49 Yale alum
50 McDowell in *Halloween II*
53 Last Supper figure
57 Code word for "A"
58 Llamrei's rider
60 Robin Hood's beneficiaries
61 Eastern VIP
62 Grown-up elvers
63 "Auld Lang ___"
64 Marry again
65 It's played on a stage

DOWN

1 Humdinger
2 Platte River tribe
3 Playing with a full deck
4 Misery befell him in *Misery*
5 Oceanfront
6 Landers and Miller
7 Ship captain's account
8 Robert on Traveller
9 27 Down, for one
10 Frank in *High Society*
11 Hero's rider
12 Country path
13 Poems that were sung originally
18 Bridle attachment
22 Nissan Leaf, for one
25 Waterproof wood
26 Shower sponge
27 Buck's rider
28 "Sexy" girl in a Beatles song
29 Narrow parts
30 Pope's crown
31 Page in *Juno*
34 Father's Day giver
40 Not false
41 Star's nightmare
42 First American in space
43 Storm chaser's target
45 "Long, long ___ ..."
47 Genus of swans
50 Results of genetic research
51 "If I Were ___": Beyoncé
52 Charades performer
53 "Miracle Mets" outfielder
54 Vincent van Gogh's brother
55 Respite
56 Celtic language
59 Innovative

Keep Going

Start on a blank square of your choice and connect as many blank squares as possible with one single continuous line. You can only connect squares along vertical and horizontal lines, not along diagonal lines. You must continue the connecting line up until the next obstacle, i.e., the rim of the box, a black square or a square that has already been used. You can change direction at any obstacle you meet. Each square can only be used once. The number of blank squares that will be left unused is marked in the upper square. There is more than one solution. We only show one solution.

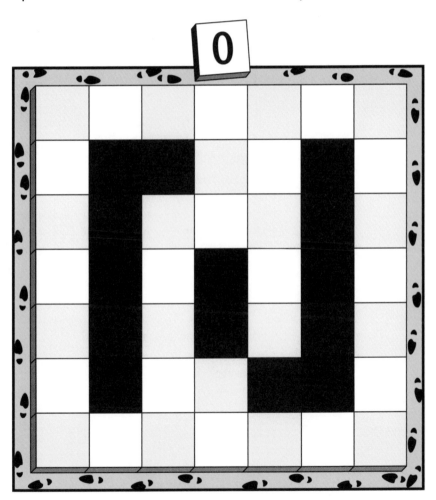

delete ONE

Delete one letter from **A FLARING END** and find the deciding game.

Plant Evidence

Here's a mixed bag of questions to challenge your mastery of the plant world.

1. Which plant flavors gin?
   a. Anise
   b. Juniper
   c. Lingonberry

2. What is a perennial plant?
   a. One that lives for more than one season
   b. One that blossoms year-round
   c. One that lives for about one month after flowering

3. Sitka and Norway are types of which coniferous tree?
   a. Maple
   b. Spruce
   c. Oak

4. Who saw: "…a crowd, a host, of golden daffodils"?
   a. William Wordsworth
   b. William Blake
   c. William Holden

5. What plant is the national flower of Northern Ireland?
   a. Wild Irish rose
   b. Marsh marigold
   c. Shamrock

6. What color are gorse flowers?
   a. Pink
   b. White
   c. Yellow

7. What does a deciduous tree do with its leaves in winter?
   a. It keeps them
   b. It sheds them
   c. Neither—this type of tree doesn't have leaves

8. From what plant is opium extracted?
   a. Poppy
   b. Crocus
   c. Willow bark

9. Busy Lizzie, jewelweed, and touch-me-not are all common names for what type of flower?
   a. Impatiens
   b. Geranium
   c. Begonia

10. What color are fresh coconuts?
    a. Yellow
    b. Green
    c. Brown

do you KNOW? In *The Winter's Tale*, which plant did Shakespeare describe as "the fairest flowers o' the season"?

CROSSWORD — On the Strip

ACROSS
1 ___ metabolism
6 European high points
10 Silicate used as an insulator
14 Plato's marketplace
15 Jim Nabors' soldier role
16 Yankee slugger
17 Perfumed powders
18 Blueprint
19 Songsmith Porter
20 Robert Louis Stevenson novel
23 Lady of Spain
24 Honeybunch
25 "___ Talkin' ": Bee Gees
28 ATM need
30 Victorian, in a way
34 "Harvest" singer DiFranco
35 Painted Desert sights
37 Acclimatize
38 What answers to clues are
41 Paid for a hand
42 Tamarack
43 Eight-ball stick
44 Units of wisdom?
46 Jacobi in *Avalon*
47 Many adoptees
48 Puppy plaint
50 Sevier Lake locale
52 Yankee Stadium song
58 Slow story
59 Musical disk
60 Pond greenery
61 Black-hearted
62 Succulent herb
63 First two-time Nobelist
64 Rolex face
65 New Jersey players
66 Success has a sweet one

DOWN
1 Cotton sheet
2 Food thickener
3 Loafer part
4 Mortal Kombat milieu
5 Calf roper's handful
6 Evaluation
7 Grammy winner Lovett
8 *Dead Men Don't Wear ___* (1982)
9 Has a gut feeling
10 Yankee Doodle's "feather"
11 Item in Tiger's bag
12 Frosty
13 Citrus drink
21 Let float, as a currency
22 Running a bit behind schedule
25 Mexican cathartic
26 Ludicrous
27 Windows 7 predecessor
29 Like SpongeBob's voice
31 Corner chair occupant
32 Tiler's mortar
33 Concurrences
35 Musical mixture
36 Mooches
39 "All right then ..."
40 Less than right?
45 Party catchphrase
47 Taxonomic division
49 Common worker
51 Flying radar station
52 *Avatar* aliens
53 "Grace Before Meat" essayist
54 Clove hitch, e.g.
55 Fiend of dreams
56 Bannister
57 Howard of *Annie Get Your Gun*
58 Guitarist Nugent

Construction

All the words are hidden vertically, horizontally or diagonally—in both directions. The letters that remain unused form a sentence from left to right.

```
T H E C O N C S F M T R U C T
I R S T E E L O T T O O N I N
D E U S M T R C C R Y R I S A
P M N E E E E R A C O T N D
L O N O M J T E M E B P I A U
A T C A O I N C P C S L E C R
S S N R H G E I T O O A E R A
T U P C I W P T S L T N H S B
E C R S O N R S E O A N T F L
R A E O I O A A G G C E U S E
E D D A T E C L D Y S R O N M
R A R K I C N P I O F F I C E
G D H O M E A S R O O F E R W
A G R A V E L R B R I C K N I
D O N A I C I R T C E L E T R
T N E M N O R I V N E H E R I
R E B M U L P S T R O U C T N
S L A I R E T A M U R C E S G
```

- ARCHITECT
- BRICK
- BRIDGES
- CABLES
- CARPENTER
- CEMENT
- CONTRACTOR
- CUSTOMER
- DESIGNER
- DRAINPIPE
- DURABLE
- ECOLOGY
- ELECTRICIAN
- ENVIRONMENT
- FOREMAN
- GRAVEL
- MATERIALS
- MORTAR
- OFFICE
- PLANNER
- PLASTERER
- PLASTIC
- PLUMBER
- PROJECT
- ROOFER
- STEEL
- WIRING
- WOOD

Sudoku

Fill in the grid so that each row, each column and each 3 x 3 frame contains every number from 1 to 9.

							5	
9		3						
					9	8		4
		4			3	2		8
		1		8				
7			9			6		
4			8	7			2	5
	2					1		
5							6	

do you KNOW?

What was the name of Henry VIII's first wife?

_____

_____

FRIENDS

What do the following words have in common?

STRUCTURE VISIT APPEAR BUILD FINANCE

Close Encounters

ACROSS

1 Uproar
6 Two-masted sailboat
10 Pintail duck
14 Division signs
15 Potpourri
16 To ___ his own
17 Green finch
18 Tick off
19 Title for a big Turk
20 Comedian encounters film director
23 Punk rock genre
24 Twitch
25 Soundtrack insertion
28 Expectant
31 Stunned and speechless
35 2011 Jay-Z/Kanye West song
37 Lacquered metalware
39 Prefix for "sun"
40 Golfer encounters business baron
43 ___ de menthe
44 Carlisle's wife in *Twilight*
45 Blackthorn fruit
46 Blanched salad green
48 Stereo preceder
50 +
51 French denial
52 Suffix for expert
54 Rock star encounters U.S. senator
63 Christmas carol
64 Award for David Mamet
65 Wanted-poster word
66 Intro to mi
67 Skywalker's teacher
68 O'Reilly of *M*A*S*H*
69 Cross-country gear
70 Blind a falcon
71 Dictation whiz

DOWN

1 *Bonanza* brother
2 Assist a prankster
3 *Billy Budd* captain
4 EVOO part
5 Stanley Kubrick's art
6 Meditative discipline
7 Banned pesticide
8 Chamberlain of basketball fame
9 Davidovich in *Hollywood Homicide*
10 "Needles and Pins" group
11 Crèche trio
12 German for "genuine"
13 Question start
21 Slogan
22 Kind of court
25 *La ___ Vita* (1960)
26 Road reversal
27 Took the Schwinn
29 Actress Skye
30 Milk whey
32 "Be-Bop-___" (1956 hit)
33 Cowell of *The X Factor*
34 Imbibed
36 Florida State team
38 *Sesame Street* Muppet
41 English cattle breed
42 Material for Strauss
47 Cherishes
49 Awards for *The Artist*
53 Standing ovation, e.g.
54 Wide receivers
55 U.S. magazine (1937–71)
56 *Burnt Toast* author Hatcher
57 Instrument of African blackwood
58 Cloak
59 Boortz of talk radio
60 Mayor's underling
61 John, in Moscow
62 *Quo Vadis?* emperor

TRIVIAL PURSUIT **1942**

Little Golden Books changed publishing history when they launched in 1942. These low-priced, high-quality books boasted sturdy cardboard covers, colorful drawings and gold-foil spines.

KIDS LOVED 'EM, AND PARENTS COULD EASILY BUY THEM AT STORES WHERE THEY SHOPPED.

1 What was the average cost of Little Golden Books in 1942?

_____

2 Which title is the No. 1 bestseller of all time?

_____

3 Which Golden Books author also wrote *Goodnight Moon*?

_____

4 Generations of children have loved *The Bunny Book*, written by this Golden Books author. Who is he?

_____

5 In 1951, the Little Golden Books titles *Nancy and Doctor Dan, The Bandage Man* came with this product glued next to the title pages.

_____

6 Which of these titles is NOT a Little Golden Book?

A) *The Little Red Hen (1942)*

B) *Soft Kitty, Warm Kitty (1965)*

C) *The Saggy Baggy Elephant (1947)*

D) *Donny and Marie: The Top Secret Project (1977)*

_____

TEST YOUR RECALL

On September 4, 1942, the movie *Holiday Inn* was released and featured Bing Crosby singing what Christmas song?

_____

Binairo

Complete the grid with zeros and ones until there are 5 zeros and 6 ones in every row and every column. No more than two of the same number can be next to or under each other. Rows or columns with exactly the same content are not allowed. There is only one valid solution.

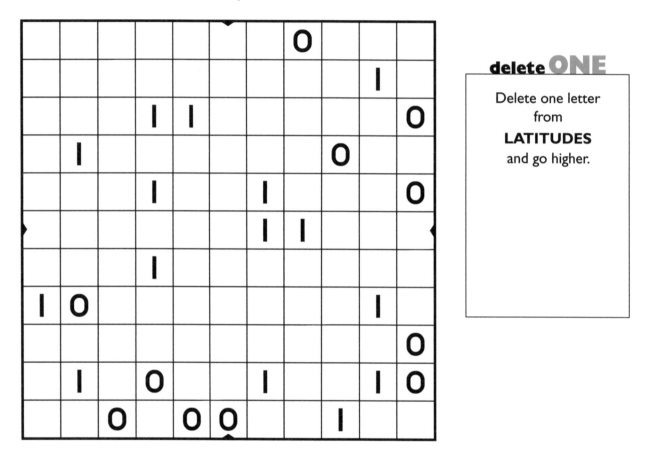

delete ONE

Delete one letter from **LATITUDES** and go higher.

ONE LETTER LESS OR MORE

The word on the right side contains the letters of the word on the left side plus or minus the letter in the middle. One letter is already in the right place.

I D E A L I S M -M D ☐ ☐ ☐ ☐ ☐ ☐

CROSSWORD Themeless

ACROSS

1 Healthy hangouts
5 Lab tube
10 Blondie drummer Burke
14 Audition goal
15 Close, in verse
16 City in Ohio or Peru
17 Decorative jug
18 Nutcracker's love
19 Burden
20 Cardinale in *The Pink Panther*
22 Elsa is a famous one
24 Gatling ___
25 Start for mature or school
26 "Heavens!"
35 Ph.D. exams
36 Buckaroo show
37 Farewell salutation
38 Sunny-___ up
39 Some skirts
40 Calm
41 Sardine whale
42 Desire wrongfully
43 Cliché-ridden
44 *Butterfield 8* Oscar winner
47 Suffix for hatch
48 USN police
49 Zorro's horse
53 "Hello, Goodbye" group
57 *The Time Machine* people
58 Like krypton
60 Mystique
61 Heaps
62 Harvest goddess
63 Itemize
64 Plaster support
65 Mardi Gras parade sponsor
66 Passenger jets of yore

DOWN

1 Blueprint stat
2 Ratchet part
3 Vicinity
4 Uphill battle
5 *Scent of a Woman* Oscar winner
6 *To Live and Die ___* (1985)
7 Shade of green
8 Spouse of a countess
9 Walks aimlessly
10 *Star Wars: Episode II* army
11 Queue
12 Six-foot birds
13 Catholic service
21 Performing pairs
23 "... ___ it seems"
26 *Damn Yankees* choreographer
27 Projecting window
28 Wheel spokes, e.g.
29 Compete at Indy
30 Trio trio
31 *Despicable Me* girl
32 Bubbling in the pot
33 City near Osaka
34 Certain fisherman
39 Whale of fiction
40 "He's a Rebel" group (with "The")
42 Buono of *The Sopranos*
43 Spanish hors d'oeuvre
45 Summit
46 Fly with a bad bite
49 Bird whose name is a color
50 Spanish stew pot
51 Carrot, e.g.
52 Humdinger
53 Make tea
54 Director Buñuel
55 Once, formerly
56 College Boards
59 Before, to Keats

Sunny

Where will the sun shine? With the knowledge that each arrow points to a place where a symbol should be, can you locate the sunny spots? The symbols cannot be next to each other vertically, horizontally or diagonally. A symbol cannot be placed on top of an arrow. We show one symbol.

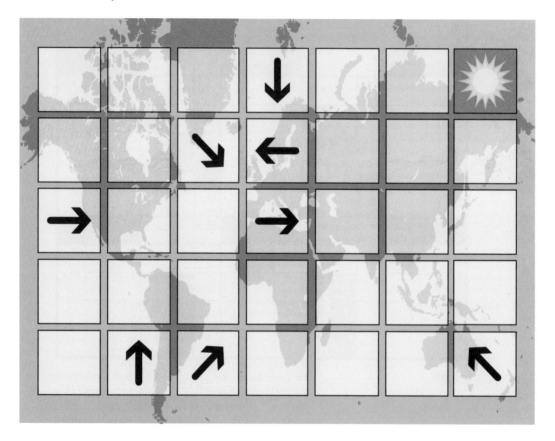

BLOCK ANAGRAM

Form the words that are described in the brackets with the letters above the grid. Extra letters are already in the right place.

A DAYDREAM (Merit for performance in motion picture)

CROSSWORD Enter Here Please

ACROSS

1 Starbuck's skipper
5 Beyond range
9 Kind of glass
14 Soccer's "Black Pearl"
15 Firebug
16 Long-tailed primate
17 1968 movie scripted by 45 Across
20 Went 60 in a 35
21 Boston Red ___
22 Former member of the jet set
23 Alpine region
25 Dogcatcher's catch
27 Museum curator's deg.
30 Where 45-A was born
34 Clumsy one
36 Mayday
37 Garden toiler
39 Giant hunter
40 Raven cry
41 Lasagna, e.g.
42 ___ avail (futile)
43 Illusionist Valentino
44 Be a backseat driver
45 *Requiem for a Heavyweight* author
48 Canada explorer John
49 Suffix for saw
50 Hirsch in *Milk*
52 Soak up
55 Super Bowl attractions
57 Timeless
61 TV show created by 45 Across
64 Bollywood locale
65 Prep a perp
66 Scottish actor Cumming
67 Commodious
68 Good Queen ___ (Elizabeth I)
69 Mesmerized

DOWN

1 Software "killers"
2 1965 Beatles album
3 Winglike processes
4 "John Brown's Body" poet
5 Kiwi genus
6 Author Dostoevsky
7 Husky utterance
8 Becomes compost
9 Solar trailer
10 Prairie
11 Sound boosters
12 Calendar abbr.
13 Once, formerly
18 Menlo Park wizard
19 ___-pocus
24 French explorer
26 Amy Winehouse song
27 Record blemish
28 Hurly-burly
29 Peptide acid
31 Heifer
32 Private reply?
33 *Murder by Death* maid
35 "Mad-Eye" of Hogwarts
38 Tear down
40 Edge or Volt, e.g.
41 Friend of Pooh
43 *Falstaff* composer
44 *Spamalot* roles
46 Shipping lane
47 Impressions
51 Neptunian chef on *Futurama*
52 Work at a gravy job?
53 "Yipes!"
54 Child, in combinations
56 Unsliced bacon
58 Orlando lake
59 Ginger cookie
60 Shipped
62 Director Burton
63 "How Can ___ Sure" (1967 hit)

Word Wheel

How many words of three or more letters, each including the letter at the center of the wheel, can you make from this diagram? No plurals or conjugations. We've found 21, including one nine-letter word. Can you do better?

Word Sudoku

Complete the grid so that each row, each column and each 3 x 3 frame contains the nine letters from the black box below. The hidden nine-letter word is in the diagonal from top left to bottom right.

A B C E H N Q R S

S						B	E	
N	E		B	R		S		
B			S			Q	C	
		H					B	
Q			N		A		S	
			Q		H			
	R			N		E		
Q	N			E				

do you KNOW?

Where do you find the Englischer Garten?

_____

_____

SANDWICH

What five-letter word belongs between the word on the left and the word on the right, so that the first and second word, and the second and third word, each form a common compound word or phrase?

WING _ _ _ _ _ PERSON

Traveling Music

ACROSS

1 Downwind
5 Wild guess
9 Hognose snake
14 Neeson in *The Haunting*
15 First-rate
16 "The Thief of Bad Gags" comic
17 Red Hot Chili Peppers song
19 Like Brown's campus
20 Rather
21 Goes through again
23 ___ *Number Four* (2011)
24 Bed bug
25 Marketplaces
29 Washington, D.C. river
32 Kind of bopper
33 Like Stephen King tales
35 Soprano Sumac
36 *Law & Order* figures: Abbr.
37 Bogus
38 Garbage boat
39 Winter boot
40 Téa in *Ghost Town*
41 1 inch = 1 foot, say
42 Classy
44 Blackened, Cajun-style
46 Tattered
47 Soul singer Shola
48 French jets
51 Champagne features
55 Related maternally
56 Song by the Lonely Island
58 Heavenly ram
59 Strawberry measure
60 "The Miracle Resolvent Soap"
61 Church belief
62 "Survey ___ ..." (*Family Feud* phrase)
63 German dam or river

DOWN

1 Asian mountain range
2 Creditor's claim
3 Cup handles
4 Love and hate, e.g.
5 Italian sub meat
6 Grahame's terrible driver
7 Shaker leader Lee
8 Ballpark beverage
9 Proficiency
10 Danny in *Get Shorty*
11 Beatles song
12 Gen. Robert ___
13 Carmine and scarlet
18 North Pole explorer
22 Atlanta campus
25 Day's march
26 Olympian's award
27 Cat Stevens song
28 Took off like ___
29 Uncontrolled fear
30 Soap plant
31 Crowed
34 Voting "nay"
37 Slant-cut pasta
38 "Words with Friends" cousin
40 Most immense
41 Ballroom dance of Brazil
43 Pointy beard
45 Frequents
48 Beef
49 Memo words
50 Mini drinks
51 Like seahorses
52 Washerful
53 Wasp nest locale
54 Asterisk
57 Broadway's *Mamma ___!*

WORD SEARCH Fast Food

All the words are hidden vertically, horizontally or diagonally—in both directions. The letters that remain unused form a sentence from left to right.

```
T H E D A N O M E L E S A S L
O W O F O O E S T U N Z K H D
M O O V B A B E K E Z C M A E
F N T I T X I M L I A R T W Y
S P O B P P O S P N E V O A R
E D A T O A F A S G V S T R T
F L O E O L D A R Y I N Y M S
L D F W H O A U L T T N H A U
T S T R O C B K E I A P T R D
S E E S E M E E F S R S L S N
O C R V A N E T A E C R A E I
T U T H R A C C L B U E E L D
I A G Y R O S H A O L G H G E
R S U G A R I U F T G A N N X
O P I O N A L P A R N N U I T
D I D R H O T D O G I E E R R
G D I O N A L L E Z T E R P A
C Y T T A F L U I S I T S N E
```

- CHEAP
- COLA
- DIP SAUCE
- DORITOS
- EGG ROLL
- EXTRA
- FALAFEL
- FATTY
- FOOD
- FRENCH FRIES
- GYROS
- HAMBURGER
- HOT DOG
- INDUSTRY
- KEBAB
- KETCHUP
- LEMONADE
- LUCRATIVE
- MEATBALL
- NUTS
- OBESITY
- OVEN
- PIZZA
- PRETZEL
- PRINGLES
- SHAWARMA
- SNACKS
- SUGAR
- TEENAGERS
- TRAIL MIX
- UNHEALTHY

Sudoku X

Fill in the grid so that each row, each column and each 3 x 3 frame contains every number from 1 to 9. The two main diagonals of the grid also contain every number from 1 to 9.

	8						9	
2			6					
	6	4	2	5		3		7
				7		6	8	
		2	5					
1								
		7	4	2	1			
				3				8
					1			

do you KNOW?

What started the Great Fire of Chicago?

LETTER LINE

Put a letter in each of the squares below to make a word which is "DIFFICULT TO SEE." The number clues refer to other words that can be made from the whole.

3 4 9 5 7 POWERFUL PERSON; 2 7 9 2 10 PLANTS WITHOUT STEMS;

9 5 7 6 ABYSS; 7 10 2 6 PLANT PART; 6 4 2 3 FROTH

1	2	3	4	5	6	7	8	9	10

CROSSWORD Winter Fun

ACROSS

1 Wood used in closets
6 Slangy hello
9 Black paving substance
12 Make amends
13 Imitate
14 *Cat ___ Hot Tin Roof* (2 words)
15 Home, for some cowboys
16 Winter fun: ___, curled up by a fire
18 Elude
20 "Would ___ to you?" (2 words)
21 Illusionist Penn's sidekick
24 Sandra Bullock movie
25 Operates
26 A single instance
29 Wager
30 Nebraska city
31 Cheer word
34 Movie pig
35 Type of wrestling
36 Illness-causing bacteria (abbrev.)
40 Choose
42 Stun
43 Curriculum ___
45 Winter fun: building ___
47 Spats
51 Long period of time
52 Baseball player "Master Melvin"
53 Ice abode
54 Brand of jeans
55 Cow's sound
56 Gangsters

DOWN

1 Automobile
2 Airport (abbrev.)
3 ___ Quixote
4 Winter fun: making snow ___
5 Superman Christopher
6 Difficult
7 Fencer's sword
8 Word of agreement, in voting
9 Type of fabric
10 Little Orphan ___
11 Carried on
17 Salsa or hummus
19 Fragrance
21 Winter fun: outdoor hot ___
22 Compass direction (abbrev.)
23 Allow
24 Word before salt or level
27 Catch
28 Treasure ___
30 ___-Wan Kenobi
31 Regret
32 Movie theater chain (abbrev.)
33 Winter fun: sipping ___ cocoa
35 Winter fun: going on a ___ ride
36 Henry Ford's son
37 Kayak's cousin
38 Atmosphere layer
39 U.S. secretary of the Treasury
41 "Weird Al" Yankovic song (2 words)
43 Reject
44 ___ *Thin Air*
46 Dad's partner
48 ___ shot
49 Ground-hugging cloud
50 Distress call

Kakuro

Each number in a black area is the sum of the numbers that you have to enter in the next empty boxes. The empty boxes that make up the sum are called a run. The sum of the across run is written above the diagonal in the black area and the sum of the down run is written below the diagonal in the black area. Runs can only contain the numbers 1 through 9 and each number in a run can only be used once. The gray boxes only contain odd numbers and the white only even numbers.

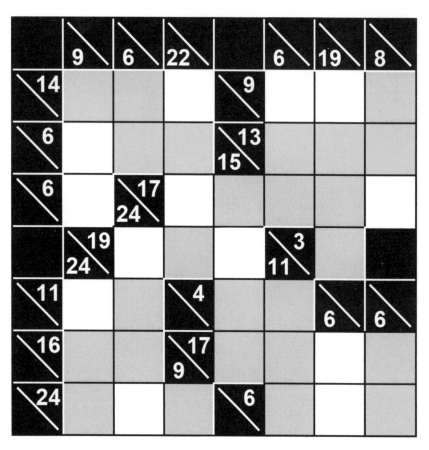

do you KNOW?

What is the capital of North Korea?

_____

_____

CROSSWORD # Invisible Ink

ACROSS

1 Strand of smoke
5 Violinist Zimbalist
10 Make an impression
14 River of Munich
15 Iris relatives
16 Result of a cobble job
17 *Dumbo* paraders
19 Matador's cloak
20 Cause of disappearing beaches
21 Indian summer month
23 Like Homer Simpson's dad
24 Leander's love
25 Many Little League coaches
27 Honesty, charity, etc.
30 River of Rome
33 Tabloid abductor
35 Hosp. patient's need
36 Grip
37 Rather remote
38 City near Mauna Loa
39 Numero ___
40 Great buy
41 ___ jury
42 Vanquishes
44 Former apple pesticide
46 Wheel connector
47 Had something to say
51 Rocky Mountain state
54 French novelist France
55 Largest dam in Germany
56 Popular potable
58 Protein-rich seed
59 Mother's-side relative
60 Rowlands of *Another Woman*
61 Olympian
62 Removed a word
63 Blue-pencil

DOWN

1 Does dish duty
2 Rhone feeder
3 Sitting room
4 Wielded a gavel
5 Me-tooed
6 Drescher of *The Nanny*
7 Gadget guru Popeil
8 Prefix for plasm
9 Shenanigans
10 Chaperon
11 "Mull it over!"
12 Handle pressure
13 "I ___ a Rhapsody"
18 Furry
22 Little gull
26 Black Friday come-ons
27 Stringed instrument
28 Old woman who wrestled Thor
29 Glasgow dweller
30 Dull sound
31 *Say Anything* ... actress Skye
32 Instant
34 Mauna ___
37 Was present at
38 Legacy
40 Reception room
41 Prairie banana
43 Actors with no lines
45 Yearned
48 Well-known
49 1985 Kate Nelligan film
50 Play the Pied Piper
51 Arizona elevation
52 Le Pew has a strong one
53 English composer (1710–78)
54 Part of A.M.
57 Ending for editor

A Walk on Wall Street

Take a stroll through the center of the financial universe with this collection of questions only an insider trader would know.

1. What term is used to describe a trader or investor who is pessimistic about a market, stock, or position, and believes that prices will drop?

_____

2. Name the only company listed in the Dow Jones Industrial Index today that was also included in the original index in 1896?

_____

3. What is the name of Dow Jones's flagship publication, founded in 1889?

_____

4. At her death in 1916, Henrietta Howland Robinson Green left a fortune that today would be worth about $17 billion, which she largely amassed through investing. What was her nickname in the finance world?

_____

5. If you were to go to 11 Wall Street in New York City, where would you be?

_____

6. What term is used to describe a trader or investor who is optimistic about a market, stock, or position, and believes that prices will rise?

_____

7. October 29, 1929, is known as the worst day in stock market history. What day of the week was it?

_____

8. Who served orange juice and brioche to traders the morning of October 19, 1999, to celebrate shares of her company being sold to the public?

_____

9. Which president was inaugurated on the steps of a building on Wall Street?

_____

10. In which city was the first stock exchange in America founded in 1790?

_____

TEST YOUR RECALL

In which year was Black Monday, when stock exchanges crashed in London and New York?

_____

BRAINSNACK® Shooting Hoops

A point is scored when the ball lands on an orange square. Give the coordinates of the last square that should be orange.

CROSSWORD # Songs of the Season

ACROSS

1 Witch
4 Cola
8 *What Child Is ___?*
12 Amazement
13 "Beware the ___ of March"
14 Zeus' wife
15 Harry Potter's best friend, ___ Weasley
16 *God Rest Ye Merry, ___*
18 Designer Calvin
20 Hammer, for example
21 River obstruction
23 Type of grated cheese
27 *___ the Red-Nosed Reindeer*
31 Elaborate house
32 Kids' card game
33 Jump
35 Peep-___ sandal
36 *___ the Jungle Girl*
39 *___ in a Winter Wonderland*
42 Unwavering
44 Principle of Eastern religion
45 Hawaiian dishes
47 Hooked up
51 *O Little Town of ___*
55 Iron ___
56 *___ Brockovich*
57 Adoration
58 Pen brand name
59 *O Christmas ___*
60 College head
61 Word screeched when spotting a mouse

DOWN

1 *___! The Herald Angels Sing*
2 Army acronym
3 Unit of heredity
4 Traffic light
5 Poetic tribute
6 Scratch
7 John Jacob ___
8 *___ & Louise*
9 Edge of a garment
10 Belligerence
11 ___ Francisco
17 Weaving device
19 Wedding words
22 Speed limit sign (abbrev.)
24 Against (prefix)
25 12 p.m.
26 State south of Wash.
27 Massages
28 Single
29 Finished
30 *___ I Met Your Mother*
34 Gentle touch
37 Girl from *Scooby-Doo*
38 No. 1 TV show *American ___*
40 Male police officers
41 Large Japanese goldfish
43 Right-of-way street sign
46 Clog, for example
48 Housecoat
49 Pennsylvania city
50 *___ the Halls*
51 Wager
52 Flub
53 Even score
54 Actress Longoria Parker

WORD SEARCH Athletics

All the words are hidden vertically, horizontally or diagonally—in both directions. The letters that remain unused form a sentence from left to right.

```
U L T R A M A R A T H O N Y A
T H E L E T S T A N D S I R C
D S R C T R A I N I N G S U I
I H S O A A S P O R T T H J A
S O S T O R W A S O R I G N I
C E N T D D Y P M U J H G I H
U S A N O I T A R A P E R P L
S L D Y P P C U L L M I A O S
T P N E I L W N O E A N V S Y
H O I L N I I A N K R D E E N
R D W K G L K E T D A O L L O
O I L T E C O J T C T O H D L
W U I V A S B M O E H R G R H
I M A R C O I R S H O T P U T
N J T O E L E R O I N U J H A
G E A B E K C L A S W S S I C
C C K O L Y M P I C G E O A E
H A M E S G E V A E R T L N D
```

- BOEBKA
- COACH
- DECATHLON
- DISCUS-THROWING
- DOPING
- GEVAERT
- GRAVEL
- HIGH JUMP
- HURDLES
- INDOOR
- INJURY
- JAVELIN
- JOHNSON
- JUNIOR
- LEWIS
- MARATHON
- MILE
- OUTDOOR
- PODIUM
- PREPARATION
- RELAY RACE
- SHOES
- SHOT PUT
- SPIKES
- STANDS
- STOPWATCH
- TAIL WIND
- TRACK
- TRAINING
- ULTRAMARATHON

Answers (Do You Know? and Trivia answers are on page 224)

PAGE 8
Signs of Spring

L	I	S	P		A	F	R	O		R	A	M
O	W	I	E		R	E	E	F		A	H	A
Y	O	R	E		D	A	F	F	O	D	I	L
		P	L	O	T			S	A	I	N	T
A	P	P	E	A	R		M	E	R	I	T	S
W	E	I	R	D		J	U	T				
E	G	G	S		B	A	D		J	E	E	R
		S	U	M		C	A	R	V	E		
B	A	N	D	E	D		S	A	C	R	E	D
A	R	O	S	E		K	I	N	K			
B	U	I	L	D	I	N	G		E	L	M	O
A	B	S		E	V	E	N		T	O	A	D
R	A	E		D	Y	E	S		S	A	N	D

PAGE 9
Sudoku

6	8	3	4	5	2	7	9	1
2	4	9	7	1	8	6	3	5
7	1	5	3	6	9	8	4	2
5	9	6	8	2	3	4	1	7
8	3	4	1	7	5	9	2	6
1	7	2	6	9	4	5	8	3
4	2	1	5	8	7	3	6	9
9	5	8	2	3	6	1	7	4
3	6	7	9	4	1	2	5	8

UNCANNY TURN •
THE DORMITORY

PAGE 10
Cage the Animal

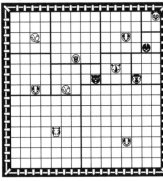

LETTERBLOCKS • KETCHUP /
MUSTARD

PAGE 11
Up and Down

A	B	I	G		O	B	E	L	I		S	H	A	W
N	A	D	A		L	U	N	A	R		T	A	L	E
T	H	E	S	A	D	S	A	C	K		E	P	E	E
S	T	O	O	G	E	S		E	S	C	A	P	E	D
			L	O	S				P	L	Y			
T	S	H	I	R	T	S		S	M	A	S	H	E	D
A	L	A	N	A		P	E	A	R	S		O	E	R
N	A	P	E		T	R	A	C	T		S	U	R	E
Y	I	P		S	O	E	U	R		A	T	R	I	A
A	N	Y	T	I	M	E		A	D	V	I	S	E	D
			F	O	G				E	E	L			
V	I	E	T	N	A	M		A	B	R	E	A	S	T
I	N	L	A		S	A	D	B	U	T	T	R	U	E
L	O	L	L		A	C	O	R	N		T	I	N	S
A	N	A	S		S	H	E	I	K		O	A	K	S

PAGE 12
Textiles

Textile means all that is woven, but the term also designates fabrics that are made in a different way.

PAGE 13
Keep Going

DELETE ONE • DELETE A AND
FIND MENTION

PAGE 14
Over the Rainbow 1

S	P	A	N			P	B	S			U	L	N	A
L	A	R	I		B	L	E	E	P		S	A	I	D
A	R	O	N		R	U	R	A	L		E	T	N	A
G	R	E	E	N	E	G	G	S	A	N	D	H	A	M
			T	O	E			C	O	T				
	A	G	E	N	D	A		L	E	M	O	N	S	
S	P	R	E	E		S	L	A	B			E	T	A
P	A	I	N	T	T	H	E	T	O	W	N	R	E	D
A	C	E			H	O	M	E		A	U	D	R	A
	E	F	F	O	R	T		R	E	V	I	S	E	
		A	R	O			R	E	S					
C	L	O	C	K	W	O	R	K	O	R	A	N	G	E
L	O	D	I		E	M	E	N	D		N	O	R	M
A	R	I	L		R	E	N	E	E		C	L	A	M
P	I	N	E			N	O	W			E	A	S	Y

PAGE 15
Maddening Maze

PAGE 16
Word Sudoku

G	R	A	U	M	S	T	D	I
S	U	D	I	R	T	M	G	A
M	T	I	G	D	A	R	U	S
A	G	M	T	U	D	S	I	R
I	S	R	M	A	G	U	T	D
U	D	T	S	I	R	G	A	M
T	A	U	D	S	M	I	R	G
R	M	G	A	T	I	D	S	U
D	I	S	R	G	U	A	M	T

SANDWICH • BACK

PAGE 17

Decorator's Delight

1. cabriole—[B] curved furniture leg. "That *cabriole* shape mimics Rufus's hind leg!" the collector's son boasted.

2. trug—[A] shallow basket. Barbara's handmade *trugs* are ideal for carrying flowers.

3. bolster—[C] long pillow. A pair of comfy *bolsters* soften the ends of a daybed.

4. pilaster—[A] column jutting from a wall. Two enormous *pilasters* flanked the entrance, dwarfing the hand-carved door.

5. torchère—[B] stand for a candlestick. "Would you mind bringing the *torchère* over here?" Dean's grandmother intoned from the dark corner.

6. grommet—[B] eyelet to protect an opening. The *grommets* jangled as I yanked open the drapes and tried to duck out.

7. pounce—[A] transfer a stencil design. Diane tried to duplicate her drawing by *pouncing* it, but the effect was lost.

8. patina—[A] weathered look of copper or bronze. "How long before the roof dulls to that fantastic *patina*?" Janice asked.

9. finial—[A] ornament at the tip of a lamp or a curtain rod. Tacky *finials* cluttered the stark window treatments.

10. organdy—[C] transparent muslin. To soften your bedroom, try *organdy* curtains—they'll filter the light.

11. newel—[B] central post of a circular staircase. The handrail is sound, but the *newel* needs replacing.

12. bergère—[A] upholstered chair with exposed wood. Invented in the 1700s, the *bergère* was designed for lounging.

13. ceruse—[C] pigment composed of white lead. Applying a *ceruse* finish may help conceal the table's flaws.

14. Bauhaus—[B] of or relating to a German school of functional design. The *Bauhaus* influence was clear in her early drawings.

15. incise—[C] engrave. A carpenter may *incise* his name into his furniture.

VOCABULARY RATINGS
9 and below: Nate Berkus knockoff
10–12: designer on a dime
13–15: HGTV design star

PAGE 18

Over the Rainbow 2

PAGE 19

Sport Maze

UNCANNY TURN • SECURITY

PAGE 20

Spot the Difference

PAGE 21

Hollywood Glamour

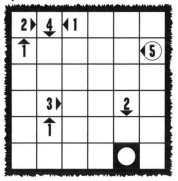

PAGE 22

Sudoku

4	2	6	5	3	9	7	8	1
8	7	9	1	4	6	5	2	3
5	1	3	7	8	2	9	6	4
9	3	7	6	2	5	1	4	8
6	4	5	8	9	1	3	7	2
2	8	1	4	7	3	6	5	9
1	6	2	9	5	8	4	3	7
3	9	4	2	6	7	8	1	5
7	5	8	3	1	4	2	9	6

TRIANAGRAM • RETRAIN / TERRAIN

Answers

PAGE 23

Roman Empire

The Roman Empire probably became too large to be properly governed and protected.

PAGE 24

Good Arrows

Tabulate the possible scores so that each set equals 142. Only three ways are possible:

50 + 40 + 40 + 6 + 4 + 2 = 142
50 + 40 + 20 + 20 + 10 + 2 = 142
100 + 20 + 10 + 6 + 4 + 2 = 142

The first score must be Robin's, as this is the only row in which 44 can be scored in two shots. The third score is Marion's, as this includes a six and we have already established that the first score is Robin's. Therefore, Maid Marion hit the bull's-eye.

PAGE 25

Target Practice

Each person's score differs by a multiple of two from everyone else's. Therefore, each score must be made up of the same number of odd and even numbers.

Alison 37 (8 + 8 + 21)
Jill 31 (8 + 8 + 15)
Keith 35 (6 + 8 + 21)
Martin 29 (6 + 8 + 15)
Charles 33 (6 + 6 + 21)
Jonathan 27 (6 + 6 + 15)

BLOCK ANAGRAM •
MERYL STREEP

PAGE 26

Petite

PAGE 27

Horoscope

END GAME •
(B O Y F R I E N D)
(E N D O S C O P Y)
(R E P R E H E N D)
(A P P E N D A N T)

PAGE 28

Sunny

BLOCK ANAGRAM •
JEAN DUJARDIN

PAGE 29

Gardening Gear

PAGE 30

Number Cluster

DOODLE PUZZLE • RINGTONE

PAGE 31

Word Pyramid

I
(1) RI
(2) AIR
(3) RAIN
(4) IRENA
(5) AIRMEN
(6) CARMINE
(7) AMERICAN

202

PAGE 32

Not So Petite

L	A	S	H		S	H	A	W	M		A	J	A	R
I	D	E	O		A	E	R	I	E		T	U	N	A
L	A	R	G	E	M	A	R	G	E		O	M	I	T
T	H	E	W	E	S	T		S	T	U	M	B	L	E
		A	R	O					R	I	O			
S	A	B	R	I	N	A		M	A	S	C	O	T	S
T	R	I	T	E		G	R	E	T	A		Z	E	E
R	U	G	S		Y	E	N	T	A		P	A	P	A
E	B	B		S	E	N	S	E		P	O	K	E	R
W	A	R	M	E	S	T		S	T	O	R	I	E	S
	O	U	T					A	P	T				
M	A	T	T	H	E	W		S	T	U	R	G	E	S
O	S	H	A		G	I	A	N	T	P	A	N	D	A
S	T	E	T		A	N	N	U	L		I	A	N	S
H	A	R	E		D	O	D	G	E		T	W	A	S

PAGE 33

A Special Occasion

1. Christmas
2. Smörgåsbord
3. Stilton
4. The oil celebrates the Hanukkah miracle of the one-day supply of oil that lasted for eight days
5. Three days
6. Gingerbread
7. "Plum" is an Old English word for dried fruit
8. Easter
9. Sweets
10. Leaving the noodles long signifies a long and happy life

PAGE 34

Sudoku Twin

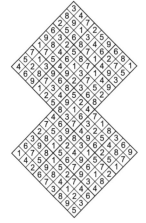

DOUBLETALK • ANT / AUNT

PAGE 35

Apple Varieties

P	A	N	G		R	A	C	E		A	R	M
O	L	E	O		I	V	A	N		L	E	I
P	E	E	L		C	O	R	T	L	A	N	D
		D	E	A	N		A	I	R	E	S	
D	E	M	E	A	N		K	I	S	M	E	T
A	G	E	N	T		G	A	L	A			
B	O	W		P	H	Y			E	R	R	
		F	U	J	I		A	G	R	E	E	
S	I	R	E	N	S		O	N	R	A	M	P
A	T	A	R	I		E	T	N	A			
M	C	I	N	T	O	S	H		N	Y	S	E
O	H	S		E	R	N	E		N	O	O	N
A	Y	E		D	E	E	R		Y	U	L	E

PAGE 36

Keep Going

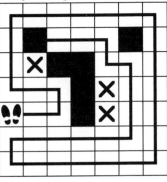

DELETE ONE • DELETE S AND FIND THE GAME OF BILLIARD

PAGE 37

Volcanos

The eruption of a super volcano can have catastrophic consequences and lead to a new ice age.

PAGE 38

'60s Hits

M	I	L	E		O	R	A	L	S		I	R	O	N
E	R	I	N		R	O	R	E	M		N	A	N	A
S	A	M	A	N	D	D	A	V	E		D	Y	E	S
S	E	A	B	E	E	S		I	L	L	I	C	I	T
			L	E	R			L	E	A	H			
A	L	T	E	R	E	D		T	E	E	N	A	G	E
D	A	H	S		D	I	V	E	D		A	R	I	D
O	T	E			C	I	S				L	A	I	
R	E	B	A		D	E	N	T	S		P	E	N	N
E	R	E	C	T	E	D		A	U	G	U	S	T	A
			A	T	O	P			G	A	L			
A	N	T	I	W	A	R		D	A	R	L	I	N	G
B	O	L	O		R	O	Y	O	R	B	I	S	O	N
A	M	E	N		T	R	A	D	E		N	E	V	A
T	E	S	S		S	Y	N	O	D		G	R	O	W

PAGE 39

Cage the Animals

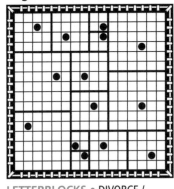

LETTERBLOCKS • DIVORCE / MARRIED

PAGE 40

Word Sudoku

D	N	I	L	V	A	M	G	E
A	E	G	I	D	M	N	V	L
V	L	M	N	E	G	A	D	I
I	G	N	A	L	E	V	M	D
M	V	D	G	N	I	L	E	A
L	A	E	V	M	D	G	I	N
E	M	A	D	G	N	I	L	V
G	I	V	E	A	L	D	N	M
N	D	L	M	I	V	E	A	G

SANDWICH • CUT

Answers

PAGE 41

The Space Race

M	A	D	A	M		B	O	N	A		W	H	A	T
A	T	A	R	I		A	M	O	K		H	E	L	I
H	O	M	E	S		C	A	N	A	V	E	R	A	L
I	M	P		S	O	O	N			A	R	O	S	E
		K	I	L	N		D	O	L	E				
P	E	R	N	O	D		F	I	V	E		T	R	I
A	L	I	E	N		R	I	V	E	T		H	A	S
C	A	P	E		L	U	N	A	R		N	E	I	L
E	T	E		R	O	M	A	N		S	E	I	N	E
S	E	N		E	N	O	L		T	H	O	R	N	S
		U	S	E	R		N	O	U	N				
S	C	O	P	E			A	I	N	T		S	H	H
A	R	M	S	T	R	O	N	G		T	E	P	E	E
T	U	N	E		O	A	T	H		L	A	U	R	A
E	X	I	T		B	R	I	T		E	R	N	S	T

CONNECT TWO •
WORK_____PARTY
MUTUALLY ___EXCLUSIVE
FREE_____LABOR
ONLY _____CHOICE

PAGE 42

Sport Maze

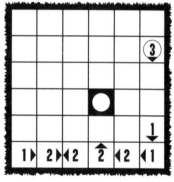

UNCANNY TURN • CONSIDERATE

PAGE 43

Futoshiki

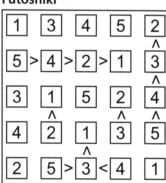

PAGE 44

Sudoku

5	8	3	7	1	9	2	6	4
6	9	4	3	2	8	5	7	1
1	7	2	4	6	5	9	3	8
7	4	8	2	5	6	3	1	9
9	3	5	8	7	1	6	4	2
2	1	6	9	4	3	8	5	7
8	6	9	1	3	7	4	2	5
3	2	7	5	8	4	1	9	6
4	5	1	6	9	2	7	8	3

FRIENDS • EACH CAN HAVE THE PREFIX POLY- TO FORM A NEW WORD.

PAGE 45

Flower Parts

L	E	A	F		M	A	O	R	I		S	G	T	S
U	G	L	I		E	L	L	E	N		H	O	O	T
G	O	O	D	F	R	I	E	N	D		A	B	B	A
E	S	T	E	L	L	E		T	I	P	P	L	E	R
		L	E	I			C	R	E	E				
S	A	P	I	E	N	T		M	A	E	S	T	R	O
A	B	U	T	S		A	D	I	T	S		P	A	X
G	A	R	Y		P	R	I	D	E		P	A	N	E
E	F	S		V	I	O	L	A		G	O	R	D	Y
S	T	U	D	E	N	T		S	C	O	T	T	I	E
		E	R	G	O			A	R	A				
I	M	P	E	A	C	H		O	N	E	T	I	M	E
D	A	R	A		H	A	L	E	Y	N	O	V	E	L
O	R	E	M		L	L	A	N	O		E	A	R	L
L	A	Y	S		E	L	T	O	N		S	N	E	E

PAGE 46

Word Pyramid

E
(1) E.T.
(2) EAT
(3) TEAM
(4) STEAM
(5) METALS
(6) AMULETS
(7) SIMULATE

PAGE 47

Trivial Pursuit 1957

1. The Whopper
2. Kentucky Fired Chicken (aka KFC)
3. Dairy Queen
4. More than 36,000
5. White Castle
6. Curbside speakers
7. Georgia

TEST YOUR RECALL •
THE QUARRYMEN

PAGE 48

Themeless

PAGE 49

St. Paddy's

PAGE 50

Spot the Amoeba

D. The figure is exactly the same shape except that large circles become small and vice versa.

PAGE 51

Meryl Streep

L	E	I	A		B	E	L	O	W		E	T	T	E
A	S	T	I		O	R	A	N	I		S	H	A	M
D	E	E	R	H	U	N	T	E	R		T	E	R	I
			L	I	R	E		R	E	C	E	I	P	T
S	H	O	A	L	S				L	E	E	R		
C	O	U	N	T	E	D		B	E	L	M	O	N	T
A	N	T	E	S		R	O	O	S	T		N	E	E
L	O	O	S		C	A	N	I	S		P	L	E	A
A	R	F		H	O	G	A	N		L	E	A	D	S
R	E	A	S	O	N	S		G	R	I	D	D	L	E
		F	O	N	T			O	B	E	Y	E	D	
C	A	R	R	E	R	A		O	U	R	S			
A	R	I	D		A	D	A	P	T	A	T	I	O	N
L	O	C	I		S	A	D	I	E		A	G	R	A
L	O	A	D		T	R	E	E	S		L	O	O	P

PAGE 52

Binairo

0	0	1	1	0	1	1	0	1	1	0	0
1	0	0	1	1	0	0	1	1	0	1	0
0	1	1	0	0	1	0	1	0	0	1	1
1	1	0	0	1	0	1	0	0	1	0	1
1	0	0	1	1	0	1	0	1	1	0	0
0	1	1	0	0	1	0	1	1	0	1	0
0	1	1	0	1	0	1	0	0	1	0	1
1	0	0	1	1	0	1	1	0	1	0	0
0	1	1	0	0	1	0	0	1	0	1	1
0	0	1	0	0	1	1	0	1	0	1	1
1	1	0	1	1	0	0	1	0	1	0	0
1	0	0	1	0	1	0	1	0	0	1	1

DELETE ONE • DELETE S AND GET REDUCTION

ONE LETTER LESS OR MORE • SEGMENT

PAGE 53

Hourglass

(1) KISSING
(2) SKIING
(3) KINGS
(4) SINK
(5) SPIN
(6) SPAIN
(7) PIANOS
(8) PASSION

PAGE 54

Planetarium 1

PAGE 55

Sudoku

7	8	2	3	1	6	4	9	5
6	3	9	5	4	7	1	2	8
1	4	5	8	9	2	7	6	3
9	2	6	1	5	3	8	4	7
4	1	7	9	6	8	3	5	2
3	5	8	2	7	4	9	1	6
8	9	1	7	2	5	6	3	4
2	6	3	4	8	1	5	7	9
5	7	4	6	3	9	2	8	1

TRIANAGRAM • STARLET / STARTLE

PAGE 56

Cage the Animals

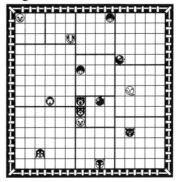

LETTERBLOCKS • AMAZON / ORINOCO

PAGE 57

Planetarium 2

A	L	M	S		T	R	U	E		S	C	A	L	E
L	A	I	C		H	I	R	T		A	L	D	E	R
A	C	T	I		E	A	S	T		H	A	V	E	N
E	Y	E	S	O	F	L	A	U	R	A	M	A	R	S
			S	P	A			I	R	O	N			
A	S	T	O	U	N	D		S	P	A	R	T	A	N
S	T	A	R	S		E	A	T	E	N		A	D	O
C	A	B	S		A	A	R	O	N		I	G	O	T
A	I	L		C	D	R	O	M		G	R	E	B	E
P	R	E	S	L	E	Y		P	R	A	I	S	E	S
		S	T	O	L			O	R	S				
J	U	P	I	T	E	R	S	Y	M	P	H	O	N	Y
E	N	O	C	H		I	T	S	A		S	L	O	E
S	T	O	K	E		M	I	E	N		E	D	N	A
T	O	N	Y	S		E	R	R	S		A	S	O	R

PAGE 58

Keep Going

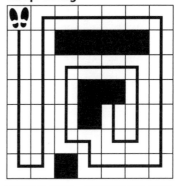

DELETE ONE • DELETE S AND FIND INVESTIGATOR

Answers

Sunny

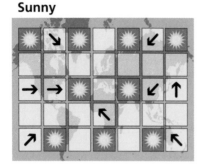

BLOCK ANAGRAM •
A SEPARATION

'70 Hits

P	A	T	S		S	U	D	A	N		O	P	E	N
A	S	I	A		P	R	O	M	O		R	I	D	E
T	H	E	B	E	E	G	E	E	S		I	N	G	E
T	E	R	R	A	C	E		S	T	R	O	K	E	D
I	N	S	I	S	T		R	O	L	F				
		N	E	E	R		B	I	B	E	L	O	T	
M	I	T	A		R	A	V	E	L		S	O	N	E
I	S	H			T	E	L			Y	E	A		
C	E	E	S		P	E	T	I	T		A	D	A	M
K	E	E	P	E	R	S		E	A	R	L			
		A	I	D	A			M	O	R	O	S	E	
V	A	G	R	A	N	T		S	A	M	O	V	A	R
A	L	L	I		C	A	R	O	L	E	K	I	N	G
I	G	E	T		E	M	O	T	E		E	N	D	O
L	A	S	S		D	E	M	O	S		R	E	S	T

Railways

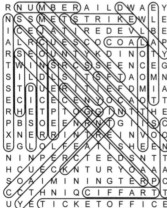

Railways were developed in England
at the beginning of the nineteenth
century as a mining technique.

Sport Maze

UNCANNY TURN •
TRANSGRESSIONS

Word Sudoku

C	E	G	M	P	R	S	H	O
R	O	S	C	E	H	M	G	P
H	P	M	O	S	G	R	E	C
O	C	R	P	G	E	H	S	M
G	S	H	R	O	M	C	P	E
E	M	P	H	C	S	G	O	R
P	H	O	S	R	C	E	M	G
S	G	C	E	M	O	P	R	H
M	R	E	G	H	P	O	C	S

SANDWICH • STREAM

Inspiring Women

C	U	R	I	E		T	S	P		C	A	N
A	S	I	D	E		R	E	A		E	C	O
P	A	P	E	R		E	A	R	H	A	R	T
		A	I	D	E	S		U	S	E	R	
K	E	L	L	E	R		O	B	E	S	E	
I	B	I	S		I	H	O	P				
T	B	D		A	V	E	R	T		E	L	I
		L	E	N	A		A	V	O	N		
T	S	A	R	S		T	E	R	E	S	A	
A	T	M	O		A	G	E	N	T			
H	E	P	B	U	R	N		D	H	A	K	A
O	R	E		P	E	A		O	U	T	E	R
E	N	D		S	A	T		F	R	A	N	K

Q&A

1. qua—[C] as, in the capacity of. Try to judge the short stories *qua* short stories, not as landmarks of literature, the student pleaded.

2. quay—[A] wharf. The passengers moaned as the new captain tried to meet the *quay* in the storm.

3. quaff—[B] drink deeply. Make three wishes and then *quaff* this mysterious elixir.

4. quasi—[B] having some resemblance. The credit offer is from a *quasi* company—there's no address, no phone number, not even an employee.

5. quahog—[A] edible clam. As the crew team's lead vanished, the coach just sat there like a placid *quahog*.

6. quantum—[B] specified amount. Showing off after physics class, Carly said, "That's an extreme *quantum* of homework, don't you think?"

7. quaver—[C] sound tremulous. Every time you try to tell a lie, your voice *quavers*.

8. quinoa—[A] grain from the Andes. When the waiter said it was tilapia and arugula on a bed of *quinoa*, Lauren asked for an English translation.

9. quondam—[B] former. As soon as Harry's *quondam* girlfriend spotted him, she burst into a quasi fit of joy.

10. quetzal—[B] tropical bird. Thinking the affair was a costume party, Andy showed up with an eye patch, a peg leg, and a *quetzal* on his shoulder.

11. quatrain—[C] four-line verse. As a hardworking poet, Jill needs to rest and raid the refrigerator after every *quatrain*.

12. quiniela—[A] type of bet. To win a *quiniela*, you need to pick the first- and second-place horses, but you don't need to specify the order of the finish.

13. quotidian—[B] occurring every day. Set in her *quotidian* routine, the puppy begged for an extra treat after breakfast and dinner.

14. quacksalver—[C] fraud or phony doctor. That *quacksalver* I go to prescribes calamine lotion for every complaint.

15. quinquennial—[C] occurring every five years. Um, darling, I think it's time for your *quinquennial* bourbon and ginger.

VOCABULARY RATINGS
9 and below: in a quandary
10–12: adequate
13–15: no equal

PAGE 66
Sudoku X

3	4	1	6	8	7	9	5	2
9	5	2	3	4	1	6	8	7
7	8	6	9	2	5	3	1	4
4	3	9	7	1	6	8	2	5
2	6	5	4	9	8	7	3	1
8	1	7	5	3	2	4	9	6
5	2	4	8	7	9	1	6	3
6	7	8	1	5	3	2	4	9
1	9	3	2	6	4	5	7	8

LETTER LINE • BUTTONHOLE; NOBLE, BOOTH, BLUE, TUBE, UNBOLT

PAGE 67
Shaker Stuff

T	E	M	P		C	O	M	A		P	I	P	E	R
A	S	E	A		O	M	A	N		A	D	E	L	E
S	A	L	T	N	P	E	P	A		T	E	P	E	E
S	U	S	T	A	I	N		S	C	R	A	P	E	D
			E	R	E			R	I	T	E			
O	P	P	R	E	S	S		L	U	C	E	R	N	E
M	I	E	N	S		H	A	Y	E	K		M	O	E
A	L	P	S		H	E	L	O	T		J	I	L	L
H	E	P		A	A	R	O	N		M	O	N	T	E
A	D	E	L	I	N	E		S	W	E	E	T	E	R
		R	E	M	O			O	R	B				
F	I	D	E	L	I	O		A	R	R	I	V	E	S
A	G	I	L	E		S	A	L	T	Y	D	O	G	S
C	O	N	E	S		S	I	G	H		E	L	A	N
T	R	E	E	S		A	D	A	Y		N	E	D	S

PAGE 68
Kakuro

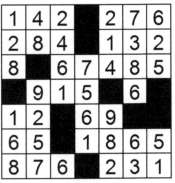

FRIENDS • EACH CAN HAVE THE SUFFIX -SCAPE TO FORM A NEW WORD.

PAGE 69
Spot the Difference

PAGE 70
George Clooney

S	H	A	H		C	R	E	E	D		W	R	I	T
P	A	N	E		H	O	R	D	E		H	A	R	E
A	S	T	A		A	T	S	E	A		E	P	I	C
T	H	E	D	E	S	C	E	N	D	A	N	T	S	
			L	E	T			B	R	C				
M	E	D	A	L	E	D		R	O	B	E	R	T	S
A	T	O	M			E	M	I	L	Y		O	H	A
T	H	E	P	E	R	F	E	C	T	S	T	O	R	M
T	O	R		N	O	O	N	E			S	T	E	M
E	S	S	E	N	C	E		R	E	B	U	S	E	S
			Y	U	K			F	U	N				
	T	H	E	I	D	E	S	O	F	M	A	R	C	H
F	I	E	F		O	V	A	T	E		M	A	R	E
E	C	R	U		V	I	N	I	C		I	R	O	N
N	O	E	L		E	L	E	C	T		S	E	W	S

PAGE 71
Resistance

Resistor A. Resistors with a red band are placed on the circuit board horizontally; those with a blue band are vertical.

QUICK WORD SEARCH •

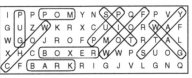

PAGE 72–73
One Among Many

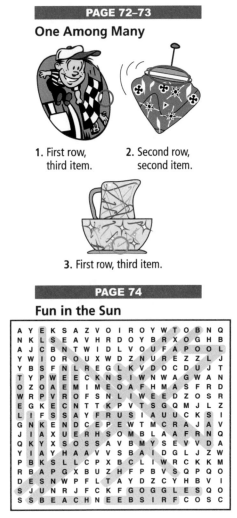

1. First row, third item.

2. Second row, second item.

3. First row, third item.

PAGE 74
Fun in the Sun

Answers

PAGE 75

Go Fly

Kite 5. All the other kites have a bow on the tail for each color on the kite. Kite 5 doesn't have a yellow panel.

QUICK CROSSWORD •

A		A		A						U	P
B	E	N	E	A	T	H		L		A	S
O		T		M				M	I	N	U	S
V		I		I				K			T	O
E			D	E	S	P	I	T	E			F

PAGE 76

Next in Line

1. c
2. b
3. d
4. c
5. a
6. d
7. b
8. a
9. c
10. b

PAGE 77

Sudoku

2	7	4	6	1	3	5	9	8
6	8	1	7	9	5	2	4	3
9	5	3	4	8	2	1	7	6
8	9	5	2	6	4	3	1	7
4	6	7	1	3	8	9	5	2
1	3	2	5	7	9	8	6	4
3	1	8	9	4	6	7	2	5
7	2	6	3	5	1	4	8	9
5	4	9	8	2	7	6	3	1

UNCANNY TURN • THE SWORD OF DAMOCLES

PAGE 78

Gridlock

7. Count the number of identically colored squares both horizontally and vertically on the axes that originate at the number. On the axes of the question mark there are 6 vertical squares and 1 horizontal square.

QUICK WORD SEARCH •

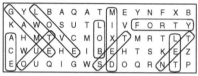

PAGE 79

'00s Hits

PAGE 80

Cool Cats

1. **b.** A tail
2. **a.** Cheetah
3. **a.** Tiger
4. **c.** Leopard
5. **c.** Ocelot
6. **a.** Its hairlessness
7. **a.** Cheetah
8. **b.** Burmese
9. **a.** Abyssinian
10. **c.** Manx

PAGE 81

Keep Going

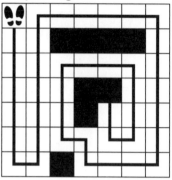

DELETE ONE • DELETE I AND FIND OPENER

PAGE 82

Sport Maze

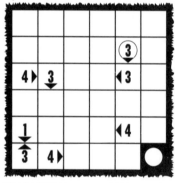

UNCANNY TURN • OPERATIONS

PAGE 83

Sticks and Stones

S	L	A	P		C	A	R	O	M		V	O	L	T
W	I	S	H		A	G	A	P	E		O	R	E	O
A	D	A	Y		N	A	S	A	L		O	L	E	S
P	O	P	S	I	C	L	E	H	O	L	D	E	R	S
		I	C	U				D	U	O				
D	E	S	C	E	N	T		A	E	R	O	S	O	L
O	L	L	A		H	A	N	O	I		T	W	A	
N	E	I	L	D	I	A	M	O	N	D	S	O	N	G
A	G	E		I	N	T	E	L		C	L	E	O	
T	Y	R	A	N	T	S		E	S	T	H	E	R	S
		L	E	R			T	A	O					
M	A	Y	B	R	E	A	K	M	Y	B	O	N	E	S
R	U	S	E		P	A	N	E	L		N	E	R	O
E	D	E	R		I	R	E	N	E		E	V	I	L
D	I	R	T		D	E	E	D	S		R	A	K	E

208

PAGE 84

Futoshiki

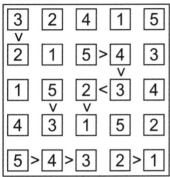

CONNECT TWO •
ALMOST _____READY
STUNTED _____GROWTH
TALK_____SHOW
UNUSUAL _____ROUTINE

PAGE 85

Word Sudoku

P	L	Z	D	I	N	A	E	Q
E	I	Q	P	Z	A	L	D	N
A	D	N	L	E	Q	Z	P	I
D	A	L	E	Q	Z	N	I	P
Q	P	I	N	A	L	E	Z	D
N	Z	E	I	D	P	Q	A	L
I	Q	D	A	L	E	P	N	Z
Z	E	P	Q	N	D	I	L	A
L	N	A	Z	P	I	D	Q	E

SANDWICH • ROAD

PAGE 86

Stormy Weather

S	L	A	V		N	A	S	T	Y		S	T	O	W
P	E	R	I		O	U	T	I	E		H	U	M	E
E	A	T	S		U	R	A	L	S		E	N	N	A
C	R	Y	I	N	G	I	N	T	H	E	R	A	I	N
			T	I	A				I	M	P			
B	A	R	I	S	T	A		A	V	I	A	T	O	R
A	G	I	N		D	E	C	A	L		E	R	E	
S	I	N	G	I	N	I	N	T	H	E	R	A	I	N
E	L	K		N	O	O	S	E		A	S	E	A	
D	E	S	A	L	T	S		D	R	Y	C	E	L	L
			N	A	H				E	E	K			
A	D	A	Y	W	I	T	H	O	U	T	R	A	I	N
B	R	E	W		N	O	O	N	S		E	L	B	E
B	A	R	A		G	R	A	C	E		N	O	E	S
A	B	O	Y		S	E	X	E	S		T	E	X	T

PAGE 87

Journalism

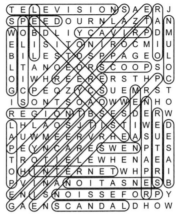

A journalistic message answers the questions who, what, where, when, why and how.

PAGE 88

Sudoku Twin

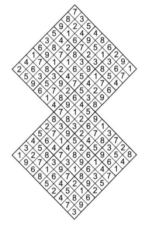

DOUBLETALK• BREACH / BREECH

PAGE 89

In the Backyard

P	A	T	H		N	E	M	O		I	M	A
I	D	E	A		O	V	A	L		T	I	S
T	E	A	M		B	I	R	D	B	A	T	H
			M	A	L	L		M	E	L	E	E
O	P	P	O	S	E		S	A	T	Y	R	S
T	R	A	C	K		R	A	N				
T	O	C	K		P	O	T		S	H	E	D
			D	A	B		C	U	B	A	N	
F	E	N	N	E	L		S	E	N	O	R	A
E	V	I	A	N		P	L	O	D			
D	O	G	H	O	U	S	E		I	O	T	A
U	K	E		T	H	A	W		A	N	E	W
P	E	R		E	F	T	S		L	O	N	E

PAGE 90

Building Blocks

A2, D3, BCE1. The building blocks always form a group of four identically colored blocks.

QUICK CROSSWORD •

PAGE 91

Binairo

0	1	1	0	1	0	0	1	0	0	1	1
1	0	1	0	1	0	0	1	0	1	1	0
0	1	0	1	0	1	1	0	1	1	0	0
0	0	1	1	0	1	0	0	1	0	1	1
1	1	0	0	1	0	1	1	0	0	1	0
1	0	1	1	0	1	0	1	0	1	0	0
0	1	0	0	1	1	0	0	1	1	0	1
1	0	1	1	0	1	1	0	0	1	0	0
0	0	1	1	0	0	1	0	1	1	0	1
1	1	0	0	1	1	0	1	0	0	1	0
1	0	1	0	0	1	1	0	1	0	0	1
0	1	0	1	0	0	1	0	1	1	0	1

ONE LETTER LESS OR MORE •
ONBOARD

DELETE ONE • DELETE S AND FIND A PATHOLOGIST

PAGE 92

Hoofers

D	A	R	N	■	M	Y	T	H	■	S	A	B	E	R
E	R	I	E	■	E	E	R	O	■	T	R	U	C	E
A	N	N	M	I	L	L	E	R	■	R	I	D	O	F
F	E	D	E	R	A	L	■	S	T	E	E	D	■	■
■	■	■	S	O	N	■	■	■	R	E	T	Y	P	E
S	P	R	I	N	G	S	■	P	O	T	T	E	R	S
T	H	U	S	■	E	A	R	E	D	■	A	B	A	T
O	R	B	■	■	■	L	I	P	■	■	■	S	T	A
L	A	Y	S	■	P	E	A	S	E	■	B	E	E	T
E	S	K	I	M	O	S	■	I	N	T	E	N	S	E
N	E	E	S	O	N	■	■	■	D	E	N	■	■	■
■	■	E	T	U	D	E	■	G	L	A	N	C	E	D
S	E	L	E	S	■	G	E	N	E	K	E	L	L	Y
S	E	E	R	S	■	G	R	A	S	■	T	I	L	E
T	E	R	S	E	■	S	A	T	S	■	T	O	A	D

PAGE 93

Intersection

7. There is always a red circle on a perpendicular T-intersection.

QUICK WORD SEARCH •

E	N	G	I	N	E	L	E	X	H	A	U	S	T	T
Q	U	A	E	C	J	L	H	G	E	A	R	L	L	X
G	T	I	L	X	B	R	Z	N	N	N	I	O	R	K
T	R	R	A	X	F	U	E	L	N	O	B	B	A	V
J	A	C	K	W	A	D	T	M	A	N	U	A	L	V

PAGE 94

Horoscope

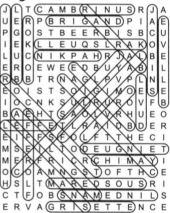

END GAME •

(ASCENDANT)
(CRESCENDO)
(BARTENDER)
(ENDECAGON)

PAGE 95

Hard Stuff

R	O	T	C	■	S	I	G	M	A	■	A	P	O	D
B	R	I	O	■	C	R	A	I	G	■	L	U	R	E
I	R	O	N	M	A	I	D	E	N	■	G	M	A	N
■	■	■	F	A	T	S	■	N	O	R	E	P	L	Y
I	N	S	U	L	T	■	■	■	M	A	R	I	■	■
R	A	T	T	L	E	R	■	R	E	M	I	N	D	S
O	G	E	E	■	R	A	M	O	N	■	A	G	E	E
N	A	E	■	■	■	C	O	B	■	■	■	I	V	E
I	N	L	A	■	D	E	P	O	T	■	B	R	I	M
C	O	W	B	O	Y	S	■	T	H	E	R	O	S	E
■	■	H	A	W	N	■	■	■	R	A	I	N	E	D
S	T	E	L	L	A	R	■	M	I	T	T	■	■	■
A	R	E	O	■	M	A	N	O	F	S	T	E	E	L
K	I	L	N	■	I	N	E	R	T	■	L	E	V	Y
I	P	S	E	■	C	A	T	T	Y	■	E	L	A	N

PAGE 96

Trivial Pursuit 1962

1. "The Ballad of Jed Clampett"; bubblin' crude, black gold, Texas tea
2. "Y'all come back now, y'hear?"
3. Ce-ment pond
4. Critters
5. Bodine; son of Jed's cousin Pearl
6. Mother-in-law
7. Mr. Drysdale
8. Jane Hathaway
9. Jed; bloodhound
10. Possum
11. Bug Tussle
12. Fancy eatin' table
13. 1921 Oldsmobile
14. Daisy

PAGE 97

City Gates

Point 9.

QUICK CROSSWORD •

T	R	A	C	K	■	■	B	■	■	D	■	■	■	■
■	U	■	H	■	■	■	A	Q	U	A	T	I	C	S
■	G	■	E	■	■	■	L	■	■	R	■	■	■	U
■	B	A	S	E	B	A	L	L	■	T	■	■	■	M
■	Y	■	S	■	■	■	■	■	■	S	O	M	B	O

PAGE 98

Metallica

S	H	E	L	■	I	R	O	N	Y	■	I	C	A	N
I	A	S	I	■	S	O	F	I	A	■	D	O	L	E
N	I	C	K	E	L	B	A	C	K	■	E	P	E	E
S	L	E	E	V	E	S	■	E	S	C	A	P	E	D
■	■	■	N	E	T	■	■	■	■	U	T	E	■	■
A	M	H	E	R	S	T	■	R	O	B	E	R	T	O
F	O	I	S	T	■	S	H	I	N	E	■	H	O	B
T	O	Y	S	■	M	A	M	A	S	■	P	E	R	E
E	L	O	■	T	A	R	O	T	■	M	E	A	T	Y
R	A	S	C	A	L	S	■	A	M	A	N	D	E	S
■	■	I	L	L	■	■	■	■	I	O	N	■	■	■
P	O	L	E	C	A	T	■	I	S	R	A	E	L	I
A	L	V	A	■	G	O	L	D	F	I	N	G	E	R
G	L	E	N	■	O	B	E	L	I	■	T	O	N	I
E	A	R	S	■	G	E	N	E	T	■	S	S	T	S

PAGE 99

Belgian Beers

J	L	T	C	A	M	B	R	I	N	U	S	R	J	A
U	E	R	P	B	R	I	G	A	N	D	P	I	A	E
P	G	O	S	T	B	E	E	R	B	I	S	B	C	U
I	E	K	L	L	E	U	Q	S	L	R	A	K	O	V
L	U	C	N	I	K	P	A	H	R	J	A	L	B	E
E	R	O	E	W	E	E	D	B	U	Y	A	B	I	L
R	B	B	T	R	N	A	G	L	P	V	P	L	N	L
E	O	I	S	T	S	O	I	G	I	M	O	E	S	E
I	O	C	N	K	S	U	L	R	U	R	O	V	F	B
B	A	E	H	T	S	A	O	L	V	R	H	U	E	O
L	E	F	F	E	T	L	R	A	I	D	B	D	E	R
E	I	F	F	S	F	O	L	F	T	T	H	E	C	I
M	S	E	I	L	T	O	D	E	U	G	N	I	E	T
M	E	R	F	R	I	C	R	C	H	I	M	A	Y	I
O	C	O	A	M	N	G	S	T	O	F	T	H	C	E
H	S	L	T	M	A	R	E	D	S	O	U	S	R	I
C	T	F	O	B	S	N	A	M	E	D	N	I	L	S
E	R	V	A	G	R	I	S	E	T	T	E	N	C	E

Trappist beer is brewed by Trappists, monks of the Order of the Cistercians of the Strict Observance.

PAGE 100

Sudoku

5	8	6	3	1	9	4	7	2
2	1	4	5	7	6	8	3	9
7	9	3	8	2	4	5	1	6
4	2	1	7	6	3	9	5	8
9	6	8	1	5	2	7	4	3
3	5	7	4	9	8	6	2	1
6	7	5	9	3	1	2	8	4
1	4	9	2	8	7	3	6	5
8	3	2	6	4	5	1	9	7

TRIANAGRAM • SHARES / SHEARS

PAGE 101

Map File

1. Corsica
2. South Africa
3. France
4. Poland
5. Iceland
6. Italy
7. Peru
8. New Zealand
9. Mexico

PAGE 102

Historic Aircraft

S	H	O	T		O	P	A	R	T		O	O	P	S
L	E	A	H		S	A	R	A	H		C	L	E	O
E	N	T	E	R	P	R	I	S	E		E	D	A	M
P	R	E	P	A	R	E		P	O	T	A	B	L	E
T	I	R	A	D	E			R	U	N	E			
		P	A	Y	S		N	I	L	S	S	O	N	
P	O	W	E	R		K	N	E	E	L		S	L	O
A	M	I	R		B	A	B	E	S		S	I	A	M
C	N	N		S	A	L	A	D		P	E	E	V	E
S	I	N	A	T	R	A		S	C	A	N			
		I	R	O	N			A	R	T	I	S	T	
S	H	E	L	L	A	C		A	B	S	E	N	C	E
H	O	M	E		C	H	A	L	L	E	N	G	E	R
O	N	A	N		L	E	A	S	E		C	O	N	S
O	G	E	E		E	T	H	O	S		E	T	T	E

PAGE 103

Sport Maze

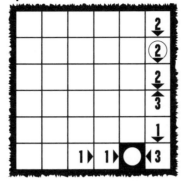

UNCANNY TURN • POTATO

PAGE 104

Keep Going

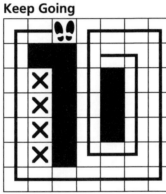

DELETE ONE • DELETE A AND FIND THE DENTIST

PAGE 105

Get Set for Back to School

D	U	B		T	I	E	R		C	H	A	T
I	T	O		A	S	T	A		H	O	P	I
B	A	C	K	P	A	C	K		A	M	E	N
S	H	A	N	E			E	A	S	E		
		O	D	I	N			N	E	R	D	S
M	U	S	T		T	O	A	D		O	I	L
A	R	C		C	A	M	P	Y		O	N	A
U	G	H		A	L	A	S		S	M	O	G
L	E	E	K	S		D	E	L	E			
		D	O	E	S			O	A	T	H	S
A	G	U	A		P	O	R	T	R	A	I	T
M	A	L	L		E	D	I	T		I	L	E
P	L	E	A		D	E	M	O		L	O	W

PAGE 106

Floor Plan

Floor plan 2. In floor plan 2, the element in the top right-hand corner is reflected on its vertical axis.

QUICK CROSSWORD •

PAGE 107

Word Pyramid

O
(1) GO
(2) EGO
(3) LOGE
(4) GLOBE
(5) BOGGLE
(6) BLOGGER
(7) GOLDBERG

PAGE 108

Word Sudoku

M	B	R	J	O	A	S	G	N
A	O	S	N	B	G	R	J	M
J	G	N	M	R	S	B	A	O
S	R	A	O	N	M	J	B	G
N	J	O	A	G	B	M	S	R
G	M	B	S	J	R	O	N	A
O	N	M	G	S	J	A	R	B
B	S	G	R	A	O	N	M	J
R	A	J	B	M	N	G	O	S

SANDWICH • HORSE

Answers

PAGE 109

Flower Power

1-2-8-15-16-20

QUICK CROSSWORD •

PAGE 110

Weather

1. inclement—[B] severe. Today's kite festival has been canceled due to *inclement* weather.

2. temperate—[A] marked by moderation. After that cold snap, we could really use some *temperate* conditions.

3. aridity—[C] drought. If this *aridity* continues, I swear I'll do my rain dance.

4. nimbus—[B] rain cloud. We took one glance at the looming *nimbus* and headed straight for shelter.

5. doldrums—[B] stagnation or listlessness. FYI, the everyday use of *doldrums* refers to the area around the equator where prevailing winds are calm.

6. inundate—[C] flood. After the storm, our tiny shop was *inundated* with water and debris.

7. abate—[A] decrease in force, as rain. "I do believe," said Noah, "that the downpour is about to *abate*."

8. convection—[B] hot air rising. Sea breezes are a common weather effect of *convection*.

9. striated—[B] banded, as clouds. You could almost climb the ladder suggested by those *striated* cirrus clouds.

10. hoary—[B] white with frost or age. Professor Parker's beard was almost as *hoary* as the windshield he was scraping.

11. leeward—[C] not facing the wind. We huddled on the *leeward* side of the island, well out of the stiff breeze.

12. graupel—[A] snow pellets. As I heaved my shovel in the winter nor'easter, *graupel* stung my cheeks like BBs.

13. insolation—[A] sunstroke. *Insolation* is a serious threat during summer football practices.

14. permafrost—[C] frozen subsoil. Excavating the *permafrost* in Alaska often requires a jackhammer.

15. prognosticate—[A] forecast. We might not always appreciate his opinion, but nobody can *prognosticate* like Punxsutawney Phil.

VOCABULARY RATINGS

9 and below: partly cloudy
10–12: generally sunny
13–15: clear blue skies

PAGE 111

At the Track

D	E	A	L		E	M	C	E	E		P	S	S	T

(crossword grid)

Across/grid entries:
DEAL · EMCEE · PSST
ERGO · MALTY · OTIS
BIRTHPLACE · SERA
SEAHOLLY · SOEVER
AMOS · GIGUE
OSPREY · WAGERING
STAID · TITHE · ROE
TARO · MOTET · TWIN
III · GOATS · WRIST
ARMCANDY · RAINES
URGES · SAGA
CUTESY · RIPOSTES
AGUE · BESTINSHOW
PLED · ANTED · IONA
OILS · GAUSS · CUSP

PAGE 112

Happy Anniversary

(word search grid)

PAGE 113

Sudoku

5	2	3	4	1	8	6	9	7
4	6	1	7	9	5	8	3	2
9	7	8	3	2	6	4	1	5
3	1	7	8	5	9	2	6	4
2	5	6	1	4	7	3	8	9
8	4	9	2	6	3	5	7	1
7	8	4	5	3	1	9	2	6
1	9	2	6	8	4	7	5	3
6	3	5	9	7	2	1	4	8

TRIANAGRAM • WHITER / WITHER

PAGE 114

Fashion Fads

(crossword grid)

Grid entries:
ZONES · PICOT · HOT
OPERA · AGORA · ONE
OILED · GOGOBOOTS
TEL · DOERS · SPOT
BLUR · ABU
REGRET · CITE · CPS
AFROS · NATAL · AOL
CLASH · ORB · LORNA
EAT · OLIVE · BLACK
RTE · EIRE · GOATEE
USE · DUTY
ASSN · POINT · ELS
MINISKIRT · ONYOU
AMI · TENET · MARDI
HIP · ENEMY · SHEET

PAGE 115

Losing Marbles

3. All non-purple marbles are in groups of five and form an angle.

QUICK CROSSWORD •

P		S	J				U	
E	T	H	I	O	P	I	A		S
R			A		P	A	K	I	S	T	A	N
U		C	H	I	N	A			
			N		N	O	R	W	A	Y

PAGE 116

Hourglass

(1) ELASTIC
(2) CASTLE
(3) STEAL
(4) TALE
(5) HATE
(6) EARTH
(7) THREAD
(8) HYDRATE

PAGE 117

High Spirits

A	H	A	B		C	R	O	A	K		S	T	O	P
N	A	V	I		A	I	S	L	E		A	H	S	O
T	H	E	G	I	N	G	A	M	E		R	E	E	L
		S	C	A	G		A	P	P	A	R	E	L
H	A	S	H	E	S			S	U	L	U
E	S	C	O	R	T	S		D	I	L	E	M	M	A
A	L	O	T		A	C	T	O	N		E	D	A	S
R	E	T			R	I	D			I	N	S
S	E	C	T		F	U	N	G	I		R	A	N	I
E	P	H	R	A	I	M		E	N	C	O	R	E	S
	B	A	R	R			L	A	D	Y	D	I
D	E	R	I	D	E	S		D	A	M	E
U	P	O	N		B	O	U	R	B	O	N	R	E	D
M	I	T	E		U	R	A	N	O		T	A	X	I
A	C	H	E		G	A	B	O	R		S	T	E	M

PAGE 118

Sunny

BLOCK ANAGRAM • TITANIC

PAGE 119

Sudoku X

8	5	3	1	6	4	7	2	9
9	6	2	7	5	8	4	1	3
1	4	7	9	3	2	8	6	5
3	9	4	5	2	7	1	8	6
6	7	1	8	4	9	3	5	2
5	2	8	6	1	3	9	7	4
7	1	5	4	9	6	2	3	8
4	3	6	2	8	1	5	9	7
2	8	9	3	7	5	6	4	1

LETTER LINE • RETROGRADE; TRADER, REGARD, GARTER, ERROR, OGRE

PAGE 120

Spot the Difference

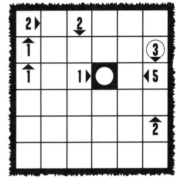

PAGE 121

In Memoriam 1

M	A	L	I		G	L	A	S	S		A	W	E	D
A	M	E	N		R	A	N	E	E		R	I	T	E
J	O	E	F	R	A	Z	I	E	R		A	N	T	E
O	L	D	L	A	D	Y		R	E	T	R	E	A	D
R	E	S	A	L	E				N	O	A	H
			M	E	S	A		C	A	R	T	O	O	N
H	O	S	E	S		T	R	A	D	E		U	M	A
A	N	T	S		A	L	I	K	E		U	S	E	S
I	C	E		F	L	A	M	E		A	N	E	N	T
R	E	V	E	A	L	S		S	O	L	S
	E	L	I	O					S	E	A	C	O	W
M	A	J	O	R	C	A		N	I	R	V	A	N	A
A	L	O	P		A	N	D	Y	R	O	O	N	E	Y
T	O	B	E		T	O	R	S	I		R	E	I	N
T	E	S	S		E	A	S	E	S		Y	A	L	E

PAGE 122

Sport Maze

UNCANNY TURN • A PARTNER

Hobbies

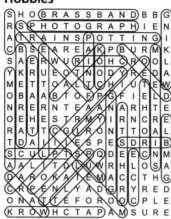

Hobbies are pursued out of interest, not as paid work; they are done for pleasure.

In Memoriam 2

A	P	A	R		D	I	M	E	S		S	P	C	A
R	E	N	O		I	L	O	N	A		Y	E	A	H
D	A	N	W	H	E	L	D	O	N		S	T	L	O
O	C	E	L	O	T	S		S	T	A	T	E	L	Y
R	E	S	A	L	E			I	G	E	R			
			N	E	D	S		H	A	R	M	F	U	L
F	O	L	D	S		I	M	A	G	O		A	L	E
I	S	I	S		S	T	E	N	O		G	L	E	N
N	E	Z		S	P	E	A	K		B	A	K	E	D
D	E	T	A	I	L	S		S	C	A	M			
		A	R	N	E			A	R	E	N	A	S	
D	A	Y	T	O	N	A		P	R	O	F	A	N	E
E	L	L	I		D	U	K	E	S	N	I	D	E	R
E	G	O	S		I	T	A	L	O		S	I	N	G
P	A	R	T		D	O	Y	E	N		H	A	T	E

Number Cluster

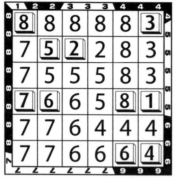

DOODLE PUZZLE • COMBINE

Great Ships

1. Vaporetti
2. *Amoco Cadiz*
3. *Lusitania*
4. *The Mississippi*
5. *The Carpathian*
6. The bow of another ship, the *Stockholm*
7. British troops
8. *Mayflower*
9. *Cutty Sark*
10. *Queen Mary*
11. *Lenin*
12. *Britannic*
13. *Argus*
14. *Flying Cloud*

Kakuro

2	4	1		9	4	5	3	2
1	2	3		5	1		9	7
	1	5	7	8		8	2	1
8	9		4	7	2	3	1	
2	3	1	6		8	9	6	4
4		4	2	8	5		8	9
1	6	3		7	6	4		6
5	9			4	1	3	2	
9	8	4	3			2	8	3

FRIENDS • EACH CAN HAVE THE PREFIX SUR- TO FORM A NEW WORD.

Keep Going

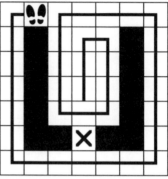

DELETE ONE • DELETE F AND FIND CONSIDERATE

A Short Distance

M	A	S	H		P	L	A	S	M		S	T	I	R
A	L	L	Y		E	A	G	L	E		T	R	O	I
S	K	I	P	S	C	H	O	O	L		R	I	N	D
C	A	M	E	L	O	T		E	S	C	A	P	E	S
			A	S	I			O	I	L				
A	S	H	O	T			L	A	N	T	E	R	N	
T	W	O	S		D	A	R	I	N	G		J	A	I
H	O	P	S	K	I	P	A	N	D	A	J	U	M	P
O	O	P		L	E	E	W	A	Y		A	M	I	S
S	P	I	R	I	T	S			G	Y	P	S	Y	
		N	A	N			A	B	A					
T	I	G	R	E	S	S		L	I	Z	A	R	D	S
O	N	M	E		S	K	I	P	P	E	D	O	U	T
O	R	A	L		N	I	C	H	E		I	D	E	O
T	I	D	Y		S	N	E	A	D		T	E	L	L

PAGE 130

Fictional Ships

B	O	M	B		P	I	N	N	A		C	R	E	E
A	L	E	A		O	R	I	E	L		H	E	L	L
B	L	A	C	K	P	E	A	R	L		A	D	A	S
Y	A	N	K	E	E	S		D	I	P	L	O	M	A
		B	L	Y			A	L	E	C				
C	A	J	O	L	E	D		K	N	O	T	T	E	D
A	G	O	N	Y		R	E	A	C	T		O	N	A
T	A	L	E		B	E	L	L	E		A	B	U	T
C	M	L		D	R	A	K	E		D	E	E	R	E
H	A	Y	S	E	E	D		S	T	I	R	R	E	D
		R	I	M	A				O	V	O			
R	I	O	R	I	T	A		S	T	A	B	L	E	S
A	A	G	E		H	I	S	P	A	N	I	O	L	A
G	M	E	N		E	R	R	O	L		C	A	I	N
E	A	R	S		R	E	S	T	S		S	N	A	G

PAGE 131

Number Maze

PAGE 132

Missing Art

F = blue and H = yellow. This work of art consists of 6 identical square areas that were each turned 45°.

QUICK WORD SEARCH •

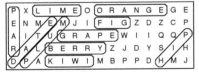

PAGE 133

Tea

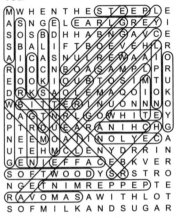

When the English have afternoon tea, they drink very strong tea with lots of milk and sugar.

PAGE 134

Sudoku

9	2	1	3	7	5	8	6	4
7	5	8	4	1	6	2	9	3
6	4	3	2	9	8	7	5	1
1	7	2	5	4	9	6	3	8
8	9	5	6	3	1	4	7	2
3	6	4	8	2	7	9	1	5
4	8	9	1	6	3	5	2	7
5	3	6	7	8	2	1	4	9
2	1	7	9	5	4	3	8	6

TRIANAGRAM • AIRMEN / MARINE

PAGE 135

Smorgasbord

M	A	S		A	S	S	E	S			P	L	E	B
A	S	P		C	A	C	T	U	S		O	O	Z	E
D	Y	E		A	M	E	R	I	C	A	N	P	I	E
A	O	N	E		U	N	E		H	I	T	S	O	N
M	U	S	T	S	E	E		R	E	N	I			
	E	N	G	L	I	S	H	M	U	F	F	I	N	
S	P	R	A	T		A	Y	E		F	L	O	E	
P	O	I		S	M	I	L	E	R	S		Y	U	M
E	L	A	N		A	D	O		A	V	I	S	O	
C	A	N	A	D	I	A	N	B	A	C	O	N		
		T	A	N	S			A	T	S	I	G	N	S
M	A	D	A	S	A		A	F	T		T	H	A	W
I	R	I	S	H	C	O	F	F	E	E		I	C	E
N	E	T	H		T	O	R	I	N	O		G	R	E
G	A	Z	A			P	O	N	D	S		H	E	P

PAGE 136

Futoshiki

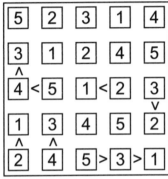

CONNECT TWO •
ETERNAL_____LIFE
GREAT _____DEPRESSION
LESSER _____EVIL
NEW_____ROUTINE

PAGE 137

Word Sudoku

E	A	B	D	S	P	N	Q	L
D	S	N	Q	B	L	E	A	P
Q	L	P	E	N	A	D	S	B
P	Q	E	L	D	S	B	N	A
N	B	S	P	A	E	Q	L	D
A	D	L	B	Q	N	P	E	S
B	E	D	S	L	Q	A	P	N
S	P	A	N	E	B	L	D	Q
L	N	Q	A	P	D	S	B	E

SANDWICH • STOP

PAGE 138

Sunny

BLOCK ANAGRAM •
JACK NICHOLSON

PAGE 139

AKA 1

PAGE 140

Trivial Pursuit 1974

1. The Conversation
2. Young Frankenstein
3. Blazing Saddles
4. Chinatown
5. The Sugarland Express
6. Alice Doesn't Live Here Anymore
7. The Great Gatsby

TEST YOUR RECALL •
MIA FARROW

PAGE 141

Spot It

6 spots. The dominoes are on an imaginary grid and the number of spots is equal to the values of the grid. The grid contains alternating rows with the numbers 4 5 4 5 4 5 4 5 and the numbers 3 6 3 6 3 6 3 6.

QUICK WORD SEARCH •

W	W	Z	C	A	N	A	P	E	S	P	I	L	L	R
K	I	Q	U	C	O	C	K	T	A	I	L	T	U	O
P	E	N	G	H	D	G	L	A	S	S	O	U	P	D
J	G	U	E	S	T	D	E	S	S	E	R	T	R	L
N	A	P	K	I	N	A	H	V	D	I	N	N	E	R

PAGE 142

Friends from the Start

C	A	S	A		E	T	A	P	E		S	P	A	M
A	L	A	N		N	A	T	A	L		K	A	L	E
P	A	L	I	N	D	R	O	M	E		I	L	I	A
P	E	A	S	O	U	P		S	P	O	I	L	E	D
			E	R	R				H	O	N	I		
E	M	P	T	I	E	D		C	A	L	G	A	R	Y
R	E	A	T	A		A	M	A	N	A		T	O	E
I	D	L	E		E	V	I	C	T		M	I	L	A
C	A	M		A	T	I	L	T		S	A	V	E	R
A	L	R	I	G	H	T		I	M	P	R	E	S	S
		E	S	A	I			A	A	R				
S	H	A	L	L	O	W		A	R	T	I	C	L	E
N	A	D	A		P	A	L	L	B	E	A	R	E	R
O	M	E	N		I	D	E	A	L		G	O	N	G
B	A	R	D		A	E	R	I	E		E	C	T	O

PAGE 143

Balls

Ball 3. The ball always turns 90° and changes color. The valve is on the top of the ball.

QUICK WORD SEARCH •

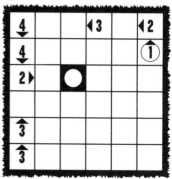

PAGE 144

Sport Maze

UNCANNY TURN •
PREMEDITATIONS

PAGE 145

Friends to the End

H	U	G	O		S	W	A	P		S	L	E	P	T
O	V	E	R		P	E	R	E		T	E	P	E	E
M	U	N	I	C	I	P	A	L		A	G	I	L	E
E	L	E	G	A	N	T		F	O	R	E	S	T	S
S	A	T	I	R	E			Z	I	N	C			
			N	O	T	E		C	O	N	D	O	N	E
S	E	P	A	L		S	L	I	N	G		P	O	L
C	U	R	L		S	T	A	T	E		R	A	N	K
A	R	I		P	E	E	V	E		S	A	L	E	S
B	O	N	D	A	G	E		S	E	M	I			
		C	O	D	A				D	A	N	C	E	R
S	W	I	N	D	L	E		P	I	C	C	O	L	O
P	A	P	A	L		B	L	A	C	K	O	P	A	L
A	G	A	T	E		O	U	S	T		A	R	N	E
S	E	L	E	S		N	C	O	S		T	A	D	S

PAGE 146

Many Thanks

```
P L Y M O U T H F F O O T B A L L S Z
L Y G N T K B B N M V X N P B I G S J
A I S T S G Y B W M V F N W I R R K N
T Z S Y E P N O V E M B E R P P A V D
T J L V V K X X O Q Y A M S X D C Y M
E Q A G R Z F R B F N E S D F F E B F
R B I U A W W A Y A D I L O H G G P M
J L P R H I E E S U W L S S P N D A H
O E O L O I K I T E V K R C I G Y R R
P S C P Z R R I T K I E S R X F D A E
I S U O U H T G M W V R E U L O G D V
L I N T B A B O N O T H R O Z N T E T
G N R Q R S D C T I T W W E I R E S T
R G O G L E L F F A F E S V B R W S G
I S C Z E W E H G F R F R Q U N A G C
M D B R C L H W H G E A U F U E A Q K
S M F H J L U E F X C N A T F A Y R F
I E X Z E I P N I K P M U P S G S D C
F X I G E G O C J U F S B C C Q B H J
```

PAGE 147

Sudoku

2	4	1	9	7	3	5	8	6
8	6	7	5	2	1	9	4	3
3	9	5	4	8	6	2	1	7
9	2	3	8	4	7	6	5	1
7	5	4	6	1	9	8	3	2
1	8	6	2	3	5	7	9	4
6	1	8	3	5	2	4	7	9
5	3	9	7	6	4	1	2	8
4	7	2	1	9	8	3	6	5

TRIANAGRAM • SAINT / SATIN

PAGE 148

AKA 2

```
O S S A   S C R A P   T H O R
C L U B   P A U L O   A U T O
T I N A T U R N E R   B L O T
A D U L A T E   S T R I K E S
D E P O R T     R U T H
    N E E R   F A T H O M S
L A D E   R E L A Y   A G A L
A M E   M A C     A R A
M I M I   D U P E D   E N V Y
B R I D G E S   D E R N
    M E E T   L O L I T A
F L O A T E D   R E T I R E S
L O O T   C A T S T E V E N S
I N R E   T R O V E   E N T E
T I E D   S T E P S   N E S T
```

PAGE 149

Seating Plan

Clockwise from bottom center:
Dave, Alice, Bob, George, Ida, Carl,
Jack, Harriet, Frank, Ella

PAGE 150

Keep Going

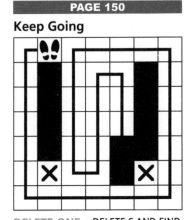

DELETE ONE • DELETE S AND FIND
TROUBLES

PAGE 151

Before and After

```
M A R Y   P O T T S   A L S O
A L E E   O S H I P   T O O L
V A N N A W H I T E H O U S E
S E T T L E   S H E E P D O G
    L O R D   E D A
D U N   U F O S   S L I V E R
I R I S   U N A S   E D I N A
J A C K B L A C K F R I D A Y
O N E I L   T R O I   G A T O
N O R M A N   A A R E   L E N
    D I S   L E A S
A C A D E M I C   A S P I R E
J A M E S B R O W N T R O U T
A P E D   L E M A T   A L D O
R E N E   E D E N S   T E E N
```

PAGE 152

Tiles

A4123B.

QUICK CROSSWORD •

```
    R             B   B
D E E P     M A R R I E D
  D   O P E N     B   O   N
      O     E   L O W   T
D E A R   A W A K E   N
```

PAGE 153

Binairo

I	O	I	I	O	O	I	I	O	I	O
I	I	O	O	I	O	I	I	O	I	O
O	I	I	O	I	I	O	O	I	O	I
O	O	I	I	O	O	I	I	O	I	I
I	I	O	O	I	I	O	O	I	I	O
O	O	I	O	I	I	O	I	I	O	I
I	I	O	I	O	O	I	I	O	I	O
I	I	O	I	O	I	O	O	I	O	I
O	O	I	O	I	I	O	I	O	I	I
I	I	O	I	I	O	I	O	I	O	O
O	O	I	I	O	I	I	O	I	O	I

DELETE ONE • DELETE S AND FIND
LATIN AMERICA

ONE LETTER LESS OR MORE •
SATANIC

PAGE 154

Themeless

```
B U M P   P E L L E   H O W L
O N E A   O R I E L   O L E O
S T E V E N S P I E L B E R G
C O T E R I E   S P O N G E S
    M A E     H B O
V A N E S S A   C A B B A G E
A L I N E   S T O N Y   B U S
L A S T   S T O A T   T E A S
E M E   S P E N T   C R A V E
N O I S I E R   S A H A R A N
    I N C     V I I
A B I G A I L   H E L P I N G
J E N N I F E R A N I S T O N
O B O E   I C I N G   E T T U
B E N D   C H O S E   D O E S
```

Answers

PAGE 155

Cookie Monster

1. **c.** A spicy hard gingerbread biscuit
2. **b.** A wholemeal cookie, sometimes dipped in chocolate
3. **d.** Twice-baked
4. **a.** A spicy gingerbread
5. **b.** The Dutch koekje, meaning little cake
6. **a.** A large spice cookie with raisins
7. **c.** A soft cinnamon-spiced cookie with a crackled surface
8. **d.** Spiced, baked in balls, and rolled in powdered sugar
9. **c.** Marzipan

PAGE 156

Number Cluster

DOODLE PUZZLE • **H**ITCH**C**OCK

PAGE 157

Garden

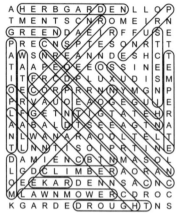

Allotments come in different sorts and shapes, including vegetable gardens, ornamental gardens and rock gardens.

PAGE 158

In the Vanguard

S	O	A	P		B	L	I	S	S		T	R	I	P
H	O	U	R		R	A	R	E	E		W	A	D	E
E	Z	R	A		A	N	A	R	M		O	V	E	N
L	E	A	D	I	N	G	Q	U	E	S	T	I	O	N
			O	D	D			M	L	I	I			
B	B	C		S	N	A	P		E	D	M	U	N	D
O	A	H	U		E	G	O	N		E	E	N	I	E
F	R	O	N	T	W	H	E	E	L	D	R	I	V	E
F	I	R	E	R		A	T	T	U		S	T	E	M
S	C	E	N	I	C		S	S	T	S		E	N	S
		G	A	L	A			H	A	H				
A	H	E	A	D	O	F	T	H	E	C	U	R	V	E
F	A	N	G		W	O	O	E	R		M	E	E	T
E	T	T	E		N	O	R	I	A		U	N	T	O
W	E	E	D		S	T	E	R	N		S	O	O	N

PAGE 159

Sudoku Twin

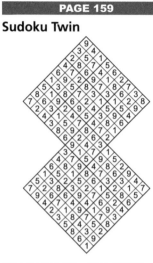

DOUBLETALK • ROLL / ROLE

PAGE 160

Melting

Ice cube 9.

QUICK WORD SEARCH •

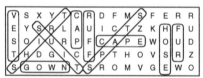

PAGE 161

Word Sudoku

P	W	D	O	T	S	A	V	R
T	A	V	W	R	P	O	S	D
O	R	S	D	V	A	P	T	W
V	P	R	S	A	D	T	W	O
S	O	T	R	W	V	D	P	A
W	D	A	T	P	O	S	R	V
D	V	W	A	S	T	R	O	P
A	S	P	V	O	R	W	D	T
R	T	O	P	D	W	V	A	S

SANDWICH • HAT

Concentration— Join the Dots

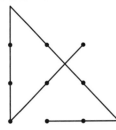

QUICK WORD SEARCH •

L	M	G	S	C	S	O	W	C	L	C	J	S	R	J
M	N	H	A	N	D	J	Q	K	O	W	Q	N	G	I
E	V	D	B	C	G	X	A	Z	S	P	J	A	E	N
R	K	I	N	G	E	Z	Y	C	E	H	R	P	P	A
K	W	H	O	C	P	L	A	Y	K	B	E	T	C	P

Night Lights

I	W	A	S	A		S	A	G	E		E	D	N	A
D	I	N	A	R		E	M	U	S		S	E	A	T
E	N	N	U	I		V	O	L	T		C	A	T	O
M	O	O	N	O	V	E	R	P	A	R	A	D	O	R
		A	S	I	N		S	T	O	L				
P	E	I		O	C	T	A		E	R	A	S	E	R
E	L	S	A		A	E	R	I		E	T	U	D	E
S	T	A	R	T	R	E	K	N	E	M	E	S	I	S
C	O	A	C	H		N	I	T	A		D	A	N	E
I	N	C	H	E	S		N	E	S	T		N	A	T
			E	R	I	C		L	E	A	S			
P	L	A	N	E	T	H	O	L	L	Y	W	O	O	D
R	I	D	E		C	U	B	E		L	I	N	G	O
A	D	A	M		O	T	I	C		O	P	A	L	S
M	A	R	Y		M	E	E	T		R	E	N	E	E

Maximize

890. The result is 128 + 79894 - 35604 = 44418.

QUICK CROSSWORD •

D		V				O		G	R	O	W	T	H
A	N	I	M	A	T	I	O	N			A		U
S		T				M					T		M
H	E	A	R	T		S	P	A	R	K	L	E	A
		L				H				R			N

Cooking Terms

1. gustatory—[B] relating to taste. Here, try my new *gustatory* experiment—beet ice cream!

2. au gratin—[C] covered with cheese and browned. Is there anything better than onion soup *au gratin* on a cold, rainy day?

3. succulent—[B] juicy. For dessert, the chef served pound cake topped with *succulent* pears.

4. mesclun—[A] mix of greens. "You call this a salad? It's just a plate of wilted *mesclun*."

5. piquant—[C] spicy. The *piquant* smells from the Mexican restaurant wafted out onto the street.

6. chiffonade—[B] shredded herbs or veggies. If you add a *chiffonade* of fresh basil, this frozen pizza isn't half bad!

7. toothsome—[B] delicious. Hattie makes the most *toothsome* cherry pie I've ever tasted.

8. sous vide—[C] cooked in a pouch. Though preparing steak *sous vide* takes time, it will cook your meat evenly and retain the moisture.

9. culinary—[A] of the kitchen. Julia Child was a true *culinary* icon.

10. umami—[C] savory taste. *Umami* is one of the five basic tastes, along with sweet, sour, salty, and bitter.

11. tempeh—[B] soy cake. Ezra, a devoted vegan, serves *tempeh* burgers and tofu dogs at his cookouts.

12. fricassee—[A] cut and stew in gravy. Tired of turkey sandwiches and turkey soup, Hector decided to *fricassee* the leftovers from his Thanksgiving bird.

13. oenophile—[A] wine lover. A serious *oenophile*, Adrienne was horrified when her date added ice cubes to his pinot noir.

14. poach—[A] cook in simmering liquid. For breakfast, Sasha loves to *poach* an egg and pair it with avocado toast topped with tomato.

15. fondant—[B] cake icing. Kelly flunked her cake-making class when she slathered on too much *fondant*.

VOCABULARY RATINGS
9 and below: apprentice
10–12: head cook
13–15: master chef

Dominator

Shape 2. In the previous series it emerged that the order in ascending superiority is: D - E - B - A - C. Green is dominant in E and F.

QUICK CROSSWORD •

T	R	U	E	G	R	I	T		P	U	S	H
I				A		H			A			
T		P	A	N	D	O	R	U	M			
E				G		R			L			
	G	I	J	O	E							

Stripes

P	A	L	M		V	O	C	A	L		I	B	A	R
I	D	E	A		A	L	O	H	A		G	A	L	A
C	A	N	D	Y	C	A	N	E	S		U	R	A	L
A	R	T	I	S	A	N		M	A	C	A	B	R	E
			G	E	T				G	O	N	E		
A	P	P	A	R	E	L		E	N	G	A	R	D	E
T	A	R	N		S	E	N	S	E		S	P	E	D
O	N	I				P	E	T				O	M	I
M	I	S	S		B	E	F	O	G		B	L	O	C
S	C	O	O	T	E	R		P	O	O	R	E	S	T
		N	A	R	A				A	L	I			
Y	A	W	N	I	N	G		S	T	A	T	U	E	S
A	B	E	D		B	O	U	L	E	V	A	R	D	S
R	I	A	S		A	E	R	I	E		I	S	I	N
N	E	R	O		G	R	I	T	S		N	A	T	S

PAGE 168

Cooking Techniques

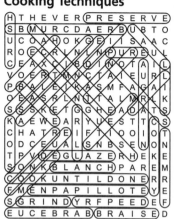

The verb "to cook" is a collective term for all the ways that food can be prepared.

PAGE 169

Sudoku

4	9	5	7	1	6	3	2	8
6	2	1	5	8	3	7	9	4
7	3	8	9	4	2	6	5	1
1	4	2	6	5	9	8	7	3
5	6	3	2	7	8	1	4	9
8	7	9	1	3	4	2	6	5
3	5	7	4	2	1	9	8	6
9	1	4	8	6	7	5	3	2
2	8	6	3	9	5	4	1	7

TRIANAGRAM • HATER / HEART

PAGE 170

Spot the Difference

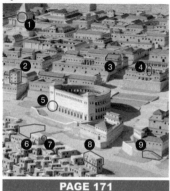

PAGE 171

Tennis Talk

E	M	I	R		P	O	L	Y	P		E	L	A	N
D	A	T	E		A	N	E	A	R		L	O	G	O
A	C	E	V	E	N	T	U	R	A		E	V	E	R
M	E	M	E	N	T	O		D	I	S	C	E	R	N
		N	O	H			S	E	T	A				
R	I	N	G	L	E	T		F	E	A	R	F	U	L
U	S	E	E		R	E	W	E	D		A	F	R	O
N	A	T		P	O	W				A	G	O		
G	A	P	S		L	I	N	E	D		P	I	E	S
S	C	R	E	W	E	D		R	E	M	O	R	S	E
	O	L	E	A			M	A	P					
D	I	F	F	E	R	S		T	O	R	C	H	E	S
A	L	I	I		N	I	G	H	T	C	O	U	R	T
W	I	T	S		E	N	S	U	E		R	E	B	A
N	A	S	H		R	E	A	D	S		N	Y	E	T

PAGE 172

Spy Relay

Character A hid the papers in the windmill.

C gave them to B;
B gave them to D;
D gave them to A.

PAGE 173

Futoshiki

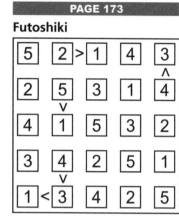

CONNECT TWO •
CLOSE_____DISTANCE
ZERO _____DEFICIT
REAL_____FANTASY
CRASH _____LANDING

PAGE 174

Sports Maze

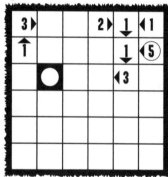

UNCANNY TURN • PARODIST

PAGE 175

Themeless

T	A	L	C		N	O	T	H		S	H	A	M	U
O	H	I	O		S	I	R	I		O	A	T	E	S
G	A	M	Y		F	L	I	N	T	S	T	O	N	E
A	B	B	O	T		O	D	E		E	M	U	S	
		T	E	T	E		U	S	B					
A	D	H	E	R	E	N	T		H	A	R	P	E	R
M	R	I		M	A	N	I	A		H	O	R	D	E
B	A	R	T		R	I	N	G	S		Y	O	G	I
E	M	E	R	Y		S	E	A	L	S		M	E	N
R	A	D	I	U	M		S	P	O	N	S	O	R	S
			M	I	T		E	P	I	C				
I	R	A	S		N	E	E		T	O	O	L	E	
B	U	L	L	W	I	N	K	L	E		O	K	A	Y
I	N	D	I	A		S	E	E	R		B	R	I	E
S	T	A	T	S		E	D	E	N		Y	A	R	D

PAGE 176

Riders

L	O	S	S		S	A	L	E	M		S	T	L	O
U	T	A	H		E	N	O	L	A		I	H	A	D
L	O	N	E	R	A	N	G	E	R		N	E	N	E
U	S	E	L	E	S	S		E	S	C	A	P	E	S
		D	I	I			H	A	T	H				
A	L	M	O	N	D	S		N	A	R	R	A	T	E
L	O	A	N		E	A	S	E	L		A	N	I	L
D	O	T		D	O	C			T	A	L			
E	F	T	S		S	I	N	K	S		T	O	R	E
R	A	D	I	A	T	E		S	H	O	W	M	A	N
	I	N	G	A			E	L	I					
M	A	L	C	O	L	M		A	P	O	S	T	L	E
A	B	L	E		K	I	N	G	A	R	T	H	U	R
P	O	O	R		E	M	E	E	R		E	E	L	S
S	Y	N	E		R	E	W	E	D		R	O	L	E

PAGE 177

Keep Going

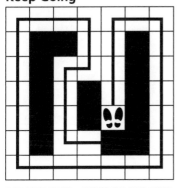

DELETE ONE • DELETE E AND FIND GRAND FINAL

PAGE 178

Plant Evidence

1. **b.** Juniper
2. **a.** One that lives for more than one season
3. **b.** Spruce
4. **a.** William Wordsworth
5. **c.** Shamrock
6. **c.** Yellow
7. **b.** It sheds them
8. **a.** Poppy
9. **a.** Impatiens
10. **b.** Green

PAGE 179

On the Strip

B	A	S	A	L		A	L	P	S		M	I	C	A
A	G	O	R	A		P	Y	L	E		A	R	O	D
T	A	L	C	S		P	L	A	N		C	O	L	E
T	R	E	A	S	U	R	E	I	S	L	A	N	D	
			D	O	N	A		D	E	A	R			
J	I	V	E		P	I	N		S	T	O	D	G	Y
A	N	I		M	E	S	A	S		I	N	U	R	E
L	A	S	V	E	G	A	S	C	A	S	I	N	O	S
A	N	T	E	D		L	A	R	C	H		C	U	E
P	E	A	R	L	S		L	O	U		P	E	T	S
		Y	E	L	P		U	T	A	H				
N	E	W	Y	O	R	K	N	E	W	Y	O	R	K	
T	A	L	E		G	O	N	G		A	L	G	A	E
E	V	I	L		A	L	O	E		C	U	R	I	E
D	I	A	L		N	E	T	S		S	M	E	L	L

PAGE 180

Construction

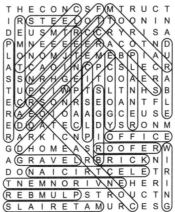

The construction industry is an economic sector that focuses on making homes and other structures.

PAGE 181

Sudoku

8	4	2	1	3	7	9	5	6
9	6	3	5	4	8	7	1	2
1	7	5	2	6	9	8	3	4
6	5	4	7	1	3	2	9	8
2	9	1	6	8	4	5	7	3
7	3	8	9	5	2	6	4	1
4	1	9	8	7	6	3	2	5
3	2	6	4	9	5	1	8	7
5	8	7	3	2	1	4	6	9

FRIENDS • EACH CAN HAVE THE PREFIX RE- TO FORM A NEW WORD.

PAGE 182

Close Encounters

H	A	V	O	C		Y	A	W	L		S	M	E	W
O	B	E	L	I		O	L	I	O		E	A	C	H
S	E	R	I	N		G	A	L	L		A	G	H	A
S	T	E	V	E	M	A	R	T	I	N	R	I	T	T
			E	M	O			T	I	C				
D	U	B		A	T	I	P		A	G	H	A	S	T
O	T	I	S		T	O	L	E		H	E	L	I	O
L	U	K	E	D	O	N	A	L	D	T	R	U	M	P
C	R	E	M	E		E	S	M	E		S	L	O	E
E	N	D	I	V	E		M	O	N	O		A	N	D
			N	O	N			I	S	E				
E	L	T	O	N	J	O	H	N	M	C	C	A	I	N
N	O	E	L		O	B	I	E		A	L	I	V	E
D	O	R	E		Y	O	D	A		R	A	D	A	R
S	K	I	S		S	E	E	L		S	T	E	N	O

PAGE 183

Trivial Pursuit 1942

1. 25 cents each
2. The Poky Little Puppy
3. Margaret Wise Brown
4. Richard Scarry
5. Band-Aids (due to tie-in with Johnson & Johnson)
6. **b.** Soft Kitty, Warm Kitty

TEST YOUR RECALL •
WHITE CHRISTMAS

PAGE 184

Binairo

I	O	I	I	O	I	O	O	I	O	I
O	I	I	O	O	I	O	I	O	I	I
I	O	O	I	I	O	I	O	I	I	O
O	I	I	O	I	I	O	I	O	O	I
O	I	O	I	O	I	I	O	I	I	O
I	O	I	O	I	O	I	O	I	I	O
O	I	O	I	I	O	O	I	I	O	I
I	O	O	I	O	I	I	O	O	I	I
I	O	I	O	I	I	O	I	I	O	O
O	I	I	O	I	O	I	I	O	I	O
I	I	O	I	O	O	I	O	I	O	I

ONE LETTER LESS OR MORE •
DAILIES

DELETE ONE • DELETE S AND FIND
ALTITUDE

PAGE 185

Themeless

S	P	A	S		P	I	P	E	T		C	L	E	M
P	A	R	T		A	N	E	A	R		L	I	M	A
E	W	E	R		C	L	A	R	A		O	N	U	S
C	L	A	U	D	I	A		L	I	O	N	E	S	S
		G	U	N				P	R	E				
F	O	R	G	O	O	D	N	E	S	S	S	A	K	E
O	R	A	L	S		R	O	D	E	O		B	Y	E
S	I	D	E		M	I	N	I	S		C	O	O	L
S	E	I		C	O	V	E	T		T	R	I	T	E
E	L	I	Z	A	B	E	T	H	T	A	Y	L	O	R
		E	R	Y			S	P	S					
T	O	R	N	A	D	O		B	E	A	T	L	E	S
E	L	O	I		I	N	E	R	T		A	U	R	A
A	L	O	T		C	E	R	E	S		L	I	S	T
L	A	T	H		K	R	E	W	E		S	S	T	S

PAGE 186

Sunny

BLOCK ANAGRAM •
ACADEMY AWARD

PAGE 187

Enter Here Please

A	H	A	B		A	F	A	R		P	L	A	T	E
P	E	L	E		P	Y	R	O		L	E	M	U	R
P	L	A	N	E	T	O	F	T	H	E	A	P	E	S
S	P	E	E	D	E	D		S	O	X		S	S	T
		T	I	R	O	L		C	U	R				
B	F	A		S	Y	R	A	C	U	S	E	N	Y	
L	U	M	M	O	X		S	O	S		H	O	E	R
O	R	I	O	N		C	A	W		P	A	S	T	A
T	O	N	O		V	A	L		K	I	B	I	T	Z
	R	O	D	S	E	R	L	I	N	G		R	A	E
		Y	E	R		E	M	I	L	E				
S	O	P		A	D	S		A	G	E	L	E	S	S
T	H	E	T	W	I	L	I	G	H	T	Z	O	N	E
I	N	D	I	A		A	B	E	T		A	L	A	N
R	O	O	M	Y		B	E	S	S		R	A	P	T

PAGE 188

Word Wheel

bad, ban, bid, bin, bio, boa, lab, mob,
bail, bald, band, bind, boil, bold,
bond, lamb, limb, blind, blond, albino,
abdominal

PAGE 189

Word Sudoku

S	C	R	H	A	Q	B	E	N
N	E	Q	B	R	C	S	H	A
B	H	A	E	S	N	Q	C	R
A	N	H	R	E	S	C	B	Q
Q	B	E	N	C	A	R	S	H
R	S	C	Q	B	H	N	A	E
H	R	S	A	N	B	E	Q	C
C	Q	N	S	H	E	A	R	B
E	A	B	C	Q	R	H	N	S

SANDWICH • CHAIR

PAGE 190

Traveling Music

A	L	E	E		S	T	A	B		A	D	D	E	R
L	I	A	M		A	O	N	E		B	E	R	L	E
A	E	R	O	P	L	A	N	E		I	V	I	E	D
I	N	S	T	E	A	D		R	E	L	I	V	E	S
			I	A	M			M	I	T	E			
E	M	P	O	R	I	A		P	O	T	O	M	A	C
T	E	E	N	Y		S	C	A	R	Y		Y	M	A
A	D	A	S		P	H	O	N	Y		S	C	O	W
P	A	C		L	E	O	N	I		S	C	A	L	E
E	L	E	G	A	N	T		C	H	A	R	R	E	D
			T	O	R	N		A	M	A				
M	I	R	A	G	E	S		B	U	B	B	L	E	S
E	N	A	T	E		I	M	O	N	A	B	O	A	T
A	R	I	E	S		P	I	N	T		L	A	V	A
T	E	N	E	T		S	A	Y	S		E	D	E	R

PAGE 191

Fast Food

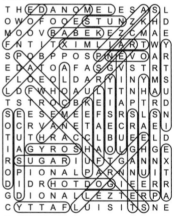

The Slow Food movement is opposed
to fast food and wants to preserve
traditional and regional cuisine.

PAGE 192

Sudoku X

7	8	5	3	1	4	2	9	6
2	3	1	6	9	7	8	5	4
9	6	4	2	5	8	3	1	7
3	4	9	1	7	2	6	8	5
6	7	2	5	8	3	9	4	1
1	5	8	9	4	6	7	3	2
8	9	7	4	2	1	5	6	3
5	1	6	7	3	9	4	2	8
4	2	3	8	6	5	1	7	9

LETTER LINE • CAMOUFLAGE;
MOGUL, ALGAE, GULF, LEAF, FOAM

PAGE 193

Winter Fun

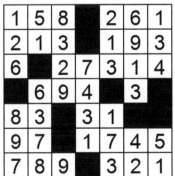

FRIENDS • EACH CAN HAVE THE
SUFFIX -AGE TO FORM A NEW WORD.

PAGE 194

Kakuro

1	5	8	■	2	6	1
2	1	3	■	1	9	3
6	■	2	7	3	1	4
■	6	9	4	■	3	■
8	3	■	3	1	■	■
9	7	■	1	7	4	5
7	8	9	■	3	2	1

PAGE 195

Invisible Ink

PAGE 196

A Walk on Wall Street

1. Bear
2. General Electric
3. *The Wall Street Journal*
4. The Witch of Wall Street
5. The New York Stock Exchange
6. Bull
7. Tuesday, a day that has come to
   be known as "Black Tuesday"
8. Martha Stewart
9. George Washington
10. Philadelphia

TEST YOUR RECALL • 1987

PAGE 197

Shooting Hoops

6F. Points are scored on intersections
where the number corresponds with
the letter's place in the alphabet.

CONNECT TWO •
FUZZY_____ LOGIC
RUBBER ___ CEMENT
SAFE_____ WEAPON
DISTANT ___ RELATIVE

PAGE 198

Songs of the Season

H	A	G	■	S	O	D	A	■	T	H	I	S
A	W	E	■	I	D	E	S	■	H	E	R	A
R	O	N	■	G	E	N	T	L	E	M	E	N
K	L	E	I	N	■	T	O	O	L	■	■	■
■	■	■	D	A	M	■	R	O	M	A	N	O
R	U	D	O	L	P	H	■	M	A	N	O	R
U	N	O	■	■	H	O	P	■	■	T	O	E
B	I	N	D	I	■	W	A	L	K	I	N	G
S	T	E	A	D	Y	■	T	A	O	■	■	■
■	■	■	P	O	I	S	■	W	I	R	E	D
B	E	T	H	L	E	H	E	M	■	O	R	E
E	R	I	N	■	L	O	V	E	■	B	I	C
T	R	E	E	■	D	E	A	N	■	E	E	K

PAGE 199

Athletics

ANSWERS TO DO YOU KNOW?

p. 9:	The Vatican (0.2 square mile)
p. 10:	8
p. 16:	Cedric Errol
p. 19:	Neil Diamond
p. 20:	Ljubljana
p. 22:	Marilyn Monroe
p. 27:	Peaseblossom, Cobweb, Moth and Mustardseed
p. 30:	Ford Torino
p. 31:	She induced an Egyptian cobra to bite her.
p. 39:	A ray
p. 40:	Sweden
p. 42:	George Gershwin
p. 44:	Edvard Munch
p. 46:	Belmopan
p. 55:	Edward
p. 56:	Mortimer Mouse
p. 62:	Fleet Street, London
p. 63:	Woody Allen
p. 66:	Grant Wood
p. 68:	Diving
p. 69:	Donald Duck
p. 77:	Robert Burns
p. 82:	Vladimir Nabokow
p. 85:	Hamlet
p. 94:	The Cars
p. 100:	John Calvin
p. 103:	Karen Blixen
p. 107:	Tiber
p. 108:	Ferdinand de Lesseps
p. 113:	Oscar Wilde
p. 119:	Richard Gere
p. 120:	Mrs. Hudson
p. 122:	Highclere Castle
p. 125:	Mark Spitz
p. 127:	Greg LeMond
p. 134:	Rudolf Hess
p. 137:	William Faulkner
p. 144:	Patricia Highsmith
p. 147:	Paul Simon
p. 155:	They are bean-based or products of beans
p. 156:	Idi Amin
p. 161:	New Zealand
p. 169:	Richard Nixon
p. 170:	A score of 2 under par on an individual hole
p. 174:	Leonardo da Vinci
p. 178:	Carnation
p. 181:	Catherine of Aragon
p. 189:	Munich
p. 192:	A cow kicked over a lantern in a barn
p. 194:	Pyongyang

ANSWERS TO TRIVIA

p. 20:	Ladybird
p. 43:	Sergio Leone
p. 50:	Hibernation
p. 69:	Aslan
p. 72:	They cool the elephant's blood
p. 84:	Chubby Checker
p. 120:	The giant squid
p. 136:	Nigel Mansell
p. 170:	The Egyptian Empire
p. 173:	Ted Danson

CREDITS

Cover photo credit:
ziviani/Shutterstock

Puzzle credits:
Peter Frank: Binairo, Kakuro, Number Cluster, Sudoku, Word Searches, Word Sudoku
Sam Bellotto Jr.: 48, 135, 187
Book Creation Services: 50, 101
Guy Campbell and Paul Moran: 15
Philip Carter: 24, 25
Emily Cox & Henry Rathvon: 65, 110, 165
Maggie Ellis: 92, 182
Linda Lather: 70, 158
Mary Leonard: 83
John McCarthy: 154
Jim Moran: 111
Anna Nilsen: 172
Brian O'Shea: 67, 195
Peggy O'Shea: 45, 51, 129, 176, 185
Karen Peterson: 14, 18, 98, 139, 148, 163
Dave Phillips: 76
Alison Ramsey: 17
John M. Samson: 11, 38, 54, 57, 60, 79, 102, 121, 124, 130, 142, 145, 151, 167, 179, 190
Michele Sayer: 26, 32, 86, 171
Mary-Liz Shaw: 140
Debra Steilen: 47, 96, 183
Tim Wagner: 95, 117
Kelly Whitt: 8, 21, 29, 35, 41, 64, 89, 105, 114, 175, 193, 198